Rice, Spice and Bitter Oranges

MEDITERRANEAN FOODS AND FESTIVALS

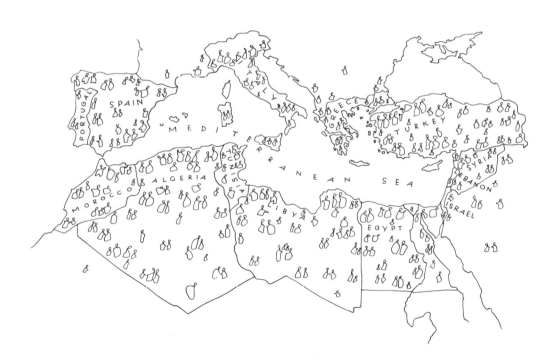

By Lila Perl

RICE, SPICE AND BITTER ORANGES:
Mediterranean Foods and Festivals

RED-FLANNEL HASH AND SHOO-FLY PIE:
American Regional Foods and Festivals

THE DELIGHTS OF APPLE COOKERY

WHAT COOKS IN SUBURBIA

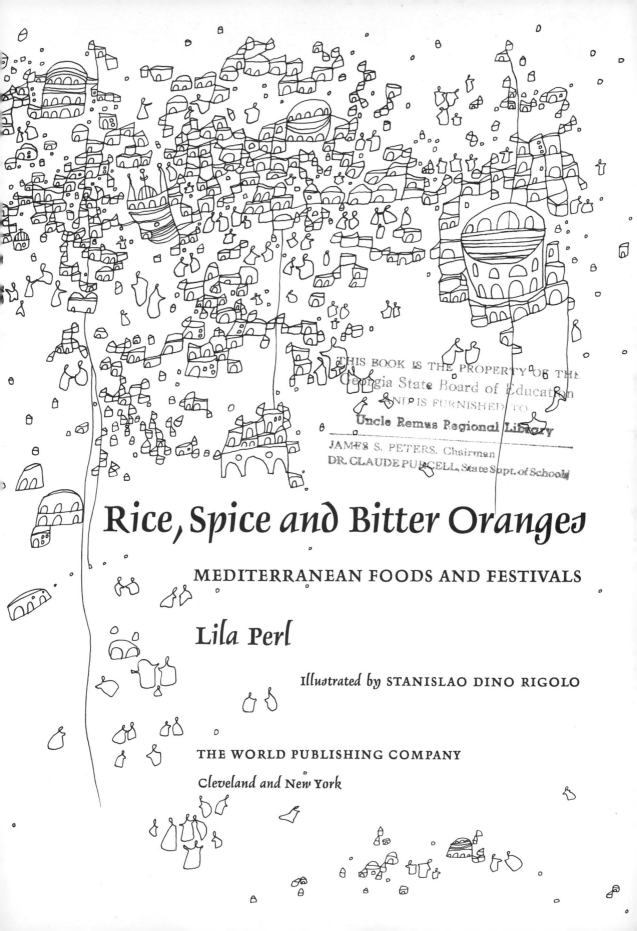

Rice, Spice and Bitter Oranges

MEDITERRANEAN FOODS AND FESTIVALS

Lila Perl

Illustrated by STANISLAO DINO RIGOLO

THE WORLD PUBLISHING COMPANY

Cleveland and New York

Published by The World Publishing Company
2231 West 110th Street, Cleveland, Ohio 44102
Published simultaneously in Canada by
Nelson, Foster & Scott Ltd.
Library of Congress catalog card number: 67–23361
Text copyright © 1967 by Lila Perl
Illustrations copyright © 1967 by Stanislao Dino Rigolo
Designed by Jack Jaget

Contents

NORTH AFRICA: EGYPT TO MOROCCO

Introduction

OUR EARTH shrinks a little each day. As it does so, its people become more aware of their likenesses and, hopefully, less concerned about their differences. The vivid patterns of a nation's customs and folkways, holidays and religious festivals, cooking methods and dining habits, all spring into focus and are appreciated for their unique quality, as well as for the historical and geographical factors that shaped them.

Americans should be especially attuned to the diverse flavors of other lands, for the United States has been the great gathering-in place of a wide sampling of the world's peoples in modern times.

Yet many Americans shudder at the mention of boiled octopus, fried squid, or goat's-milk cheese. They are dismayed by the Spanish family that subsists on garlic soup, and by the Portuguese who lives on dried cod and grilled sardines, never tasting meat from one year's beginning to another's end. They are shocked at the Bedouin practice of serving sheep's eyes to honored guests, of eating with the fingers at fancy dinner parties, and of making loud appreciative noises to compliment one's host for his generous table.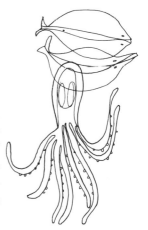

These are some of the people of the Mediterranean world. To this world, rimming and admirably served by the Mediterranean Sea, all of Western civilization is indebted. In ancient times, one brilliant culture after another rose on Mediterranean shores. Although, physically, each of these worlds was eventually ground to dust, it is their collective heritage that enriches each of our lives today.

Naturally the life of the Mediterranean world has changed over the centuries, but the changes have come rather slowly. Daily customs like the charming Spanish *paseo* are as deep-rooted as the great yearly Moslem fast of Ramadan. The Spanish bullfight, the Greek Easter, the Italian *palio*, a Syrian wedding, Israel's folk dances and the rich Hebrew ritual of the orthodox Jewry of that land—all are viewed in these pages. An insight into a way of life still very different from our own is the reward of a lingering look at the folk and religious festivals of the Mediterranean lands.

Equally rewarding is an appraisal of the foods of these lands each of which, though bound in tradition by similar geographical factors and crisscrossed by common trade routes, has a cookery stamped with its own special style and flavor. In addition, the details of a nation's dining hours and table etiquette, its cooking utensils from Italian *polenta* pots to Turkish *shishkebab* spits, all come under the gaze of the curious Mediterranean traveler.

Undeniably a country's cuisine is a clue to dozens of factors in its past, to the changing nature of its present, and to that elusive element perhaps best tagged as its personality. To peek into the bake ovens of pharaonic Egypt and ancient Rome is no less revealing than to peer into the cooking pots of present-day Spain and Portugal, Italy, Greece, Turkey, Syria, Lebanon, Israel, and North Africa.

A typical menu and a sampling of recipes are given for each Mediterranean country visited. Most of the recipes are simple, all are authentic, and all employ ingredients easy to obtain throughout the United States, or easily substituted, be the dish a Portuguese bread pudding, a Greek *moussaka,* a Syrian-Lebanese *tabbouleh* salad, or a North African *couscous*.

You are about to embark on a Mediterranean cruise, a journey in time that will take you back to the era of antiquity; a journey in space commencing at the Iberian Peninsula and rounding the Mediterranean coast until you regain the Atlantic at Morocco.

Buen viaje!

Rice, Spice and Bitter Oranges

MEDITERRANEAN FOODS AND FESTIVALS

The Mediterranean Basin
of Prehistory

B LUE IS THE COLOR of the inland sea—a blue so intense that the waters of this sea, the Mediterranean, may be said to resemble jewelers' velvet, violet-tinged and marvelously smooth. This is the fine-weather Mediterranean. It is the Mediterranean of antiquity, the sea of the ancient Egyptians who ventured forth from the Nile delta in frag-

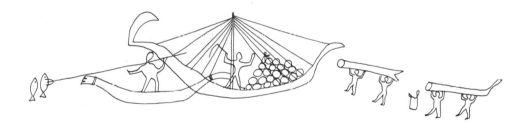

ile barks to cut lumber in the cedar groves of Lebanon. It is also the sea of Phoenician commerce, of Greek legend, and of Roman conquest.

In later years the Mediterranean became a treasured link in the land-and-sea chain that brought rich goods from the Orient to western Europe and gilded the coffers of Italian merchant princes. But after the Portuguese, Vasco da Gama, discovered the long-sought all-water route to India, a lull descended upon the inland sea. Mediterranean blue may be said to have gone out of fashion for a time.

Then in 1869, with the opening of the Suez Canal, the Mediterranean attained a brisk new commercial and military importance. Soon after this, in the 1880s, there began an era of luxury travel that, although interrupted by wars, has continued into the present.

While twentieth-century winged transport offers incomparable speed and efficiency between land points everywhere, an undispellable magic still clings to the seaborne tour known as the Mediterranean cruise. Nor is there any better way to gain an understanding of the countries of the Mediterranean world than from the sea that is their common heritage. To come to know the Mediterranean as the transmitter of early civilizations, as the cradle of world navigation, and as the source of man's widespread enrichment, we must cruise these waters in both space and time.

The space we shall cover is vast, 2300 miles in length, equal to nearly two-thirds the distance across the Atlantic from New York to Gibraltar. The inland sea has 14,000 miles of shoreline, and as we travel this shore in a clockwise direction, we will call at ports in more than a dozen countries.

Nor will the Mediterranean always be an unruffled blue. The vivid, cloudless sky reflected in placid waters through a dry and dustless atmosphere is chiefly a phenomenon of summer. But the Mediterranean has other moods. These are incited by the dread winds that blow from surrounding land areas—the hot, dust-laden African sirocco, the violent chilling French mistral, and the wild Adriatic bora.

Gales can quickly chop the Mediterranean into a series of short steep waves, and an oyster-colored sky drains every ounce of azure from the unhappy waters. Perhaps even more dramatic than the storms themselves are those dusky brooding clouds that hang ominously over the Mediterranean in hot, still weather. These are the clouds that stain the water a thick, flushed purple and recall to us the wine-dark sea of Homer and the ancient Greek heroes.

Nonetheless, the Mediterranean was the ideal training school for the first seafarers, men from the lands along its shores. In ancient times many must have advanced timidly into its waters from sheltered coves and silent beaches; others, deriving confidence from their experience of river navigation, set out more boldly. In any case, the invitation to explore the inland sea could not be resisted, for here was a body of water that touched on three continents—Europe, Africa, and Asia—at a time when land travel was an appalling hardship.

Warmed by the desert breezes of Africa and Asia, and protected by mountains from the chill northern winds of Europe, the climate of the Mediterranean Sea was for the most part ideal. In addition, tides were almost nonexistent and small-craft harbors, provided by islands, peninsulas, and the jagged northerly coast, were abundant.

Fishing was but one of the many enterprises that drew men of early civilizations to the sea. As early as 2700 B.C. the ancient Egyptians, as we have mentioned, sailed to Lebanese shores for cedarwood so that they might build larger and sturdier boats than the river craft supplied by the sparse timber of their own country. Later they made regular trips to this coast to take from its forests resin, which they used in their highly developed art of embalming. By 2000 B.C. the Phoenicians, who lived on the strip of land between the Lebanese mountains and the Mediterranean, had been spurred to seafaring for purposes of trade. In time their incredible fearlessness took them to the western end of the sea and through the Pillars of Hercules (the Strait of Gibraltar) into the unknown Atlantic.

However, no civilization could even begin to take shape until man's basic needs were met, and the search for food was frequently a primary motive in setting out upon the sea. The Mediterranean abounds in fish, although many of its over four hundred species are inedible —weird, nightmarish creatures of garish color and even stranger contour. Among food fish, the Mediterranean deeps offer varieties ranging from the undersized anchovy to the hefty tuna; bewhiskered red mullet and pancake-bodied sole; the fiercely shaped needlefish, the perchlike sea bream, and the coin-dotted John Dory, which the Spanish call *dorada* and the Italians call *pesce San Pietro* (Saint Peter fish).

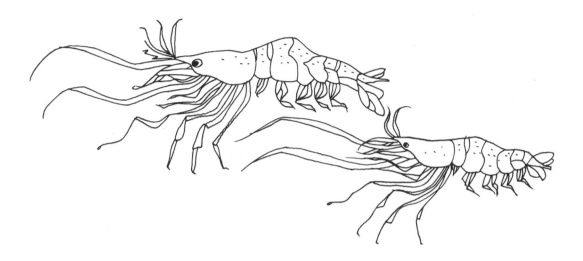

The shellfish family is represented by the clawless *langouste*, or spiny lobster, and a bevy of relatives diminishing in might to those delicate thumbnail-size shrimp that are stirred whole into beaten eggs for omelet. Most terrifying, perhaps, of all the Mediterranean's edible submarine inhabitants is the ten-tentacled squid, served neatly sliced, swimming, in its own black ink—or perhaps it is the octopus, whose weaving white tentacles are boiled and served up dressed with oil and red pepper.

All of these fish and many others have long existed in Mediterranean waters. The ancient Romans feasted on lobster, and one banquet-giving Roman nobleman is reputed to have paid 6000 sesterces ($240) for a six-pound mullet brought directly from the sea by relays of runners.

On the other hand, the food picture on the shores of the Mediterranean has enlarged gradually over the centuries. Hillsides once covered with scrub have been planted with groves of scintillant gray-green olive trees. Marshlands have been transformed into rice fields, their bright shoots, of an almost poisonous green, contrasting vividly with Mediterranean citrus trees—oranges, bitter and sweet; pale lemons; and the aromatic citron.

From the dry soils of the Mediterranean countries, almond trees burst into a miraculous snow of blossoms each spring, and grapevines thrive as their elongated roots manage somehow to find the necessary moisture. These soils also support the feather-duster date palm, and the lobe-leafed fig tree ready to survive on a trickle of water provided only that it is protected from cold.

Because in summer Mediterranean rainfall is almost nonexistent, field crops are limited to winter-planted wheat and barley, and to beans. But a little irrigation brings fat melons and poppy-red tomatoes to the fields, and a really good irrigating system makes Mediterranean farmlands as luxuriant as those of southern California.

These food plants of the Mediterranean shores date to the comparatively recent past. The tomato is one of the newest arrivals, having been brought to southern Europe from America by the Spanish conquistadors in the sixteenth century. The tomato has changed the accent of cookery in several Mediterranean lands in the past four centuries. How different, for example, the present-day cuisine of Italy is from that of ancient Rome or of Italian Renaissance times. The sixteenth century also saw the introduction of the sweet orange, brought to Europe from China by Portuguese explorers and carried early into Spain where it supplanted the bitter orange of the Moslem invaders.

It was the Moslem invaders, however, inspired by their new religion of Islam in the seventh and eighth centuries, who brought the greatest single influx of new foods to the Mediterranean area. From Arabia, the land of the prophet Mohammed, Islam spread, rapidly gathering zealous followers from the Middle East, taking Cyprus, Rhodes, and Sicily, sweeping across North Africa and then by way of Gibraltar into Spain and Portugal.

This massive invasion was also something of a massive gift offering, for the Moslems diffused through Mediterranean lands a wealth of foods, many previously unknown, that had originated in China, India, and western Asia: sugar cane and rice; figs, dates, almonds, mulberries, and pome-granates; the lemon, the citron, and the bitter orange that flourishes to this day in Spain, its glowing fruits falling from dark-leaved trees to lie untouched in the streets of Córdoba and Valencia.

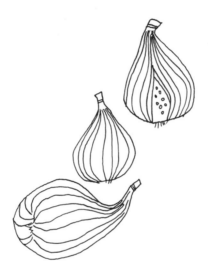

Among the Romans and the Greeks of earlier times, honey was the universal sweetener, for sugar was unknown; and wheat, barley, and legumes were the starch counterparts of the rice of the Orient. Nor were citrus fruits known.

The populace of imperial Rome, reputed to have lived on bread and circuses, subsisted largely on *pulmentarium*, a porridge of boiled dried peas, beans, lentils, or chick-peas. These seeds of leguminous plants are known as pulses, and give their name to the cooked dish. In ancient Greece, a porridge of barley, one of the first cereals cultivated by man, was a staple food along with wheat bread, olive oil, and wine. The rice and the lemons that are the hallmark of modern Greek cookery were not to be seen for yet a thousand years. However, the Greeks and the Romans did have the two food plants still characteristic of Mediterranean cuisine today—the vine and the olive.

Salt fish was known to all of the ancient civilizations, and vegetables included onions and garlic, lettuce and asparagus, cabbage, beets, radishes, turnips, and other simply cultivated plant foods. Melons and several kinds of tree fruits were grown.

The ancient Egyptians were, however, more restricted in their diet than the Greeks and Romans. Until the invasions of the Hyksos, an Asian people, in the 1700s B.C., the olive tree, the apple, and the pomegranate were unknown in Egypt. And it was not until Roman times that Egypt made cheese or grew peaches, pears, cherries, or almonds. The staple of the poor was a crude barley bread, and although wine was drunk, the most common beverage of ancient Egypt was beer brewed of a mixture of fermented grains and a liquid extracted from dates.

We have now roughly traced Mediterranean foods back to the dawn of recorded history, or to about 3000 B.C. If we step just a little further into time, we cross this threshold and find ourselves in the vast prehistoric era. Here the eons seem limitless, for our earth is roughly four billion years old. But we need not go that far into the past to trace the beginnings of the Mediterranean world. A backward jaunt of, let us say, one million years brings us to a meaningful point in the evolution of man in the Mediterranean basin.

Beginning about one million years ago, the great ice age known as the Pleistocene Epoch descended upon the earth. The Pleistocene had been preceded by other ice ages, and was itself not one single period of glaciation, but rather four such periods interspersed with eras during which the earth warmed up for a time. It has been theorized that we are even now living in such a warm interval, that in the future the earth will once again grow very cold, and we shall see the formation of still another great southward-moving icecap.

THE ICE AGE

AND THE

MEDITERRANEAN

BASIN

While many theories have been advanced as to the cause of these intense climate changes, no single explanation is as yet generally accepted.

The ice sheets of the Pleistocene Epoch were miles thick and moved slowly but steadily southward from the polar region, covering northern Europe, practically all of Canada, and a large part of the United States. In Europe, ice covered the British Isles and the Scandinavian countries. The Mediterranean region, while not frozen, was colder than it is now, so that the woolly mammoth and the woolly rhinoceros stalked the plains of southern Europe and of North Africa.

The formation of the icecap had a strong secondary effect on the Mediterranean basin, for as huge quantities of water were taken up to be frozen, the level of the world's oceans was lowered by several hundred feet. In the Mediterranean region, the water level of the Atlantic dropped sufficiently to permit the Gibraltar land bridge to emerge from the sea. The protrusion of this strip of land, connecting what are now Spain and North Africa, made of the Mediterranean a completely landlocked sea. It is by means of this land bridge that the forebears of the Barbary apes, found today on Gibraltar and nowhere else in Europe, are believed to have made their way northward from Africa.

Due to low rainfall and limited river inflow, the Mediterranean (deprived of its principal water source, the Atlantic) now began to evaporate, and finally shrank into two smaller seas or lakes, with a second land bridge emerging between Italy and Tunisia, by way of Sicily. Were the Atlantic water supply to be artificially withdrawn from the Mediterranean Sea today, this same condition would result.

Of the two landlocked seas, the western sea was the more densely laden with salt, for it had held the salt water of the Atlantic and received little fresh-water inflow. The eastern sea is believed to have been less salty for it was fed by the Nile and the Po, two major fresh-water sources. It is even possible that at times the eastern sea grew higher than the western sea and overflowed into it. Nevertheless, the land masses of the Mediterranean basin were now linked, and the last glacial period of the ice age saw primitive man and early animals inhabiting this valley down to the shores of the inland seas, and wandering freely from one continent to another.

It was during the Pleistocene Epoch, beginning about one million B.C., that early man (often referred to as "true" man) began to evolve, for the ice age coincides roughly with the Old Stone Age (or Paleolithic Period). But forms of *pre-man* can be traced back *ten* million years. It is interesting to note that studies reveal these pre-men, who were really a species of advanced ape, to have been vegetarian just as apes and monkeys are today. Insects, it is believed, were the only nonvegetable matter they ate. By four million B.C., a transition stage had begun during which the advanced ape developed into a composite ape-man who learned to kill for his food and became a habitually meat-eating creature. By the time the Old Stone Age had arrived, man's diet was highly diversified. Old Stone Age man inhabited Asia, Africa, and Europe—and, later in that period, America.

Comic strips and movies have vividly perpetuated the image of Stone Age man dressed in animal skins and armed with a club, pursuing a dinosaur or even doing hand-to-hand combat with such a creature. Nothing could be more erroneous, for the two were destined never to meet. The dinosaurs vanished from the earth sixty million years ago—a full *fifty million* years before even the earliest form of pre-man, the advanced ape, came upon the scene.

Nor is it likely that Old Stone Age man, whose tools were limited to roughly shaped chipped stones, acted the individual aggressor with the mammoth or bison of his day. Early man was more likely the hunted than the hunter with regard to large, fierce animals. Men of the Old Stone Age, acting as a group, probably stampeded giant sheep or other animals over a cliff or into a bog through harassment and rock throwing, as did their descendants, the American Indians, in the case of the buffalo. Or they might track aged,

EARLY MAN ON THE MEDITERRANEAN SCENE

sick, or weakened animals, often eating the putrid flesh of the already dead and half-rotten.

Otherwise, early Mediterranean man hunted smaller game such as the rabbit and the rat. He gathered birds' eggs, ate reptiles, grubs, worms, insects, as well as snails and frogs, which are still daily food in France. Shellfish were dug on the coasts of Spain and Portugal with a picklike tool formed by chipping a beach pebble to a sharp point.

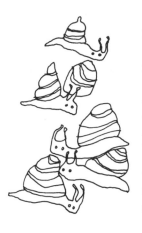

Plant life, too, provided sustenance. Nuts and berries, crab apples and other wild fruits, leaf buds and roots, mushrooms and other fungi, seaweed, and wild honey were probably all gathered by the women and the young. Fire was known in the Old Stone Age, although food was but lightly cooked at first. Heaps of animal bones have been found on early campsites, cooked just enough so that they could be split and the marrow sucked out.

As the Old Stone Age progressed, tools became more skillfully shaped to provide scrapers, chisels, and other more specialized bladed instruments. Two important developments mark the closing centuries of the Old Stone Age. First, Stone Age people living in Asia began to cross the Bering Strait land bridge to North America. This migration is thought to have begun twenty to fifteen thousand years ago. These men, who were the ancestors of the American Indian, took with them their Stone Age culture which they preserved (long past that of man of the Mediterranean basin) due to their complete isolation, their lack of contact with other early civilizations. For example, the North American Indian was *still* boiling his food in bark or skin containers in the sixteenth century A.D., just as Old Stone Age man in Europe had done tens of thousands of years earlier!

A second development of the Old Stone Age was man's artistic self-expression and representation of the world around him, as seen in the cave paintings of over thirteen thousand years ago. France, Spain, and Italy provide examples of such cave art. Especially interesting are the caverns of Altamira in northern Spain, where a ceiling area over forty feet long is decorated with about twenty-five animals, some reindeer and many bison, for southern Europe was still cold enough at this time to support herds of these species.

The Stone Age artists worked with four basic colors, a white pigment derived from pipe clay, a black from charcoal, and reds and yellows extracted from iron ore. The pigments were mixed with grease and then applied to the rough, fissured cave ceilings, either from crude scaffolds or with the artist lying flat on his back on a rock couch (the same position from which the paintings are best viewed by visitors today). Since the caves were totally dark, light for the Stone Age artist was supplied by torches or by stone lamps filled with oil.

Remarkably, the caves at Altamira remained sealed until the late 1800s, when a Spanish huntsman followed his dog, which had chased a fox into the caves. His deeper exploration of the caves, some seven years later, revealed the paintings. They were in an excellent state of preservation, their lifelike animal figures depicted in rich, warm sepia tones accented with blacks and grays. While it is uncertain whether the Stone Age artists were specialists or huntsmen

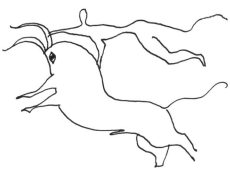

as well, the cave paintings show that the hunting civilization of this period and in this region fed man well enough to afford him leisure time for pursuits beyond mere subsistence. The motive of Stone Age man in depicting the animals upon which he preyed was probably a religious or magical one, calculated to insure the continuance of successful hunting.

TOWARD THE BEGINNINGS OF MEDITERRANEAN CIVILIZATION

About ten thousand years ago, or roughly 8000 B.C., the Old Stone Age, and along with it the ice age, came to a close. Now the earth began to grow warm again. Slowly the ice melted and the glaciers withdrew from northern lands, leaving great boulders and other rock rubbish in their wake. As the water taken up by the ice was released, the oceans of the world began to rise. In the Bering Sea, the land bridge over which Stone Age man had trekked onto the American continent sank beneath the waters. Migration ceased and the American continent was sealed off from further contacts until man should master the sea in ships.

In the Mediterranean Basin, too, the waters began to rise as the swelling Atlantic flowed first into the western sea, over the Gibraltar land bridge, and then into the eastern sea. The hunting grounds of the valley dwellers who lived on the shores of the two great lakes were flooded, and the Mediterranean became the sea it is today, with only a few minor differences.

At this time, man entered a transitional era known as the Middle Stone Age (Mesolithic Period), which lasted from about 8000 B.C. to 6000 B.C. As the climate grew warmer, the open plains of the Mediterranean basin became forest lands, and the plains animals—the bison, the mammoth, and the reindeer—gave way to forest animals such as the deer and the boar. Most of these Mediterranean forests have since been denuded by man, but the Middle Stone Age people of this region were sometimes referred to as "forest folk."

Since forest hunting required greater skills and better weapons than plains hunting, Mesolithic man developed more efficient tools during this period: the bow and arrow, and hunting as well as fishing spears with barbed heads. He also began large-scale preservation of foods, smoking fish and meats over fire or drying them in the sun.

Most significant, however, are the three thousand years that now followed, known as the New Stone Age (Neolithic

Period). During this time (6000 B.C. to 3000 B.C.) man turned from hunting to herding, and from food gathering to agriculture.

Domestic cattle are believed to be descended from the aurochs or great ox, which is said to have stood as high as an elephant, was never domesticated, and finally became extinct. Similarly, sheep and goats are derived from wild forms. Domestication probably began when man isolated weak or defective animals from their fiercer fellows, gradually developing them into relatively amenable herds.

The growing of plant foods was the most vital step in the evolution of early civilizations. Wild grasses that developed into barleys and wheats may have been cultivated as early as 6000 B.C. or 5500 B.C. in the Middle East. Pod-bearing plants (legumes), such as peas, beans, and lentils, also lent themselves to very early cultivation. The last of these is mentioned in the Bible, Esau having sold his birthright for a "pottage of lentiles."

Since farming required rich soils and a source of irrigation, the river valleys of the Nile in Egypt, the Euphrates in Mesopotamia (now Iraq), and the Indus (in what is now West Pakistan) became the sites of permanent villages and later of cities. In Central and South America, civilizations began to grow up around the cultivation of corn, squash, and potatoes; in eastern Asia the cultivation of rice became the basis of a highly developed economy.

Once man was assured of a regular food supply and even endowed with a surplus for trade, his social organization could begin to develop on several levels. More complex tools, finer weaving and pottery, the working of metals, industry, commerce, and growth in the arts all ensued. Thus by 3000 B.C. the Egyptians were already a unified kingdom on their way to building the great pyramids, and the Mesopotamians had learned to alloy copper with tin to make bronze.

Copper, the earliest metal used by man, had been mined and beaten into shapes from very early times, possibly by 8000 B.C. in the Tigris-Euphrates valley and by 6000 B.C. in Egypt. Even the North American Indian had mined and worked some copper, found in the vicinity of the Great

Lakes. However, the weapons and tools made of this soft reddish-gold material were not strong or durable enough. The discovery that copper could be melted and alloyed with tin to produce a harder, more resistant metal resulted in a new historical period for man known as the Bronze Age.

The Bronze Age came early to the Mediterranean basin. In other parts of the world, as for example Northern Europe, this stage of development was not reached until hundreds of years later. Having begun thus with Mesopotamia and Egypt, Mediterranean civilization now burst into flower on the island of Crete, set in almost the very center of the Mediterranean Sea.

Crete had fertile soil, timber, natural harbors for trading and fishing, and the all-important deposits of copper. From about 3000 B.C. to 1100 B.C., Cretan civilization (often called Minoan civilization after Crete's legendary King

Minos) flourished. This was a true Bronze Age civilization, for it corresponded in time to the Mediterranean Bronze Age, and Crete's metalwork was one of its finest achievements.

It was during this time, too, that the adventurous Phoenicians, searching for both copper and tin, made their sea journeys to Spain, past Gibraltar, and up the coasts of western Europe, bringing elements of eastern Mediterranean civilization to these remote and primitive places.

From Crete, the center of Mediterranean civilization was to shift to the Greek mainland, and then spread westward to southern Italy and Sicily. Early in this period (about 1100 B.C.) man began to cast tools and weapons of a metal that was cheaper and more abundant than the copper and tin required for bronze. This material was iron. While the smelting and forging of iron are believed to have begun in Asia Minor (now Turkey), this skill was already known in Greece by 1000 B.C. By the time Rome was founded, the Mediterranean world was in the Iron Age, the same era that gave rise to formidable industrial development, and in which we still find ourselves today. (Many, of course, would say that we are now in the Atomic Age, and this too is true, for all ages of man's development have overlapped—and the achievement of one age nurtures the aspirations of the next.)

The Mediterranean stage was now set for the giant era of Roman conquest which saw the Mediterranean basin, from Iberia to Arabia, united under a single power for the first time in history. While Rome acted as a great and valuable diffuser of language and of law, of custom and cuisine, of architecture and engineering, and even of religion, the countries of the Mediterranean were destined each to pursue a separate course.

This then is the panorama that will henceforth concern us—the unique flavor and color, the foods and the festivals of these countries, set upon an amethyst sea, against a backdrop of history as old as the ice age.

Portugal and Spain

T HE BULL'S HIDE —this is how early mapmakers
described the land mass of southwest Europe that
lay beyond the Pyrenees. Looking at a map of Europe today, we agree that their image was apt, for the Iberian
Peninsula does truly resemble the stretched hide of a great
bull. It is apt, too, that this huge shape reaching, nose to
tail, from Portugal's southwest tip to Spain's northeast edge,
should comprise the only two countries in Europe where
bullfighting prevails.

Bullfights and fiestas, against a background that is at once
Roman, Visigothic, Moorish, and Christian, are part of the
common heritage of Portugal and Spain. This heritage lives
in the white Moorish houses traced with black wrought-iron
work, or trimmed with colorful building tiles known as
azulejos. It lives, too, in the ancient Roman bridges and
aqueducts, many still spanning or carrying water eighteen

35

hundred years after their construction. In the fields of both countries may be seen olive trees and grapevines that descend from Roman times, the heavy wooden ox-drawn plow of the Germanic invaders who followed the Romans, and the Moslem water wheel or *noria* that irrigated the lands of southern Iberia and made them fruitful.

Dried salt cod, prepared in any of over a hundred different ways, is a staple food in both Portugal and Spain—and the windows of pastry shops from Lisbon to Barcelona glitter with gemlike cakes and sweetmeats, many of them filled with a velvety confection of egg yolk and sugar that is seldom found outside Iberia.

Portugal, on the western edge of Iberia looking seaward to the Atlantic, took shape as a separate nation in the twelfth century. Although her boundaries give her no Mediterranean coastline, one cannot help but consider Portugal a Mediterranean country. Historically, agriculturally, in many of her customs and traditions, and in much of her cuisine, she is inescapably bound with Spain to the geographical land mass from which both countries developed. France, on the other hand, although she does have a Mediterranean coastline, is not generally thought of as being a Mediterranean land, for her focus has always been a northerly one.

Iberia takes its name from the dark, wiry Stone Age people known as Iberians who migrated to Europe from North Africa, probably across the Mediterranean land bridges of the ice age. These people eventually streamed across Spain and into what is now Portugal. The Basque people of northern Spain and the French Pyrenees are believed to be directly descended from the Iberians. Centuries of isolation produced their highly unusual language. Totally unrelated to French or Spanish, the Basque tongue may be the only living language to contain prehistoric Iberian words.

Late in the Neolithic Period, the Iberians of Spain and Portugal were living in fortified hill villages known as *castros*, their huts and village walls built of granite or other local materials. By 2500 or 2000 B.C. the Iberians had collected animal herds, cleared fields by burning away virgin forest, and learned to mine and to work copper.

From the eastern end of the Mediterranean, the land that is now Lebanon, the Phoenicians in the twelfth century B.C. sailed westward to Spain. So thoroughly did the Phoenician galleys dominate trade at this time that the Mediterranean Sea was termed a "Phoenician lake." Nor did the Phoenician ventures cease at Gibraltar, for the crescent-prowed vessels were to sail into the Atlantic, up the coast of Portugal, and as far north as the Cornish coast of England.

PHOENICIANS, GREEKS, AND ROMANS BEAR GIFTS TO IBERIA

At the present sites of Cádiz and Málaga on the southern coast of Spain, the Phoenicians established ports. Here, copper extracted from the Spanish mines and salt evaporated from the coastal marshes were traded for woolen and linen cloth that the Phoenicians wove and had learned to dye a deep, rich purple. Phoenician-manufactured goods of glass and metal were also taken in trade for Spanish copper and salt. Thus the first glimmerings of Middle Eastern civilization began to reach Iberia.

The Phoenicians are believed to have brought to Spain, among other eastern Mediterranean foods, one of the world's oldest legumes, the chick-pea, which the Spanish call *gar-banzo. Garbanzos* were destined to become a mainstay in the Spanish diet, the basis of *sopa de garbanzos* (*garbanzo* soup) which the conquistadors later brought to Florida and to New Mexico, and of *olla podrida,* the stew also known as *cocido* or *puchero* that is to this day the national dish of the

Spanish people. Ingredients for an *olla podrida* vary with the region—rice or potatoes, blood sausage or *chorizo* (a hard, paprika- and garlic-spiced sausage), chicken or rabbit, green cabbage or squash. But the two invariable ingredients are *garbanzos* and some form of pork.

The meaning of *olla podrida* is "rotten pottage," an unattractive name resulting no doubt from the peasant custom of simmering soups and stews on a low fire for days, adding ingredients to the pot as they came along. Since the stew was never either refrigerated or brought to a healthy boil, its pleasantly warm temperature rendered it an ideal medium for bacterial culture. By the time the stew gave off a sufficiently unsavory odor to be discarded, many who had eaten it had no doubt suffered digestive upsets!

A good *olla,* however, is a hearty feast. By the 1600s, at country fairs and on market days, portions of this rich, garlicky stew were sold from a three-legged pot kept simmering over a fire. The clergy of Spain were said to indulge themselves on feast days with very special *ollas* prepared with turkey and sweet potatoes (delicacies recently introduced from the New World), several varieties of sausage, and of course *garbanzos*. For the very poor, however, even a meager stew was out of the question if fuel was scarce, for a proper *olla* requires at least three to four hours to cook.

It must have been an underdone stew that the horrified Alexandre Dumas sampled when he visited Spain in 1846. *Garbanzos,* the noted French novelist wrote to a friend in Paris, "are hard bullet-sized peas, quite beyond my powers of digestion. But," Dumas added, "if you were to begin by eating one on the first day, two on the second, and on the third day, three, it is just possible that you might survive!"

The heritage of the early Phoenicians is most vividly seen today in Portugal, where the daring and colorful fishermen of the coastal villages of Nazaré and Peniche are believed to be of Phoenician descent, and even their brightly painted fishing boats resemble those of ancient Phoenician design.

By the time Greek trading vessels visited Iberia in about 600 B.C., another people had begun drifting onto the peninsula by land routes from the north. These were the Celts, a pastoral folk, fair-haired and blue-eyed, who were to merge with the dark-haired native Iberians to produce a people known as Celt-Iberians.

The Greeks brought settlers to Iberia and founded colonies. Lisbon, originally Ulyssipo (or Ulissipo), is said to have been named after Odysseus, the wandering king of Greek legend whom the Romans called Ulysses. Although the Phoenicians had brought stock of the vine and the olive to Iberia, the Greek and Roman influences were greater in terms of cultivation, and also in developing the arts of wine making and olive pressing.

As in other Mediterranean lands, olive oil was to become the bath oil, the lamp oil, the cooking fuel, and the butter of Spain and Portugal. Today, Spain outstrips all other countries in the production of olives, with Italy running a close second. Many of the silver-leaved trees growing in Spanish soil are hundreds of years old. It is said that one plants olive trees not for one's children, but for one's grandchildren and great-grandchildren. Twenty years may pass before the olive tree matures and bears fruit, but to compensate for this the olive is one of the longest-living fruit trees.

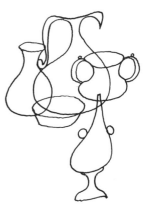

Only ripe olives (nearly black) are used for oil. These are harvested in December or January. Green, or unripe, olives are harvested in the fall, but both varieties must be pickled, or otherwise processed, before eating. The fresh green olive has a violently disagreeable taste.

In some rural Mediterranean areas olives are crushed just as in ancient times, between two large stones, to extract the oil. Often the grindstone is turned by a blindfolded mule. The highly prized virgin oil is that which comes from the first pressing. Fruit that is not bruised or otherwise blemished, and that is crushed soon after picking, yields the purest, palest oil with the most delicate aroma. "Two hours from tree to mill" is the boast of modern processors who use machinery for pressing the fruit and employ advanced refining, bleaching, and blending methods.

As the pulp is pressed a second, third, and fourth time, the quality of the oil deteriorates. Dark, almost greenish oils containing impurities that hasten rancidity are sometimes used in the poorer homes and cheaper restaurants of Spain and Portugal, while the better grades are apt to be exported. Richard Ford, an Englishman who both traveled and lived in Spain in the mid-nineteenth century, remarked that olive oil was "used indifferently for lamps or stews," so poor was the general quality at the time.

Good olive oil, however, properly refined, is a flavor enhancer and a cooking fat of tremendous value. It gives Iberian food its unique character—a few drops in *gazpacho* (the refreshing cold salad-soup of southern Spain) and in other vegetable-base soups for "meatiness"; a nutty-flavored frying base for the crisp-edged Spanish *tortilla;* a dressing for shrimp or vegetables, or in *ali-oli,* a potent garlic-and-oil sauce served on baked or poached fish.

Olive oil has other advantages too. It is healthful, considerably more so than animal fats; it does not require refrigeration (which does not exist, even today, in most Spanish and Portuguese homes); and even the pulverized olive stones that remain after the final pressing are useful as a heating fuel, burned in an Eastern-style brazier. For Spain, most of which has little grazing land for dairy cattle, olive oil is the ideal butter substitute. In Galicia, however, in northern Spain where there are few olive trees but where many pigs are raised, lard and salt pork are the principal fats. In Portugal, which today has a declining yield of olive oil, less costly peanut oil imported from that country's African colonies is frequently substituted for the expensive high-grade olive oil.

For the renowned wines of Iberia, especially Spanish sherry and Portuguese port, much credit is due both the Greek colonists and the Roman conquerors who followed them. From the third century B.C., when Spain became a Roman province, until the Germanic invasions of the fifth century A.D., a Roman-directed civilization flourished in Iberia.

Wine making and olive pressing; the cultivation of pear, plum, quince, walnut, and fig trees; of beans, peas, lentils, and chick-peas; and of wheat and other grains were all vastly expanded. Spain became the granary of Rome. Spanish horses performed in Roman circuses, and Spanish mines produced gold and silver and the copper that provided bronze shields for the Roman legions. The Roman soldiers in turn brought the informal, non-classical speech of ancient Rome (known as vulgar Latin) to the provinces. From this tongue developed the Portuguese language, Castilian Spanish, and the various Spanish dialects such as Catalan and Gallego. Roman law and a new religion, Christianity, were also gifts of the Roman conquerors.

Cities sprang up. At one point the Roman provincial administrator listed 360 cities in Spain. Nor were all of these mere settlements. Roman bridges and roads wove networks that linked the cities, Roman aqueducts provided them with water, Roman amphitheaters and baths offered their inhabitants recreation and relaxation. The *thermae* (hot baths), open to public use as in Rome, were the pride of the larger Spanish towns, only to be destroyed later by the Visigoths. Even sewer systems and central heating existed in some Roman cities in Spain.

Today the vestiges of a great Roman complex—baths, amphitheater, circus maximus—may be seen just outside the dusty Spanish city of Mérida. At Segovia, north of Madrid, the remarkable Roman aqueduct, constructed only of dressed stones without a binding of cement or other mortar, not only stands as an impressive monument to the past, but still supplies the city with water as in Roman times.

The Roman name for Spain was Hispania, derived from the Carthaginian word *sphan* (rabbit) and meaning literally "land of rabbits." The area that is now Portugal and western Spain was called Lusitania, after a tribe of particularly fierce guerrilla fighters led by the legendary Portuguese hero Viriathus, who resisted the Roman legions to the death.

Yet these very Romans are largely responsible for the port wine industry that Portugal enjoys today. Port wine is named for the city of Porto, where this wine has been bottled and shipped since the seventeenth century. The port wine grape grows in the valley of the Douro River where the finely layered rock formations in the soil, the frosty winters, and the furnacelike summers are just right for the vines. So

intense is the summer heat in the narrow channel of the Douro valley that it is said "the blood of the vine boils in the grapes."

In late September the grapes are harvested and crushed locally in granite tanks. Although machinery is now commonly used to extract the juice from the grapes, the Portuguese have long believed that the human foot exerts just the right pressure for this job. Trampling breaks the skins and frees the juice, yet does not crush the pits which give the wine a bitter flavor due to their tannin content. So for centuries, trousers tucked up, feet scrubbed, the men have stepped into the vats to tread the grapes, which are chill and unyielding at first but which grow warmer as fermentation sets in.

Fermentation is checked by the addition of grape brandy of high alcoholic content. A short fermentation period means a sweet wine; a longer fermentation, not so sweet. Thus a pale, dry port such as the Portuguese like to sip before dinner and the dark, sweet dessert port that the English prefer may be developed from the same grape.

The English at once became so fond of port wine that in 1703 they signed a treaty with the Portuguese providing for the import of port wine and the export of English woolens on favorable trade terms. England has long termed Portugal her "oldest ally"—and as to the great wine of that country, the English simply say, "Any time you are not drinking port is a waste of time!"

Spain was also to produce a great many wines of the vine stock planted in ancient times, the most notable of which is sherry. Spanish sherries come from a small area near the town of Jerez de la Frontera, a name bestowed by Spanish Christians centuries ago when this was a frontier village in the campaign to repel the Moors. Jerez, once spelled Xeres, was in English pronunciation "sherris." Soon this was regarded as a plural form, and the singular came to be sherry. The correct Spanish pronunciation of Jerez, however, is "Hereth."

Spanish sherries are produced by a special blending method known as the *solera* system. In the *bodega* (wine cellar) the barrels are piled four deep and the wine trickles down from cask to cask. The lowest tier of barrels, however, is never emptied, so that some trace of old wine (perhaps sixty to eighty years old) goes into each bottle. For example, a sherry marked Solera 1850 would mean that the newer wine is blended with a mellowed wine that is over a hundred years old.

Sherry may be very pale and dry (*fino*), medium dry (*amontillado*), or full-bodied, dark, and somewhat sweet (*oloroso*). "Milk" sherries were developed in England in the sixteenth and seventeenth centuries, by adding sweet syrupy wines to sherry. It is thought that the name milk sherry derived from the fact that these sweet wines were sometimes given to children. Cream sherry is an even richer dessert or after-dinner wine.

Other Spanish dessert wines, as well as brandies, champagnes, and non-sweet table wines, are produced in great variety and quantity. A refreshing drink, especially in the dry summer heat of southern and central Spain, is *sangria*— dry red wine, slices of lemon, orange, and often peaches, sugar just to sweeten, ice, and fizzing soda water to fill the pitcher.

However, the drink preferred by most Spaniards is dry sherry, which is enjoyed as an apéritif (a pre-dinner drink) along with innumerable *tapas*—bite-size appetizers such as olives, toasted and salted almonds, whole shrimp in the shell, tiny crisply fried sardines, slices of black sausage rich

with pine nuts, or squares of thinly sliced dark-red mountain ham known as *jamón serrano*. Beer or dry wine may substitute for sherry among the less well-to-do, but *tapas* are indispensable. Some *tabernas* in the larger cities have as many as fifty different varieties, and since dinner in Spanish cities is late (ten-thirty in Madrid), bars and taverns do a thriving business from seven o'clock on, when most stores and offices close. In fact, so satiated can one become with the constant nibbling that accompanies a glass or two of sherry that some Spaniards do not go on to dinner at all!

The Spanish and Portuguese, like other Mediterranean peoples, have long known how to make proper use of their wines—to whet the appetite, to enhance the flavors of foods at meals, and to make for amicability, relaxation, and lively discussion at almost any hour. But drunkenness, which is often found in non-wine-drinking countries, is almost never seen in Mediterranean lands. The Spaniard whose behavior suggests that he is under the influence of alcohol is considered to be *sin virguenza* (without shame), a condition of great disgrace, for good manners, careful grooming, and innate dignity are the hallmarks of the people of Iberia.

Many of the stone and marble edifices of the Roman empire in Spain were to totter and crumble under the heel of the invaders from the north. The excessively brutal Vandals were among the earliest Germanic tribes to overrun Spain. They gave the word vandalism to our language, and the name Andalusia to the southern part of Spain. Later they were forced into North Africa by their cousins, the semicivilized Visigoths who, having no superior culture of their own, ruled Spain and Portugal according to Roman law, and permitted both Christianity and the Latin-based languages of the various regions to develop.

An important contribution of the Germanic tribes in Spain and Portugal was their custom, as a wood-using people, of keeping wine in wooden casks rather than in earthenware jars smeared with flavor-impairing pitch, as the Romans had. Thus most Iberian wines, including port and sherry, are today kept in the wood and have been for centuries.

THE GARDEN
OF ALLAH
IN IBERIA

From the fifth century A.D. to the eighth, the Germanic kings and overlords held sway in Iberia, frequently squabbling among themselves and giving way at last to the irrepressible force of the Moslems sweeping northward across the Mediterranean from North Africa.

The Moslem religion was founded by the prophet Mohammed, in Arabia in A.D. 622. It is astounding that in less than a hundred years (by A.D. 711) this religion, which Mohammedans call Islam, had gathered sufficient force not only to penetrate Iberia, but to retain powerful holdings there for the next eight centuries!

The Moslems were a mixture of peoples—from Arabia, Asia Minor, Persia, Syria, and from Egypt and other North African lands. The word Moor applies only to the native Berbers of western North Africa who were converted to Islam and intermarried with Arab Moslems. The Moors were not Negroes, as is often erroneously supposed.

Among the Berbers and among some Arabian desert tribes there *were* fanatic elements, but these were definitely a minority. The Moslem invaders of Iberia, despite different national backgrounds, were united in their worship of one God, Allah, and they brought with them a tradition of religious tolerance toward other nonpagans. The Moslems of the Middle East were the most cultivated elements in the so-called Moorish rule, and they endowed Iberia with all that was richest and most progressive in Eastern culture.

From Damascus in Syria came the art of inlaying steel with gold and silver thread. In Spain, the craftsmen of Toledo made the creation of exquisite damascened swords, jewelry, and other articles their very own. Beautifully worked leather and wrought iron (formed into delicate and complex shapes by heating, but not smelting, iron strips and bars) were Moslem-taught crafts. Paper, textiles, and the decorative glazed tiles (*azulejos*) still seen today in Portuguese and Spanish buildings were brought by the Moslems.

Nor would Spain's music have its exotic coloring and unique dramatic quality were it not for the influence of the East. Even the Spanish "*olé*," that expression of excitement and approval, is believed to be derived from the word Allah.

The Moslems, like all people from arid lands or desert habitats, had a tremendous reverence for water. They made much of washing and bathing, and it was part of their religion to perform daily ablutions. They loved the sight and the sound of water, and fountains and pools such as those seen at the Alhambra in Granada are part of their heritage. They appreciated the importance of water in agriculture, too, and they brought to Iberia, just as they had to Egypt and the rest of North Africa, the *noria* or water wheel. This device consisted of a large wheel with pots or buckets attached to the outer rim. The wheel was operated by an ox or a donkey, and as the wheel creaked round and round, the buckets lifted water from a cistern or pool and poured it into irrigation ditches that ran into the dry fields.

The Moslems were the true possessors of "green thumbs," for with their attention to irrigation, their knowledge of soil fertilization and crop rotation, their skill in fruit-tree grafting, and their innate love of gardens and orchards as well as fruitful fields, they both increased the productivity and enriched the cuisine of Iberia.

Paella, a mound of saffron-gold rice decorated with swatches of vermilion pimento, is almost the national dish of Spain—and indeed bears the very colors of the Spanish flag. Its main ingredients, however, are not of Spanish origin. It was in the marshy lowlands along the Valencian and Catalonian coasts that Moslem-introduced rice was first planted and is still being grown. The Moslems also brought saffron, produced to this day from the violet crocus flowers that bloom on the slopes of the Spanish province of Murcia.

Saffron is a costly spice prepared from the dried stigmas of the autumn crocus. It is sold either in powdered form or as frail little threads which are the dried stigmas themselves. Since each blossom has only three stigmas, it takes about four thousand flowers to yield one ounce of commercial saffron. Saffron had long been used in the East for the bright yellow coloring and the slightly bitter but pleasing flavor that it gave to foods.

Paella takes its name from the large two-handled frying pan in which the dish is cooked. Clams and mussels in the shell, good-sized tidbits of chicken, shrimp, squid, *chorizo* sausage, and often artichoke hearts are liberally distributed throughout and atop the rice. Peas, and in more recent times, tomatoes, are added. Arguments flare and fizzle as to the proper ingredients for, and relative merits of, *paella a la valenciana, paella a la catalonia,* and others. But in truth almost anything tastes good in a properly prepared *paella*.

Like the *cocido*, the *paella* is a perfect catchall for the leftovers or the small quantities of meat, poultry, or shellfish that come the way of the Spanish family and must be stretched to feed many people. *Paella* is sometimes served as a first course at a festive Sunday dinner. *Arroz con pollo* (rice with chicken) is simply another type of *paella*, one that uses chicken exclusively, no shellfish. In northern and western Spain, which do not have rice-growing regions, potatoes or beans are the basic starches, and *paellas* are not so frequently encountered. It is also interesting that, compared to Italy, macaroni and other forms of *pasta* are little found in Spain and Portugal, appearing, when they are used, chiefly in soups.

The "honey-bearing reed," sugar cane, was another Moslem introduction, and was soon being grown on plantations in southern Spain. For more than two hundred years Spain was the sole sugar-growing country of Europe, supplying all of Iberia and other lands as well with the principal ingredient of an entire realm of new desserts, pastries, and sweetmeats.

Sugar cane was native to India and had long been used in the marzipans, the crystallized fruits, and the syrup-drenched pastries of Persia and other lands of the Middle East. It was known to few in Europe before the Moslem invasion of Iberia. However, a Greek physician living at the time of the Roman emperor Nero wrote about "a sort of hard honey . . . found upon canes in India." It was "grainy like salt and brittle between the teeth, but of sweet taste withal."

Today Spain and Portugal appear to be one huge pastry shop. Every moderate-sized town and every city is studded with *pastelerías* and tearooms displaying *dulces* (sweets) of endless variety—tiny rich cakes filled with cream, custard, or almond paste; pastries stuffed with jams or with velvety egg-yolk confection; plump fruits preserved in sugar. While fresh fruits such as melons, oranges, pears, plums, figs, bananas from Spain's Canary Islands, or pineapples from the Azores are the usual mealtime desserts, sweets seem to be in constant demand.

Not only Sundays and feast days send people scurrying to the *pastelería* or stopping on the way home from mass to make mouth-watering purchases. Spanish and Portuguese ladies of some leisure spend afternoon hours at smart tearooms, congregating at six or seven (halfway between lunch and dinner) to drink tea, coffee, or chocolate and to eat dainty, rich cakes. The tearoom is to the Iberian woman what the male-patronized café is to her husband.

Pastries and sweetmeats are luxury items, seldom prepared at home in Iberia, for many homes do not have ovens. In early Christian times, soon after the Moslems were driven out, the preparation of sweetmeats was the province of the nuns. The popular Spanish egg-yolk confections known as *yemas* are said to have been created by Santa Teresa of Ávila, a nun born in 1515 who reformed and built up the Carmelite order. But *yemas* are undoubtedly of Eastern origination.

Yemas are prepared by slowly adding raw egg yolks to a sugar-and-water syrup, beating all the while to ensure a smooth mixture. The confection, sometimes flavored with lemon or with ground almonds, is cooled, shaped into balls or little cakes, and rolled in sugar. Eggs are fairly plentiful in Spain, but poorer families may prefer *yemas económicas*, which are made with a mashed-potato base and thus use fewer eggs. In Portugal a similar sweet, to which port wine is sometimes added for flavor, goes by the name of *toucinho do céu* which translates as "heavenly bacon" or "little bacon from heaven."

In Spain and Portugal almost every region seems to have its own sweetmeat or pastry specialty. At Ávila, a town completely walled just as it was in medieval times, the little

round golden *yemas* of melting goodness are still made by the nuns of Santa Teresa. Toledo is almost as well known for its intriguingly shaped marzipan sweets as for its delicate damascene work and its keen blades used in bullfighting. Almonds, also the gift of the Moslems, are crushed to a paste and combined with sugar and egg to make this toothsome confection which the Spanish call *mazapán*.

In Portugal, the university city of Coimbra features *ovos moles*, flaky elongated pastries crammed with a custardy *yema*-like filling. The border city of Elvas is renowned for its moist, plump preserved plums, while the southern Algarve coast produces fig-and-almond confections.

Nor did the Moslem reign in Iberia furnish food only for the stomach. The great Moslem cities of Spain were, in their order of flowering, Córdoba, Seville, and Granada. Córdoba was the largest city in Europe during the Middle Ages. While the rest of the continent languished in poverty, servility, ignorance, and crude warfare, libraries and a university flourished in Córdoba. Its people knew the highest standard of living, and its scientific pursuits in medicine, astronomy, and mathematics were the most advanced in all of Europe. Maimonides, the great Jewish physician and philosopher, was born in Córdoba—and indeed the Jews, who had been in Spain in large numbers since the second century A.D. and who had known oppression under the Visigoths, enjoyed freedom and were able to make rich cultural and economic contributions under the tolerant Moslem rule.

Seville, which grew to prominence after the decline of Córdoba, was so great a center of wealth and abundance that it was said, "If one were to ask for birds' milk in Seville, he would be able to get it." When the Christians besieged this city, as part of their reconquest of Spain, they burned the fertile fields that lay outside its walls and cut down the orchards of almond, orange, and pomegranate trees. In 1248, when Seville fell, its great mosque was demolished leaving only its minaret which stands today beside the Gothic cathedral that has replaced the mosque. In Córdoba the great Moslem mosque, begun in the eighth century, has fortunately been preserved.

Granada was the last of the Moslem strongholds in Spain. Its Alhambra, a palace complex that is a miracle of stone lacework and fine intricate decoration, had flush toilets, running water, and deep stone bathtubs in the royal apartments, with three spigots that provided water—hot, cold, and perfumed.

In what is now Portugal, the chief center of Moslem culture was Silves on the Algarve coast. It was inhabited largely by the descendants of Arabs from Yemen, and was in those times known by the Arabic name, Shelb. Today Silves is an undistinguished small town, its airy palaces and richly stocked bazaars gone, its river silted up and no longer navigable to the sea. But the fig and the almond trees descended from Moslem times are still much in evidence.

The fall of Granada, to the Christian forces of Ferdinand and Isabella in 1492, marked the end of Moslem power in Spain. The reconquest had been going on intermittently for eight hundred years. Much of the time it had bogged down in petty wars between rival Christian rulers and between rival Moslem rulers. Even El Cid, the national hero of medieval Spain who lived from 1043 to 1099, fought for the Moslems against the Christians as well as vice versa. He is more celebrated as a soldier of fortune and a heroic leader than as a Christian partisan, and his very name comes from the Arabic word *sidi*, meaning leader or lord. Victory for its own sake, and for the spoils of war—booty, slaves, domination—was the motivation of El Cid that later fired the conquistadors.

The unification of Spain under the Christian monarchs Ferdinand and Isabella unleashed the terrible force of the Inquisition, which was to burn, torture, and hound the Moslems and the Jews from Spain in the name of "purification." The confiscated Moslem lands were doled out to indifferent absentee landowners, and Spanish agriculture even centuries later was to lag far behind that of Moslem times. As to the Moslems beaten back to North Africa, so bitter was the loss of their beloved Granada that even in modern times their evening prayers have included the plea to Allah, "Restore to us Granada!"

Americans do not think of the year 1492 as marking the end of Moslem power in Spain, or as the start of the Spanish Inquisition (which was to last until 1820). To Americans, this is the year of Columbus' great discovery, an event that was to enrich both continents beyond the imagination of even the boldest and most adventurous of the conquistadors.

Columbus had an audience with the Portuguese king as early as 1484. But his plan was rejected. The Portuguese (who had acquired the status of an independent nation through their expulsion of the Moslems in western Iberia) had plans of their own regarding the sea route to India. As it turned out, the Portuguese plan was the right one, for five years after Columbus accidentally found America, Vasco da Gama executed his expressed intention of rounding Africa and, in this way, reaching India.

As a result, Iberia and the rest of Europe were to reap a double harvest. From Columbus' New World came gold and silver, precious stones, featherwork, chocolate, vanilla, the tomato, pimento, pineapple, white potato, sweet potato, maize (Indian corn), tobacco, many varieties of squash, and

THE CONQUISTADORS RETURN WITH MORE THAN GOLD

the turkey, a game bird that was unknown in Europe. From India and the Far East, the Portuguese brought silks, gems, ivory, porcelain ware, the fan, the walking stick, and the firecrackers that were to become an indispensable part of all Spanish and Portuguese festivals. They brought the long-sought spices needed for food preservation and flavoring (pepper, nutmeg, cinnamon, cloves); coconuts, bananas, and mangoes from India and southeast Asia; and sweet oranges from China.

In the 1500s the English began to import sweet oranges from Portugal, referring to them as "portyngales." As to spices, these had become so vital in Europe by the late 1400s that a pound of cloves in England was worth two cows. Pepper from India, brought via the old overland route and then shipped through the Mediterranean by Italian merchants, had been so inflated in price due to middleman profits that its cost was forty times its original value by the time it reached Portugal. Da Gama's all-sea route to India changed all this and greatly diminished sea commerce in the Mediterranean.

The Portuguese genius for the sea had been much advanced by Prince Henry, known as the Navigator. Son of one of Portugal's early kings and an English-born queen, Henry devoted his life to planning and directing the exploration of the African coast and of Atlantic waters. At Sagres, near Cape St. Vincent at the southwest tip of Portugal, he established a school of navigation where he assembled the most prominent geographers, mapmakers, mathematicians,

astronomers, and sea pilots of his day. Oddly enough, Prince Henry never went on a sea journey himself, nor was he to share the thrill of da Gama's discovery of the route to India, for he died in 1460. Nevertheless he was largely responsible for this achievement, as he also was for the Portuguese acquisitions of Madeira, the Azores, and Brazil.

The Spanish conquistadors who followed Columbus to the New World were often cruel and rapacious, but their courage and vigor were remarkable. With a mere handful of soldiers—Pizarro is reputed to have taken the Incas of Peru with only four hundred men—they tramped through steaming jungles and scaled towering peaks, garbed in leather and weighted down with clumsy armor. Most of the Spanish conquerors were lowborn men who, in the tradition of El Cid, rose quickly to fame and wealth through heroic deeds.

They disdained menial labor. Cortez, in speaking of his conquest of Mexico, said, "I did not come to America to till the soil like a peasant."

The Aztecs whom Cortez subdued were sometimes cruel and savage, too. They practiced human sacrifice, tearing out the hearts of their victims. Although they worked metals such as gold, silver, and copper, they knew nothing of iron. They had no beasts of burden—their only domesticated animals were the dog and the turkey—and the first wheel they ever saw was that on Cortez' cannon. In return for all they took from the Americas, the Spanish conquerors brought to the New World horses, sheep, cattle, pigs, chickens; basic crops such as cotton, wheat, and sugar cane; citrus fruits, apricots, peaches, grapes, olives, and other fruit and vegetable plants too numerous to list.

Of the foods brought back to Spain from the New World, chocolate attained the most instant and lasting popularity. It was adopted as a breakfast drink, served thick and foamy and accompanied by a roll or crust of bread. It was also taken as an afternoon refreshment. The chocolate pot at the palace of Charles III, who ruled Spain in the 1700s, was said to hold fifty-six pounds of hot chocolate and to have been continually replenished for the pleasure of the court.

When that renowned novelist and intrepid traveler Alexandre Dumas visited Spain in 1846, he and his party, arriving famished for breakfast one morning at a small-town café, ordered a meal. They were able to command only the typical Spanish breakfast of a thimble-sized cup of thick black fluid, a glass of water, and a little basket of bread sticks. "From our earliest days," Dumas wrote, "we had heard of the wonderful chocolate one gets in Spain, and we hardly dared raise the cups to our lips lest this impression should vanish like so many other illusions of childhood. But no! The chocolate was excellent. Unfortunately, there was only just enough to taste."

Although the Spanish people are intensely fond of chocolate, they have not developed it as a confection in the way the Dutch, the Swiss, and some other European people have. Nor is chocolate a much-used ingredient in typical Spanish desserts. Aside from its use as a beverage, it is most likely to be found as the pungent seasoning ingredient in a veal or partridge stew, just as the Aztecs included bitter chocolate in their *mole* sauce for turkey.

The festive bird in Spain and Portugal, particularly at Christmas time, is turkey as in the United States. Many families buy their turkeys live from itinerant vendors weeks before the holiday. Thus they can fatten the turkey themselves and will be assured of a freshly killed bird for the Christmas feast. This is important in countries where neither home refrigeration nor commericial freezing is widespread.

The Portuguese and Spanish frequently bone their turkey before roasting and stuff it with a mixture that may include rice, sausage, ham, mushrooms, bread crumbs, hard-cooked eggs, and chopped livers. The turkey, which is sometimes basted with an orange sauce like that used for duck, comes to the table looking like a glistening golden football, ready to be sliced.

The tomato, native to Central America, was destined to become the sensation of southern Europe. The Spanish were quick to devise a sauce of tomato, onion, garlic, green pepper, pimento, herbs, and seasoning, which was especially good with eggs or fish and most welcome in a country where meat was not very plentiful. The Italians, too, heralded the arrival of the tomato, for here was the perfect sauce ingredient for spaghetti and other forms of *pasta*.

There is some confusion, however, regarding the dish known as "Spanish omelet." It is usually described in American cookbooks and served in American restaurants as an omelet doused with a few tablespoons of the tomato sauce described above, and then folded over on itself. While this is a perfectly good egg dish, it is not what the Iberian would call a Spanish omelet and is rarely if ever served in Spain.

To a Spaniard, an omelet is known as a *tortilla*. The Spanish *tortilla* is very different, therefore, from the thin corn-meal pancake of Mexico that goes by the same name. The Spanish *tortilla* may be a plain omelet or it may have bits of meat, vegetable, or seafood mixed with the beaten eggs before frying. Most often a *tortilla* includes diced onions and diced potatoes. It is fried crisp, golden, and nutty-flavored on both sides, in olive oil. A *tortilla de patatas* may be served as a first course at dinner, a main course at lunch or supper, or it may be taken cold to the fields or down to the sea to be eaten by the farmer or fisherman who must have his meal away from home. This is the true "Spanish omelet."

A typical Spanish egg dish that *is* prepared with tomato sauce is *huevos a la flamenco* (eggs flamenco). For this dish the sauce, possibly with bits of *chorizo* or ham in it, is spooned into small, shallow baking dishes. Eggs, broken atop the sauce, may be surrounded with cooked peas, asparagus, or fried potatoes, and the dish is then baked just until the eggs are set.

It is important, too, to distinguish between Spanish tomato sauce and the classic *salsa española,* which the French call *sauce espagnole*. Deemed one of the three or four great basic sauces from which most other sauces are prepared, *sauce espagnole* is a brown sauce prepared with meat trimmings, meat stock, vegetables including onion and carrot, but no tomato. Despite being best known by its French name, this sauce originated in Spain and came to France with Queen Ana, the Spanish wife of Louis XIII. But whatever the sauce, the Spanish say, "The best sauce is hunger and a good appetite."

Perhaps no dish shows off the tomato better than *gazpacho*, the cold soup of Spain and Portugal. In Andalusia, in southern Spain, where the sweetest sun-ripened tomatoes are grown, *gazpacho* is prepared by pounding garlic, salt, and stale bread crumbs to a paste in a wooden bowl. Puréed tomatoes, cucumbers, sweet peppers, onions, olive oil, vinegar, and seasonings are then added. Served well chilled with garnishes of fried bread croutons, diced vegetables (cucumbers, onions, peppers, tomatoes), or diced hard-cooked eggs, a *gazpacho* is the most refreshing and satisfying dish imaginable on a parching summer's day.

The name *gazpacho* is thought to come from *posca*, a vinegar-and-water drink of the Roman soldiers. A pale green *gazpacho* (consisting of thin slices of cucumber, onion, and small chunks of bread, all soaked in garlicky oil and vinegar) seems to be an earlier version of this soup, one that predates the introduction of the tomato. This type of *gazpacho* is often served in Portugal.

Whether in a sauce or salad, or served whole as *entremeses* (appetizers) stuffed with ham, anchovy, or other mixture, tomatoes seldom taste as good anywhere else as in Iberia. Even sweet jellies and marmalades are prepared from the tomato, sometimes combined with quince. Or the sweetened tomato pulp may be flavored with very thinly sliced lemon rind.

The corn of the American Indian began, in the sixteenth century, to replace other Iberian crops, particularly millet, and is today grown extensively in Spain and Portugal. Corn is seldom, however, eaten on the cob as in the United States. One reason is that no part of the corn plant is permitted to be wasted. The kernels are ground for meal, the cobs serve as fuel, the inner husks are used to stuff pillows and mattresses, and the dry outer husks serve as bedding for cattle.

The equivalent of the old-fashioned American husking bee is a regular event on the *quintas* (farms) of northern Portugal. The *esfolhada* (from the word *esfolhar*: to deleaf) is held in October. It is attended by the people of the immediate

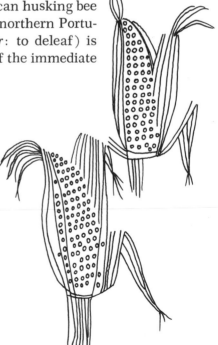

countryside and is a gay event marked by laughter, singing, and much flirtation. It is said that if a young man finds a rare red or purple ear of corn, he may kiss all the girls present; if a girl finds one, she may kiss any man she chooses.

The *esfolhada* concludes with dancing and a late supper of thick soup, wine, and *broa*, a hearty maize bread to which a little rye flour is added. In Minho, the region of northwestern Portugal where little wheat is grown, *broa* is a staple, dipped in coffee at breakfast and in soup at lunch or dinner. The most popular soup of the Portuguese Minho is *caldo verde*. This translates as "green soup," for the dish contains tall green Portuguese cabbage, finely shredded. But the basis of *caldo verde* is the South American white potato that was brought to Iberia in the sixteenth century and was later introduced to England and to Ireland, where it was to become the sustaining food of the Irish people.

While vegetables are frequently served as a separate course in Iberian meals (*before* the main dish), potatoes almost always accompany a serving of fish or meat. Nor is it unusual to be served, at the very same meal, a fish course with boiled potatoes followed by a meat course with those delicate homemade chips known in Portugal as *batatas fritas a la inglesa*. While the fried potatoes of Portugal are not really like English chips, they are beautifully crisp, flaky, and greaseless, and the Portuguese justly consider them elegant enough to be served with the important meat dish of the meal.

When pineapple first appeared in Europe, it was so highly thought of, but so scarce and so difficult to grow, that it came to be known as the "fruit of kings." Because no European climate seemed right for this tropical American fruit, pineapple had to be hothouse grown. The Azores, a group of volcanic Atlantic islands colonized by Portugal in the fifteenth century, today grow pineapples under glass, using a unique smoke method to make the plants bear fruit at any season. Smoke forcing was discovered by accident when an Azorean grower built a fire for warmth in his pineapple hothouse. Pineapples from the Azores are exported fresh, rather than canned as is so much of the Hawaiian fruit.

Fresh pineapple is often served as dessert in Portugal, sliced and drizzled with a delicate syrup.

Even an incomplete roundup of the native American foods that were introduced during the sixteenth century in Iberia reminds us of how comparatively limited European cuisine was before the time of the discoveries. As to the other riches of the discoveries—the gold and silver of the Americas, the spice trade of the Indies—no lasting benefits were brought to the people of Spain and Portugal. Much of this wealth was squandered on pomp and display, or on wars, or drained into the hands of foreign merchants who intervened in the trade between the mother country and her colonies. In Portugal, while triumphal processions rode the streets and royal diversions occupied the court, people died of hunger in the byways of Lisbon. There was a famine in 1503–1504, and this was followed by a plague in 1505.

In Spain, which at that time had the greatest empire the world had seen since Roman times, things were no better. Here, too, the wealth that should have been turned to the development of agriculture and industry was dissipated. Sheepherding, which had been a principal occupation since Moslem times, had begun to overrun former agricultural lands to the detriment of field crops. Had Spain established a thriving textile industry based on sheepherding, she might have built up her economy. But most of the wool was exported for ready profit to Flanders and Britain. These countries both processed Spain's wool and wove it into the finished product, creating employment for their people and reaping further profits. The Spanish people lived humbly during this golden era on a diet of coarse bread, sheep's- or goat's-milk cheese, wine, and *olla podrida*.

The 1800s found conditions little improved. While the aristocracy kept vast tracts of land uncultivated to be used for bull raising, itinerant peasant families roamed the countryside during the olive harvest in December and January looking for work. Wretchedly poor, they celebrated Christmas away from home and huddled in rags, with a dinner of sardines fried in olive oil. Meat and even poultry were far too costly.

The inns of the day were infamous. Meals were served at a rough wooden common table, with a knife chained to it for the use of the diners, who passed it along from one to the other. It was so widely believed that innkeepers served cat, passing it off as hare, that the phrase *"vender gato por liebre"* (to sell a cat for a hare) came into general use to describe any sort of deception.

Even today in Spanish markets, rabbit is often displayed with the furry paws left on to prove that it is not cat. Rabbit is very popular in Spain, fried, grilled, or stewed. But hare, that larger cousin of the rabbit, has never been too well liked, for it is feared that it may be rabid. Alexandre Dumas berated the Spanish for their "unaccountable age-old superstition that hares which, jugged or roasted, are so highly esteemed by us [the French], must not be served at table because they are supposed to prowl around like scavengers in graveyards." In Spain, Dumas joshed, "hares die of old age, watching Spaniards eating rabbits."

Despite thin times, the reverses and ravages of war, and the eventual loss of most of her colonial empire, Spain has retained and developed an appealing and colorful cuisine. She has also contributed to the great classic cuisine not only *sauce espagnole* but mayonnaise, which the Spanish call *salsa mahonesa*. Originally prepared with Spanish olive oil, egg yolks, and garlic, this creamy, many-purpose dressing is named after the city of Port Mahon on the Spanish island of Minorca. Non-Spanish adaptations use gentler seasonings than garlic, but the origin of mayonnaise is Spanish despite an occasional French claim to the contrary.

Still another classic dish that owes its origin to Spain is *duckling bigarade*, prepared with a sauce of the bitter Seville orange, which was native to India and was brought to Iberia by the Moslems. *Duckling bigarade*, often thought of as a French dish, is really *pato con naranjas* (duck with oranges), believed to have been brought to France in 1660 when the daughter of Philip IV of Spain married Louis XIV. Bitter oranges, often called *bigarades*, are also used to make marmalade and to flavor liqueurs such as curaçao.

Many Americans think of Spanish food as being as "hot" and spicy as Mexican food. There is, however, a distinct difference between the two. Latin-American dishes are based on the bland cornmeal, beans, and squash of the native Indian, so zestless that fierce, peppery flavors were added to give them interest. Iberian cuisine is based on a broader range of native foods, and while garlic and herbs play an important role in both Spanish and Portuguese cooking, the dishes of these countries do not sting the tongue.

What is typical Spanish cuisine? Is it the *paella* of Valencia, the roast suckling pig of Castile, or the *bacalao a la vizcaina* (dried salt cod in tomato sauce) of the Basque provinces? Spain, it has been said, is not one country, but eight or nine separate countries, each with its own dialect, customs, dances, cuisine—and some, even in modern times, with a desire for independence based on separate government.

This regionalism can be traced to Spanish geography. Spain is made up of a series of mountain ranges with craggy peaks, ringing a high central plateau that is known as the *meseta*. A fringe of lowland lies between the mountains and the seacoasts. Additional mountains and wilderness areas, radiating like the wobbly spokes of a wheel, further divide the regions surrounding the *meseta*.

Before the union of Ferdinand of Aragon and Isabella of Castile in 1469, Spain was a bevy of small kingdoms ruled by Catholic monarchs and, before that, by Moslem or Visigothic overlords. Even a hundred years after Spain's so-called unification, she was still so loosely organized that Philip II decided to move the capital to Madrid, in New Castile, since its geographical position in the very center of the country made this site a fine hub from which to rule the nation. Thus in 1561 this rather drab country town, with no waterway of any consequence, no historical, economic, or

REGIONAL CUISINES OF SPAIN AND PORTUGAL

military importance, began to develop into one of the major capitals of the world.

The regions of Old and New Castile, along with the region of León, occupy the central *meseta*. Although in ancient times Castile was crowned with thick oak forests, man later stripped this landscape, cutting lumber ruthlessly to supply and finance wars. Today—dry, dusty, and treeless, cut off by mountains and by its inland location from the tempering effects of the sea—most of Castile has scorching summers and freezing winters.

In Madrid, which at two thousand feet above sea level is the highest capital in Europe, the saying goes "nine months of winter and three months of hell." Despite the winter cold, few homes in Madrid have heat. Many depend on the *brasero*, a portable stove that burns ground olive pits or charcoal and is carried from room to room wherever it is most needed. In summer well-to-do families go to private villas or to hotels in the higher sierras outside Madrid. Or they forsake Castile entirely to bathe at San Sebastian on the Bay of Biscay, or at La Coruña on the Galician coast.

Nonetheless, Madrid with its broad avenues, innumerable plazas and fountains, and magnificent parks is a handsome city and a cosmopolitan one. Not only may regional dishes from most of Spain be sampled here, but European and American foods as well. "Snack bars" with sidewalk tables serve excellent toasted club-style sandwiches and even *perros calientes* (hot dogs), while American-type restaurants specialize in the *combinacion plato*. Such a plate might hold a "hamburger *de ternera*" (of ground veal rather than the scarcer beef), a *tortilla*, and a portion of fried *calabicines* (zucchini squash).

Probably the most typical foods of Castile are roast suckling pig and baby roast lamb. So small are these young animals that an entire piglet serves only four, and half a

baby lamb only two or three at the most, with the hind-quarter leg no larger than a moderate turkey drumstick. Due to both limited grazing land and limited cooking fuel, the Spanish long ago adopted the practice of raising small animals and of slaughtering them young. The results in terms of succulence, flavor, and delicate crispness are unlike anything one is likely to experience in the United States where larger breeds and deferred slaughtering are the rule. The *cochinillo* (suckling pig) served in Segovia, north of Madrid, is especially notable.

The poor of Castile, however, do not eat this well. Breakfast is likely to consist of *churros* bought for a few *céntimos* from the street vendor who, with a sort of pastry gun, pipes long thick ropes of dough into a cauldron of boiling olive oil. The dough quickly fries crisp and brown, and this Spanish version of the doughnut is sold in semicircles about six inches long, to be eaten with coffee.

The high cost of cooking fuel would make frying a few *churros* at home impractical. For the same reason, bread is seldom baked at home in central or southern Spain. The donkey cart from the local *panadería* makes daily deliveries of the crusted white loaves, usually shaped into rounds like pumpernickel. The peasant who has no *churro* vendor handy outside his door will probably start his day with a meal of bread dipped in olive oil.

Sheepherding and wheat growing are important occupations in Castile. Here, as in Andalusia to the south, wheat must be sown in the fall and watered by winter rains. It is harvested in summer by hand, then threshed by dragging a flinted donkey-drawn sled over the wheat. Finally, the wheat is winnowed by the age-old method of flinging the grain into the air for the wind to carry away the chaff.

The main meal of the day in Castile, if it is not a *cocido* or other stewlike mixture with snippets of meat or poultry, may quite possibly be garlic soup. This "soup of the poor" consists of garlic fried in olive oil, combined with boiling water, and poured into a bowl over bread. More prosperous families may have "lightning soup." A raw egg is placed on top of the slice of bread or toast, and the boiling-water-and-garlic mixture is poured over the egg, causing it to coagulate slightly. For those lucky enough to have some chicken or veal broth on hand, this same soup, with plump floating eggs, becomes a *consommé con huevos*.

We have already spoken of the *gazpacho* and *paella* of the southern regions, Andalusia and Valencia. Typically Mediterranean in climate, with long dry summers and rainfall mostly during the mild winters, these regions grow olives, grapes, figs, irrigated crops of oranges and melons, tomatoes and other vegetables—and in the coastal lowlands of Valencia, rice. Murcia, which lies between Andalusia and Valencia, produces saffron and is the principal date-growing region of Europe.

Andalusia's city of Granada is famous for *jamón serrano*, a dark-red ham of pungent flavor, cured in the sun upon the mountain snows of the Sierra Nevadas which loom to the south of the city. This ham is cut in very thin translucent slices and makes an excellent *tapa* with a glass of dry sherry (from Jerez de la Frontera, still another Andalusian city). Andalusia, the home of flamenco dancing, of the Spanish guitar, of the traditional bullfight costume, and of the high comb and the lace mantilla, is also the home of a large gypsy population.

In Granada the gypsies live in the Sacramonte caves, remarkable whitewashed and electrified mountainside caverns. The gypsies of Spain, like those of the rest of Europe, are believed to have come from India, drifting into Europe by way of the Balkans in the 1400s.

Traveling northward in the eastern section of Spain, we come to the region of Catalonia. Its capital is Barcelona, a Mediterranean port and a wealthy mercantile center. It was in Barcelona that the first Spanish cookbook, and surely one of the first in Europe, was printed in about 1500. Written in Catalan, the regional tongue which is a little like French Provençal, it was later translated into Castilian Spanish and is said to have been reprinted more times during its first hundred years than *Don Quixote* was during its first century. Many Catalonians still speak their native dialect at home, although Castilian Spanish is taught in the schools.

Catalonia, with its rich soil, sea-tempered climate, and prosperous European outlook has a rich cookery. Although all of Spain, including inland Madrid, is well and speedily supplied with fresh fish daily, Catalonia's *zarzuelas de pescado* or *de mariscos* (souplike stews of fish or shellfish) are outstanding.

A *zarzuela* in Spain is also an operetta with a romantic theme and light melodic music. Perhaps this name has been applied to the Catalonian fish stew because of its rhapsodic flavor. Somewhat like *bouillabaisse*, which is perhaps the most distinctive dish of nearby Mediterranean France, the Spanish *zarzuela* begins with onion, pimento, garlic, and tomatoes, lightly sautéed in olive oil. Crushed almonds and white wine are often added. The fish may include almost any variety from filets of halibut and sole to squid and the incredibly ugly monkfish.

Catalonia is also famous for its *ali-oli* (oil-and-garlic sauce) and *salsa romesco*, another garlicky sauce prepared with tomatoes and crushed toasted almonds. These are served with fish or shellfish and are potent to say the least, their recipes calling for proportions of as many as four cloves of garlic to four tablespoons of olive oil.

A refreshing beverage that is a favorite in Barcelona, and may also be found in Valencia and in Madrid, is *horchata*. This drink can be obtained at a milk bar known as a *horchatería*, but while it looks like milk and tastes of almonds, it contains neither. It is prepared from a root known as the *chufa*.

The influence of the Moslems was not strong in Catalonia, for they occupied this region for less than a hundred years. The dance of Catalonia is the *sardana*. Very different from

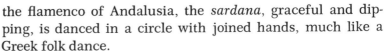

the flamenco of Andalusia, the *sardana*, graceful and dipping, is danced in a circle with joined hands, much like a Greek folk dance.

Along the Bay of Biscay, northern Spain is moist and green in contrast to the dry Mediterranean south and the harsh central region. Summers here are comfortably cool and rainy. Winters are fairly cold and damp, although roses often bloom at Christmas. In many parts of the northern coast, country people wear *zuecos*, wooden sabots, for the ground is almost always muddy.

In the Basque provinces at the eastern edge of this northern coast, food is taken so seriously that there are all-male gourmet societies—dining clubs for men only, to which wives may be invited no more than once a year. The Basques also hold eating contests at which prodigious quantities of food and wine are consumed.

Much lamb is raised on the good grazing land here, and charcoal-grilled lamb is a specialty. Even good beef is occasionally found in the north. This is a rarity throughout most of Spain, where such cuts as "bullfighter's steak" must be tenderized before cooking by marinating them in olive oil and citrus fruit juices. (Incidentally, bulls killed in the Spanish arenas are butchered and their meat is sold, but as might be expected its texture and flavor are very inferior, for this is a special type of cattle, bred strictly for the bull ring.)

A Basque specialty that has spread to the rest of Spain is *bacalao a la vizcaina. Bacalao* (dried salt codfish) is a staple in Spain, as it is in Portugal, Poland, Russia, and Japan— and was for many years in New England. To prepare it for drying, the codfish (which may be boned or not) is slit, opened out, and flattened so that the dried cods sold at market look like large, whitish flaps of leather. At home, the *bacalao* is usually beaten a dozen or so times against a hard surface to break the fibers. It is then soaked overnight, and lastly it is cooked by baking or by simmering in water.

The Basques have a great many ways of preparing *bacalao. A la vizcaina* (named for the Basque province of Vizcaya) means in a sauce of onions, garlic, pimento, and tomatoes. Often the cooked cod is shredded and made up into a pudding, a soufflé, dumplings, or into croquettes similar to New England codfish cakes or Boston codfish balls.

Another specialty of the Basque country is *angulas*, tiny silvery eel spawn, so small that a dozen fit on a teaspoon. *Angulas* are generally cooked in olive oil, garlic, and red peppers. Boiled octopus is also dressed with this sauce, while squid or the closely related cuttlefish may be cut up and fried crisp, or served in its own black ink. While this last dish has the unfortunate appearance of India ink poured over strips of white gum erasers, the flavor is appealing and the texture delicate. Octopus and squid are eaten almost everywhere in Spain.

The Basque provinces have their own language, unrelated to the Latin-derived Romance tongues spoken all around them. Basque has its own grammar, about twenty-five different dialects, and a highly complex spelling, as is demonstrated in the following family names: *Zumalcarregui, Goicoechea,* and *Azpilkoeta.* The Basques, like the Catalonians, have had independence movements in modern times. The fierce and strenuous sport of the Basques is *pelota,* a kind of handball played on a cement court enclosed on three sides, with the players wearing a long, curved basket attached to the wrist to catch and hurl the ball. Another name for *pelota* is *jai alai*, from the Basque, meaning "merry festival."

Asturias and particularly Galicia in northwestern Spain are the wettest regions of the country. While most rivers of Spain are reduced to little more than trickling streams in summer, Galicia has fjords, called *rías*, along its coast, and actually resembles parts of Norway. Asturias, the neighboring region to the east, has been compared to New England.

The Galician coast has many poor fishing villages, with the boats going out to sea each night and the men taking along their "lunches" of *tortilla de patatas*, bread, fruit, and wine. In the morning, a conch shell is blown to alert the villagers to the return of the fishing boats. The women go with plates and baskets to buy the freshly caught fish, for no wrapping will be provided. The main portion of the catch is auctioned off to commercial buyers, and the men, chilled and weary, return to their homes to sleep by day. Because life is so hard in these villages, many men leave to seek work elsewhere, often as far off as South America, and the female population remains to do much of the heavy farm work.

Seafood, as might be expected, is a specialty of Galicia, with a great many fine fish soups and stews. There is also the mouth-watering *empanada de mariscos* (seafood pie), which is served in a huge wedge, like a slab of apple pie, crammed with fish and shellfish, onions, green peppers, and pimentos. The staple soup of Galicia is *caldo gallego*, thick and hearty with kale, beans, and bacon.

Galicians speak a dialect called Gallego, which resembles Portuguese. This is not surprising since Galicia lies directly north of Portugal. Many Galicians are descended from the fair-haired blue-eyed Celts, and some look like the Scotch or Irish, just as their countryside resembles those green and misty lands.

In neighboring Asturias, the regional specialty is *fabada asturiana*, a stew of white beans and pork sausage, seasoned with garlic, and possibly including chunks of salt beef and ham. The dining ritual, as with most Spanish stews, is to make an entire two-course meal of the dish, eating first the broth (in this case, the bean soup) and then the meats and sausages. Because fat hogs are raised here, lard and salt pork are used in place of olive oil. Corn and apples are grown in Asturias, as in other parts of the northern coast, and apple cider is a favorite drink. Smoked trout caught in the local streams, and occasionally smoked bear hams (from wild bears found in the mountains), are great treats of the region.

Portugal, too, has its regional specialties—the *broa* and *caldo verde* of Minho in the verdant north; the tripe and bean dishes of Porto, whose inhabitants have long been tagged "tripe-eaters"; the succulent pork-and-clams of Alentejo, the great south-central wheat-growing region. But the over-all specialty of Portugal is fish, from good-sized grilled sardines to meaty white fish steaks bathed in a superb tomato-and-vegetable sauce.

Fish soups and fish stews abound, as does dried salt cod. Cod is still fished for every summer off the chill, fogbound Newfoundland and Greenland coasts by intrepid Portuguese fishermen. Spelled *bacalhau* in Portuguese, this staple is said

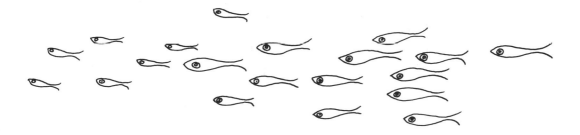

to be prepared in 125 different ways by this ingenious people. Canned fish, especially sardines, is second in importance only to cork among the country's principal exports.

Meat, as in Spain, is relatively expensive. Poor families may taste meat as infrequently as twice a year, living almost exclusively on fish, soups, and bread. A *bife* in Portugal refers to a filet cut or small steak of *any* meat—veal, pork, beef, even fresh tuna. Kid is popular, roasted or in goat's-meat stew. The black pigs of Alentejo which eat the acorns that fall from the cork oaks provide a variety of very rich, flavorful sausages. These are generally eaten in stews, omelets, and rice dishes, but seldom by the piece.

A favorite meat dish in Portugal is *iscas*, pork liver sliced into strips, marinated in wine, garlic, and herbs, and fried crisp. *Iscas* (which translates as "bait," probably because of their shape) are usually served in a casserole with pickled vegetables, fried potatoes, and fresh watercress (which is plentiful in Portugal and seems to taste better there than anywhere else).

A dish that is liked by Portuguese children, and is economical as well, is *açorda* (garlic-bread pudding). Into a bowl of broken, stale bread seasoned with salt, pepper, and chopped garlic, hot water is slowly poured until it is absorbed by the bread. Olive oil and chopped parsley are then stirred into the mixture and it is baked until a golden crust forms. Hollows are now made on the surface, and into each of these an egg is broken. The pudding is baked a little longer, just until the eggs set. Black olives are sometimes added to this dish.

Cheeses in Portugal are generally made from sheep's or goat's milk, as in Spain. These may be eaten as dessert with fruit or with *marmalada*, a firm quince jam molded in an oblong block from which servings are sliced. A Portuguese dessert similar to the Spanish custard dessert *flan* is *creme queimado* (burned cream). This dish consists of a custard baked in a mold, inverted, and decorated with an intricate design, made of caramelized sugar and cinnamon and skillfully applied with a glazing iron.

FESTIVALS OF IBERIA   Whether a Spanish *fiesta* or a Portuguese *festa*, an Iberian celebration is sure to be one of the most glittering in the world. In a land where few people get a two-week vacation with pay, own a family automobile, or have enough money to travel, the local saint's day, Holy Week, or other religious occasion is a time for pomp and processions, followed by all-out merrymaking with dancing, eating, drinking, and frequently bullfighting.

Spain's most impressive *fiesta* is undoubtedly *Semana Santa* (Holy Week), particularly as it is celebrated in Seville. From Tuesday to Good Friday, the various parish churches each send to the great cathedral in the heart of Seville a *paso,* a giant platform holding religious figures—the Virgin exquisitely garbed and radiant with jewels; a scene from the Last Supper; or a statue of *El Señor.* Each *paso,* opulently decorated, is so heavy that a multitude of men must carry it, and even so they must stop to rest frequently, so that a procession to the cathedral and back may take as long as ten hours. The streets are lined with spectators, and on Good Friday and Holy Saturday most people wear black, traffic is stilled, and places of amusement are closed as a sign of penitence and mourning.

Very soon after Easter, however, Seville breaks out in its annual *feria*. Booths and tents are set up, there are livestock shows, dancing, eating and drinking, and, of course, the bullfight season opens. The *feria* originated as the weekly fair or market that took place outside the town walls in medieval times. Many country *ferias* are still held for the purpose of buying and selling, exchanging news, and providing an opportunity for recreation. The *feria* differs from the *fiesta* in that it is not a church festival and the clergy do not officially participate. *Ferias* often run two to three days; the one at Seville lasts a week.

Another highlight of Spanish life is the great pilgrimage made every year to the city of Santiago de Compostela in Galicia. Its purpose is to visit, on July 24 and 25, the tomb of Santiago (Saint James), the patron saint of Spain. In medieval times this *fiesta* drew pilgrims from all over Europe, and Santiago was almost as great a shrine as Rome or Jerusalem. A solemn cathedral procession, violent barrages of fireworks, a parade of papier-mâché "giants" and "large heads" with painted, grinning faces, all characterize the feast of Saint James. Probably the most popular food here, equivalent to the hamburger or hot dog at an American event, is the boiled octopus in olive oil, sprinkled with red pepper, that is sold from street booths.

The very famous, albeit more subdued, pilgrimage of Portugal is that to the shrine of Fatima where on May 13, 1917, three shepherd children claimed to have seen the Virgin. She appeared to them several times again, and then for the last time on October 13. Just before these two dates, and also prior to the thirteenth of each of the summer months, the roads leading to Fatima are crowded with pilgrims, staff in hand. The women, walking gracefully, carry their travel belongings on their heads, balancing them with great ease, just as Portuguese women always do whether the burden be crockery, vegetables, or eggs.

In northern Portugal, particularly in August, there are *festa*s in almost every country town, with brilliantly costumed processions and handsome ox-drawn floats depicting the scenes of harvesting, lacemaking, woodworking, and other crafts and endeavors that make up the lives of the people.

The *romería* of Spain is a pastoral activity, generally a picnic outing with dancing and singing, to some country shrine. In Portugal this is spelled *romaria*. In both cases the word implies "going to Rome," or setting forth on a religious expedition, although a short one.

Spain's Valencia is famous for its *fallas* in mid-March. Although first created by carpenters to honor the patron saint of their trade, Saint Joseph (whose day is March 19), the *fallas* is now a sort of week-long contest and display of large, elaborately constructed wood and papier-mâché figures lampooning personalities of the day. On Saturday night, in an atmosphere of gaiety and abandon, the figures go up in flames—and on Monday morning the collection is taken up to finance next year's *fallas*.

One of the quieter and most charming customs of Spain is the *paseo* or evening stroll. After sunset, in warm weather especially, in roadside hamlet or bustling city the entire population seems to pour into the streets to promenade. In towns so small that their main street is the through road, families and young people neatly and attractively dressed walk the road oblivious to passing vehicles. In the towns and cities many stop at sidewalk cafés for cooling drinks, ice cream, or the tiny cups of black coffee served with sugar that is the standard after-dinner beverage.

Others, particularly the prim yet flirtatious young girls, simply stroll round and round the plaza, arm in arm, appearing to take no notice of the softly murmured *piropo* (compliment) of a passing youth. Here too the engaged couple, *novio* and *novia,* may walk together or sit at a café table, but they are seldom beyond the surveillance of the family group, for long engagements are very much the rule in Spain, and the betrothed pair is not usually permitted to spend time alone together.

Christmas is primarily a family and religious holiday in Iberia, with much less stress placed on the exchange of gifts than in the United States. On Christmas Eve, Portuguese families may eat a late supper of boiled codfish and potatoes, followed by a sweet rice pudding. On Christmas Day the festive dish is usually turkey with a rich stuffing. A Christmas cake made with candied fruits is served, as well as the popular small pastries and sweetmeats. In Portugal a large bean is sometimes concealed in the cake, as well as tiny gifts. The one who gets the bean must buy the cake next year.

At New Year's it is customary in both Portugal and Spain to eat twelve grapes or raisins at the twelve strokes of midnight. These are believed to bring luck for each month of the coming year.

It is impossible to leave the festivals of Iberia without mention of the bullfight, for this is not considered a sport but rather a spectacle dealing with skills and bravery. Indeed, this ritual is never called a "bullfight" in Spain, but simply a *corrida de toros* (running of the bulls). The ceremony displaying man's assertion of personal courage and of power over the beast goes back to ancient times, probably to the Minoan culture of Crete from which we have frescoes showing men vaulting and "playing" the bull.

The fighting bull is the direct descendant of the wild bulls that once roamed Iberia. His great forward weight gives added thrust to his perilously sharp horns. Six bulls are generally dispatched by three matadors at an afternoon's *corrida*. Each matador has a company consisting of picadors (horsemen who drive a long pike into the bull's shoulder muscles to weaken them), *banderilleros* (who on foot plant yard-long wooden sticks with sharp steel points, two at a time, into the bull's neck), and cape men who play the bull to test him and to divert him in time of danger. The kill, which is the province of the matador, must be well and cleanly done. If it is an exceptionally good kill, the matador may be awarded an ear of the bull, and in some cases, both ears and the tail.

Many people condemn bullfighting because of its danger and cruelty. But one need only look at British fox hunting, or American prize fighting (through which many men have died), to realize that other countries, too, have legally and socially sanctioned activities that may be open to question.

Nor is the "sport" of hunting a defenseless animal with a gun a fair contest.

Until the late 1600s, only noblemen fought the bull. Mounted on a fast, spirited horse, the rider repeatedly speared the bull with a lance until it was near death. The bull was then finished off by lackeys. Royal displeasure gradually did away with this practice, but it gave rise to the professional bullfighter, usually from the lower classes, who fought the bull on foot.

In Portugal today the bull is still fought on horseback, in an exhibition of grace and skill by both rider and horse. But in Portugal the bull is never killed. Instead he is subdued and finally brought to a halt in somewhat comic fashion by a group of bold *campinos* (cowboys), some riding his horns (which are blunted and padded), others jumping on his back or tugging at his tail. This symbolic overpowering of the bull concludes the exhibition and the bull is led away in the company of a herd of young bulls ushered into the arena for this purpose.

In Vila Franca da Xira, in Portugal's bull-raising country, it is customary to turn the bulls loose to run through barricaded streets just before the *corrida,* giving amateurs the opportunity to try their skills. In Spain, too, such brave but foolhardy skirmishes take place every July at the week-long Festival of San Fermín in Pamplona. As the bulls are driven from the station to the bull ring through a street route marked off with wooden barriers, hundreds of young men run this same route only a snort ahead of the charging bulls. Each year some are gored or trampled, while the populace looks on from balconies and upper-story windows. This is followed by a solemn procession bearing the statue of San Fermín as well as colorful and grotesque papier-mâché figures, and then by dancing and merrymaking—for, after all, San Fermín comes but once a year.

IBERIAN DINING CUSTOMS, MENUS, AND RECIPES

Dining hours in Spain, especially in the larger towns and in the cities, are always something of a shock to the visitor. Breakfasts are small, whether a *churro* and coffee or a cup of thick chocolate and a sweet roll with jam. No Spaniard would dream of eating eggs for breakfast, much less pancakes or hot oatmeal. Nor is fruit juice generally a part of the morning meal except at hotels catering to tourists. Oranges, although they grow luxuriantly in Spain, seldom appear as morning orange juice. They are usually eaten as a dessert fruit that the native Spaniard expertly peels and slices at table with his knife and conveys to his mouth with his fork.

Although breakfast is eaten quite early, lunch is seldom served before two in the afternoon, and sometimes as late as three or even four. This is generally the main meal of the day and is followed by a siesta. Business hours for offices and shops in Spain are usually from nine to one-thirty, and from three-thirty or four-thirty to seven or eight, depending on the time of year, with the longer siesta and later closing hour in summer. In Portugal, too, there is a long lunch-hour closing, so that it is customary in both countries for people to go home for lunch if at all possible.

During the long morning between early breakfast and two-o'clock lunch, most Spaniards stave off hunger by nibbling on the toasted sunflower seeds, pine nuts, and other tidbits that are sold on every street corner. Some Spanish business offices observe the custom of *las onces* ("elevenses"), having rolls or *tapas* and beer or other beverage brought in at about eleven o'clock.

The evening meal resembles lunch, but since it is often preceded by apéritifs of sherry or beer with *tapas,* and since most families have already had their principal meal of the day, it is quite likely to consist only of soup and perhaps an omelet. This meal may be served at nine or nine-thirty. Theaters and cinemas, therefore, usually schedule a seven o'clock pre-dinner performance and a ten forty-five after-dinner performance.

In large cities such as Madrid it is considered unfashionable to eat dinner before ten or ten-thirty, or even eleven, and dinner is often followed by leisurely coffees or brandies at a café. Foreign visitors who marvel at the Spaniard's capacity for keeping late hours and yet reporting promptly for work the next morning overlook the value of the midday siesta. This schedule is not, of course, characteristic of the farms and simple villages, where late hours are not kept and life is still lived by the sun.

The preparation of the large midday meal is likely to occupy the mistress of the house for the greater part of each day, beginning with the early morning. This is surely one reason for the late hour at which this meal is served. For one thing, almost all food is purchased fresh each day. Except for the luxury-class *supermarcados* in the larger cities (where canned and frozen products are featured), most food shopping is done at open markets, markets as gay and as gorgeous as flower stalls.

Here are vegetables and fruits all freshly picked and as accurate as the calendar in revealing the season—wild strawberries and white asparagus in spring; fresh figs, peaches, purple-bronze eggplants, ruddy pomegranates, sweet peppers, artichokes, and, as the summer progresses, grapes in many varieties, sweetly perfumed melons, and small round watermelons with fiery red flesh and delicate, papery texture. Prickly pears, too, appear in late summer, so sweet that one immediately craves water. Women vendors often sell these in the streets standing behind their baskets, one of fruit and one of peelings, knife in hand, idly removing thorns from their fingers as they await customers.

Fish are a miracle of freshness, even hundreds of miles from the sea, for the catch is rushed inland daily. Red mullet resting on vine leaves, ringed with silvery sardines and edged with a ruffle of shrimp, makes a worthy still life at any Spanish or Portuguese fish stall. Here, too, are spiny pink creatures of the sea, tentacled gray squid, and hefty tuna sliced up like beef.

Meat markets are perhaps the least attractive, for they often display entire carcasses, the butcher being reluctant to cut these up too far in advance, for meat may not sell readily due to its high cost and there is the refrigeration problem. Poultry is usually kept live in the more rural markets and sold live or slaughtered to order.

Thus the gathering of the ingredients for a meal is a slow process that must be repeated each day. But the indescribable quality of freshly picked and freshly caught foods adds greatly to the savor of Iberian meals.

A midday meal in Spain is likely to begin with *entremeses* (hors d'oeuvres or appetizers) or soup. On festive occasions both *entremeses* and soup may be served. Foods served as *entremeses* and as *tapas* are frequently interchangeable, but usually the latter are finger foods to be eaten conveniently with drinks, while *entremeses* either hot or cold are designed to be eaten with a fork. A variety of *entremeses* might include rings of fried squid, tiny meat balls, crusty little finger-shaped cakes of shredded *bacalao* and mashed potatoes, *chorizo* or other sausage or cold meat, anchovies, *bonito* (tuna), and cold raw or cooked vegetables in a

piquant sauce or dressing. In Portugal hors d'oeuvres of a similar nature are termed *acepipes*.

The next course consists of a fish, egg, or vegetable dish—or a *paella* might be served at this time, particularly at a Sunday dinner. The meat course follows—veal, lamb, pork, poultry, or parts such as liver, kidneys, brains, or tongue, usually served with potatoes. If no meat is to be served at the meal, an egg or vegetable course will usually be followed by a fish course.

Dessert at a family dinner usually consists of a variety of cheese, such as the popular ewe's-milk *manchego* (from La Mancha in Castile), and fresh fruit in season. On special occasions, a sweet such as *flan* (custard), *budín de pan* (bread pudding, called *pudim de pão* in Portugal), or *tarta* (cream-filled spongecake) will be served instead of cheese. The meal will close with fresh fruit which, incidentally, is never eaten out of the hand in Spain and Portugal. The fruit is dipped into a bowl for washing, then pared and sliced on the plate and eaten with the fork.

Beverages such as milk, tea, or coffee do not usually appear at the family dinner. In restaurants and hotels, black coffee served in small cups may be ordered from the bar (it is not a kitchen item), but many people prefer to go on to a café for this after-dinner beverage. Dry table wine, red or white, accompanies the meal and may even be given, sometimes diluted, to children. A midday meal in Portugal follows the same pattern as in Spain.

A Typical Spanish Menu

Entremeses   or   *Gazpacho*   or   *Sopa de Garbanzos*

*

Merluza al horno   or   *Huevos a la flamenca*
(Baked Hake)   (Eggs Flamenco)
or *Alcochafas salteadas*
(Sautéed Artichokes)

*

Chuletas de cerdo   or   *Rinones de ternera al jerez*
(Pork Chops)   (Veal Kidney in Sherry)

*

Flan   or   *Queso manchego*
(Custard)   (Cheese of La Mancha)
Frutas del tiempo
(Fresh Fruit in Season)

A Typical Portuguese Menu

Acepipes   or   *Caldeirada a pescadora*
(Fish Soup)

*

Linguado grelhado   or   *Omeleta de tomate*
(Grilled Sole)   (Tomato Omelet)

*

Iscas or *Bifes de porco*
(Marinated Fried Liver) (Filets of Pork)

*

Pudim de pão or *Queijo com marmalada*
(Bread Pudding) (Cheese with Quince Jam)
Ananás
(Fresh Pineapple)

Spanish and Portuguese Recipes

GAZPACHO

(*Spain*)

6 medium-sized very ripe tomatoes
1 cucumber, pared
1 green pepper, cut in chunks and seeded
1 small onion
2 medium cloves garlic
1 heel of dry bread (or medium-sized roll)
¼ cup olive oil
3 tablespoons red wine vinegar
2 teaspoons salt
¼ teaspoon freshly ground black pepper
⅛ teaspoon liquid hot-pepper seasoning (Tabasco sauce)
1 cup cold water

Cut out stem ends of tomatoes. Put tomatoes, cucumber, green pepper, onion, garlic, and dry bread through the fine blade of a food chopper. Set a strainer over a large bowl and put the ground mixture through the strainer, pressing out as much liquid as possible. Retain the mash in the strainer.

Add the remaining ingredients to the liquid in the bowl. Now add to this mixture, a tablespoon at a time, enough of the mash from the strainer to obtain a soup that is the consistency of thick cream. Discard the rest of the mash.

Chill the *gazpacho* and serve it with accompanying bowls of the following garnishes: diced cucumber, diced green pepper, diced onion or scallion, diced tomatoes, and croutons. To prepare the croutons, trim crusts from 4 slices of white bread, cut the bread into ⅜-inch dice, and fry golden in a mixture of 2 tablespoons of olive oil and 1 minced clove of garlic. Makes 6 servings.

TORTILLA DE PATATAS

(*Potato Omelet—Spain*)

3 tablespoons olive oil
1 small onion, diced small
1 medium-large potato, diced small
    Salt and pepper
2 eggs

Heat 2 tablespoons of the olive oil to medium hot in an 8-inch frying pan. Add the onion and the potato, cover the pan, and cook over low heat until tender. They should not brown. Add salt and pepper to taste. Remove from heat and cool slightly.

Add 2 tablespoons of water to the eggs and beat well. Add the potatoes and onions to the egg mixture. Clean the frying pan, add and heat the remaining tablespoon of olive oil. When it is medium hot add the egg mixture. When the omelet has fried crisp and golden on the bottom, invert a plate over the skillet, turn the omelet out onto the plate, and slide it, moist side down, back into the skillet to cook golden on the other side.

Serve hot. The *tortilla* may be sprinkled with finely cut fresh parsley. To serve as two separate omelets, divide the mixture in half and cook in two 6-inch frying pans. Makes 2 servings.

ARROZ CON POLLO

(*Rice with Chicken—Spain*)

     1   large broiling or frying chicken (3 to 3½ pounds)
         Salt
         Pepper
         Flour
     1   tablespoon olive oil
     1   tablespoon butter
     1   medium onion, cut fine
     1   clove garlic, minced
     1   medium green pepper, cut in 1-inch squares
    ¾   cup long-grain rice
     1   1-pound can tomatoes, or 3 very ripe fresh tomatoes, skinned and cut in chunks
    1½   cups hot chicken stock, or 2 chicken bouillon cubes dissolved in 1½ cups boiling water
    ½   teaspoon saffron
     2   tablespoons dry sherry (optional)
     2   bay leaves
     2   tablespoons diced pimento-stuffed green olives
    ½   10-ounce package frozen green peas
     1   small jar pimentos

Cook this dish in a large, deep skillet or chicken fryer that has a tight-fitting lid.

Cut chicken in eighths. Wash chicken pieces and dry thoroughly. Sprinkle with salt and pepper. Dust lightly with flour. In a large skillet heat the olive oil and butter to sizzling. Add the chicken pieces in a single layer, skin side down. Brown lightly. Turn pieces and brown other side. Remove chicken pieces and set aside.

Add onion, garlic, and green pepper to skillet. (If necessary, add 1 more tablespoon olive oil before adding vegetables.) Cook the vegetables lightly and add the rice. Cook, stirring, a few minutes longer, or until rice grains are translucent. Add the tomatoes.

Add saffron to hot chicken stock and let steep a few minutes. Add stock, sherry, bay leaves, olives, and green peas to skillet. Blend ingredients and arrange chicken pieces in skillet. Cover and cook over low heat until rice and chicken are tender, about 35 to 40 minutes.

Just before serving, arrange slices of drained pimento atop chicken and rice. *Arroz con pollo* may be served from the utensil in which it was cooked or transferred to a heated serving dish. Makes 4 to 6 servings.

CALDO VERDE

(*Green Cabbage Soup—Portugal*)

    3   medium potatoes, pared and cut in large cubes
    1   medium onion, peeled and cut in large cubes
    3½ cups water
    2   tablespoons olive oil
    1½ teaspoons salt
    ¼   teaspoon white pepper
    2   cups very finely shredded green cabbage leaves

In Portugal, this soup is made with the tall, leafy loose-headed Portuguese cabbage that is a little different from the white hard-headed cabbage grown in the United States. Use only the tender, green outer leaves for *caldo verde*.

Combine in a large saucepan the potatoes, onion, water, and olive oil. Boil 30 to 40 minutes, or until vegetables are very tender. Purée by putting the entire mixture through a strainer.

Add seasonings and cabbage, and simmer just until cabbage is limp and beginning to be tender, no more than 10 minutes. Adjust seasonings and serve hot. Makes 6 servings.

PUDIM DE PÃO

(*Bread Pudding—Portugal*)

    ½   cup sugar
    2   cups milk
    6   tablespoons sugar
    1   tablespoon grated orange rind
    2   tablespoons butter
    2   cups very finely crumbled, crustless white bread (6 to
        7 slices)
    4   eggs

Use a fine-textured good quality bread rather than a puffy, elastic white bread for best results in this dessert.

Pour the ½ cup sugar into a heavy pan and caramelize it by stirring it with a wooden spoon over medium-high heat until it has become a light golden-brown liquid. Pour the caramel into the 1½-to-2-quart mold or baking dish in which the pudding is to be baked. Tilt the mold quickly to spread the caramel evenly over the bottom.

Combine the milk, the 6 tablespoons of sugar, and the grated orange rind in a saucepan. Heat until the mixture scalds (tiny bubbles will appear around the edge). Add the butter and the finely crumbled bread. Remove from heat and cool slightly.

Beat the eggs. Add the milk and bread mixture and blend thoroughly. Turn into the caramelized mold. Set the mold into a pan containing an inch or more of hot water. Bake at 350 degrees for 45 to 50 minutes, or until a sharp knife inserted into the center of the pudding comes out clean.

Cool *pudim de pão* thoroughly. Loosen edges with a sharp, thin knife, place an inverted plate over the mold, and turn over. Jolt to release pudding, if necessary. Chill. Generously spoon caramel sauce remaining in pan over individual serving portions. Makes 6 to 8 servings.

Italy

O THER COUNTRIES border the Mediterranean; Italy
appears to immerse herself in it. The boot dangles
far into the blue waters of the inland sea, creating thereby
two large watery inlets—the Tyrrhenian Sea on Italy's long
west coast and the Adriatic on the east coast. But both of
these are one with the Mediterranean expanse. Seagirt as
she is, Italy has no land point on the "leg" of the peninsula
that is more than sixty-five miles from one of the surrounding waters.

Like the Iberian Peninsula, which is separated from the
rest of Europe by the Pyrenees, Italy is marked off by the
barrier of the Alps, the peaks of which stand like sentinels
on her northern border. Although the Alpine heights did not

prove impassable to Hannibal in the third century B.C. or to the barbarian hordes that overwhelmed Rome in the fifth century A.D., it is interesting to note that English land travelers to Italy in the eighteenth century were always much relieved once the Alps were well behind them. The practice in those days was to detach the traveling coaches and transport them over the passes on muleback. The passengers meantime, wrapped in furs and strapped into armchairs, were carried across the difficult heights by fearless mountain people.

The Italian peninsula, because of this Alpine barrier, has tended to look seaward rather than landward, so it is not surprising that the Roman civilization, and the Etruscan before it, developed on Italian shores with their command of the Mediterranean and of the lands accessible from that sea. The Mediterranean, which in the twelfth century B.C. had been termed a "Phoenician lake," became known in Roman times as *Mare Nostrum* ("Our Sea") for at the height of the Empire, Rome ruled the entire Mediterranean shoreline from Iberia to Asia Minor, and from the Middle East to western North Africa. Using these territories as springboards, she went even farther, penetrating northward to Britain and eastward to the Persian Gulf.

This greatest of empires since the beginning of time was, in the second century A.D., equivalent in size to about five-sixths of the United States. It included people of many races, religions, and national backgrounds. It sent Roman roads and bridges, law and language, architecture and agriculture, into the hinterlands, and it saw the birth and establishment of Christianity. Although the empire was doomed to eventual disintegration, Rome left something indelible of itself in every land from which it exacted tribute.

The founding of Rome by the twin brothers Romulus and Remus is legendary. Nevertheless the year 753 B.C. has been assigned to this imaginary event. While the true origin of Rome is uncertain, we do know that at about that time Rome was a small farming community with a fortified marketplace, situated on the Tiber River. The Etruscans who lived to the north of the Tiber extended their rule over Rome and held it until the 500s B.C., at which time the Romans drove out the Etruscans and established a republic. The Roman republic, now a city rather than a village, was destined to expand steadily and to become, in its mightiest and final phase, the Roman Empire.

"Let the Alps sink," Cicero had exclaimed soon after Caesar's conquest of Gaul; "the gods raised them to protect Rome from the barbarians, but now they are no longer needed." In 27 B.C. Octavian, adopted son of the murdered Caesar, took the name of Augustus and became the first Roman emperor.

Augustus, unlike most of his successors, lived frugally, and being of a sickly constitution, or perhaps merely a hypochondriac, restricted his diet to bread, fruit, cheese, and fish. He lived to be seventy-seven, his reign marked by peace, progress, and the expansion of the Roman economy.

MORNING, NOON, AND NIGHT IN IMPERIAL ROME

The visitor to modern Rome is likely to think of this great noisy city with its vigorous street life and frantic vehicular traffic as a far cry from the placid wide thoroughfares, the white marble edifices, and the distinguished toga-clad citizens of first- and second-century Rome. He is, however, mistaken. Imperial Rome had a population of a million and a half crowded into a small geographical area. Like modern Manhattan, it was in many ways a vertical city, for the

favorable land area was severely limited and, to make matters worse, there was no system of public transportation.

Tenement-like buildings called *insulae* rose five and six stories; their flats of cubicles, reached via stairways from an interior court, housed most of Rome's citizens. Like the early tenement buildings of New York, many were hastily and shoddily constructed and offered hazardous dwelling conditions. The *insulae* of Rome were built of wood and concrete, and almost every day reports of another fire or building collapse circulated through the city.

Streets, except for a few main routes, were mere lanes so thronged with humanity that vehicular traffic, except for the carts of contractors engaged in building and wrecking, was prohibited during daylight hours. Most people rose at dawn to make full use of natural light, for artificial lighting was primitive at best and there was no public street lighting.

Breakfast (*ientaculum*) was a light meal. Many people took only water on rising. Others ate bread dipped in wine, or bread with honey. Cheese and a few olives, or a handful of raisins, might be added to the meal. The kitchens in the homes of the wealthy had their own bake ovens and a hearth of masonry equipped with a grid for grilling, a spit for roasting, and a crossbeam from which kettles could be suspended. The fire was of charcoal, and a great variety of cooking utensils of copper and bronze were at hand.

In the *insulae*, cooking facilities were very different, for not even the simple fireplace of the rudest country dwelling was practicable here. Cooking was done over an open stove similar to the portable outdoor grill of modern times. This brazier, which could also be carried from room to room to provide heat, created a permanent atmosphere of smoke and was the cause of many of the fires that burned the *insulae* to the ground. Needless to say, none of the *insulae* had central heating, although the private dwellings of wealthy citizens and the rooms of the public baths were warmed by a beneath-the-floor furnace known as a *hypocaust* that piped heat to the rooms directly above through hollow tiles.

Although Rome had an excellent water supply because of its aqueducts, again it was only the ground-level dwellings, public baths, and fountains that received the direct benefits of it. *Insulae* dwellers had to fetch their water at the public fountain and carry it upstairs to their apartments.

Rome's public sewers were also commendable, but only the homes of the wealthy and the public latrines were connected to the sewer systems. At a minimal cost the poor could use the public latrines, but many chose to carry their chamber pots and other refuse to a disposal trench, while others dumped them unceremoniously from their windows —a forerunner of life in the medieval cities.

Few among the more humble citizens washed in the mornings, for they would go off later to the public baths that were open to everyone. For the wealthy who resided in the private dwelling (*domus*) with its gardens, its rich decoration, and interior plumbing, the elaborate morning toilette administered by members of the household staff was a ritual. Most Romans, however, went almost daily to the barbers who plied their trade in the streets. Here they had their hair curled with a hot iron and (during the long period in ancient Rome when it was fashionable to go beardless) were shaved with a dangerous razor-like instrument.

While working people went off at an early hour to their various callings, many Romans idled in the streets all day, for a sizable portion of the citizenry was on the bread dole and needed only occasional earnings to subsist. Visitors from all parts of the Empire roamed the city in wonderment, and the hangers-on of the rich strolled about when they were not dancing attendance on their patrons. In addition, money-changers, trinket sellers, schoolmasters and their pupils, coppersmiths and stonemasons all conducted their affairs in the open streets. Cookshops, wineshops, bakeries, and cheap restaurants were everywhere—and the human clamor, to judge from the writers of the day, was almost as bad as the motorized clamor of present-day Rome.

Lunch (*prandium*) was a rather light meal of cold meat or eggs, cheese, fruit, and wine. It was eaten at about noon. In the homes of the idle rich, lunch might be heavier and more elaborate and was often followed by a siesta. The rest of the afternoon was spent at the public baths where the appetite for dinner would be stimulated by sports, games, and gymnastics topped off with successive plunges into pools of hot, warm, and cold water.

The poor and the street crowds often bought lunch at the cookshops where cauldrons of stew or the boiled porridge of lentils, peas, or beans known as *pulmentarium* steamed over charcoal fires. The food was served in little cups dipped directly into the cauldrons and was eaten on the spot, standing up. Hot sausages were also for sale at the cookshops; and bread in flat round loaves about two inches thick, ranging in quality from fine to coarse, was always to be had at the baker's.

POSCA

At hot-drink establishments known as *thermopolia* one could obtain *calda*, a spiced wine-and-water beverage that was popular in cold weather. The soldiers and the very poor, including the slaves, drank *posca*, a mixture of vinegar and water. *Posca* is said to have been the drink offered to Jesus on the Cross.

There were no public dining places in Rome that came anywhere near meeting the lavish standards of the aristocracy. Although somewhat better restaurants sent vendors to the public baths with trays of sausages, eggs, and sweet cakes to be offered for sale to habitués of the special rooms devoted to relaxation and recreation, the inns and restaurants of Rome were on the whole crude and dirty. The wealthy dined only in their own homes or in the homes of friends.

Dinner (*cena*) was the serious meal and the high point of the day. It usually began at four in the afternoon and, if it was a banquet with invited guests, lasted at least three or four hours. A really ostentatious banquet might go on until dawn, and these have been so vividly recorded that one can easily fall into the error of assuming that all Roman dinners were prolonged gluttonous affairs.

On the contrary, the ordinary dinner of the poor was a meal of salt fish or goat's meat, bread, olive oil, and wine mixed with water. For the more prosperous there were eels or pike caught in the Tiber, or shellfish transported live in tanks from the sea seventeen miles away. The very wealthy had fresh mullet or turbot brought inland by wagon transport or by slave runners, at enormous expense. In addition, dinner might include pork or poultry, rabbit, hare, or venison. Beef was not popular, as it posed the problem of preserving a large quantity of fresh meat in a warm climate. Asparagus was a favorite Roman vegetable. Lettuce, cucumbers, beets, cabbage, radishes, and turnips were all plentiful. Dessert at an everyday dinner would be fruit such as apples, pears, grapes, or figs. Pastry or small cakes might appear if the family had one or more slave-cooks.

On non-festive occasions, the citizens of Rome retired at dark or soon after, for going about in the narrow unlit streets was considered dangerous. Nor was it very long before sleep was broken by the increasing rumble of wagons to which the streets were forbidden by day—a sound that grew louder as the night progressed and ceased only at dawn.

ROMAN COOKS, GLUTTONS, AND BANQUET GIVERS

One of the very first cookbook writers and teachers of cookery was a Roman, Marcus Apicius. He lived during the early days of the Empire and set such an example of opulence in his own banquet giving that, having squandered a fortune, he committed suicide rather than go on living in a style less grand than that to which he had become accustomed. The ostentation and gastronomic excesses of Apicius, and of the Roman emperors and other nobles who were his disciples, could only have flourished in a Rome that was both immensely rich in food resources and liberally supplied with slave labor.

As the Romans conquered the lands about them, they took slaves. By the second century A.D., roughly half the city's population was slave. The remainder consisted of freedmen (former slaves), ordinary citizens (plebeians), and first- and second-class nobles (senators and equites). Slaveowners held from ten to two hundred slaves in their city houses, and many more on their country estates. Most highly esteemed and commanding enormous prices at market (particularly from the time of Apicius) were those slaves who were expert cooks and pastry chefs.

In the early days of the republic, even prosperous Romans had lived contentedly on simple foods like those of the Greeks—bread, wheat porridge, green vegetables, and the fruits of the vine and the olive tree (which the Greeks had brought to Italy). Meat such as pork and lamb was usually reserved for feast days or special occasions when there had been a public sacrifice. As Roman power grew, however, food supplies not only increased but became more varied. There were dates and pomegranates from North Africa, plums from Syria, pepper and ginger from India, sausages and venison from Gaul, wheat from Egypt, and oil from Spain.

Non-perishable foods were stored in tall concrete warehouses on the outskirts of the city, and Rome became the grain storage center and the fancy pantry of the world. She was never to know, of course, certain foods that existed beyond her realm—the potato and the tomato, oranges, lemons, and other citrus fruits; and, as had the Greeks, the Romans used olive oil instead of butter, and honey in place of sugar.

The cookbooks attributed to Apicius gave recipes for innumerable new dishes, for the seasoning and saucing of foods, and for savory morsels, cakes, and sweetmeats to tempt even the most jaded of appetites. Revised and rewritten, tattered survivors of the Teutonic invasions and of the fall of Rome, the Apician recipes were somehow preserved and passed on through the centuries. A printed edition of a cookbook said to contain genuine Apician writings was published in Milan in 1498.

A popular seasoning of Apicius' time, although not necessarily of his invention, was *garum*, which has been called the Roman soy sauce. Although onions, garlic, salt, and spices were all available in imperial Rome, flavorings and sauces of new piquancy were constantly in demand. To prepare *garum*, the Romans salted small whole fish along with the gills, the intestines and other internal parts of larger fish. These were then allowed to sit in the sun in an

open vat for several days until the mixture had putrefied. The liquid from this compound was then strained off and was blended to taste with spices and herbs, wine, honey, vinegar, and oil.

Garum, which probably had a biting anchovy-like tang, was used freely on fish, flesh, and fowl by the rich as well as by the less prosperous. It was available in many grades. The finest *garum* was said to come from Spain and was prepared from mackerel. But excellent imitations of Spanish *garum* were made in Italy, particularly at Pompeii.

The setting for the Roman banquet was the *triclinium* or dining room, which took its name from the couches or *triclinia*, each with three reclining places, on which the guests reposed. The Roman custom of lying crosswise while dining, sandals off, feet at the foot of the couch, and left elbow resting on a pillow, seems to us highly uncomfortable. It was also a most inefficient position from which to convey food to the mouth, and required constant attendance by servants.

While guests at a Roman banquet were provided with ivory-handled knives and spoons (dining forks were unknown), most food was taken with the fingers, and eating was a sloppy affair even among the elite and the delicately bred. To preserve the costly silks and gold embroidery of the richly inlaid couches, decorative coverlets were spread upon them. To increase their own comfort while dining, the guests put aside their togas and donned a special loose-fitting gauzy garment, gay in color, called the *synthesis*. This they wore directly over their tunics, sometimes changing one *synthesis* for another between courses.

Although the guests were provided with napkins, and even had their hands washed frequently with perfumed water by the slaves who passed among them, it was not unusual for a guest to bring his own napkin as well. In this he generally took away tidbits from the banquet—a practice that was not considered bad manners. Toothpicks, freely distributed and used at Roman banquets, were sometimes of silver. But the jewel-encrusted drinking goblets had to be watched lest the guests pluck out the gems with their finger-nails.

The standard number of diners at a banquet was nine. In royal or very wealthy domiciles, additional *triclinia* and tables were brought in to accommodate twenty-seven guests or even thirty-six. The extremely wealthy upstart, Trimal-chio, was said to have had five dining rooms, the guests often shifting from one to another for the various courses at a banquet. A moderately wealthy noble might have two, a summer and a winter *triclinium*, both richly decorated with painted walls, marble columns, statuary, and sideboards laden with silver serving pieces.

In a satire by the Roman writer Petronius of a feast given by Trimalchio, the ceiling appeared to crack open and "a vast circle was let down, all round which hung golden garlands and alabaster pots of sweet ointments." Between courses, at most banquets, there was entertainment—jugglers and buffoons, mimes and acrobats, dancers, musicians, and even gladiators were sometimes engaged to perform before the diners. Such banquets lasted eight to ten hours. Belching was considered polite, a sign that the host had fed his guests well. More violent reactions to overeating were also com-

monly indulged in at the Roman banquet, thus permitting the diner to begin feasting all over again. Women sometimes attended banquets, particularly from the time of Augustus on, and those who did were reported to be no more delicate in their manners than the men.

The Emperor Vitellius, who reigned for less than a year in A.D. 69, was said to have eaten four hearty meals a day, made possible through his use of emetics. So extravagant were his requirements that none dared offer him a banquet valued at less than $16,000. Peacocks' brains and flamingoes' tongues, supplied in the thousands at enormous cost, gratified the wasteful gluttony of this man who was a culinary disciple of Apicius. Nor were these tidbits more than side dishes at the meals he ingested.

Lucullus, who was for a time the Roman governor of a province in Asia, was another lavish host and diner. He so enriched himself with spoils that when he returned to Rome he dwelt in a mansion with several dining rooms, vast gardens, well-stocked fish ponds, and pens in which he bred thrushes and other small birds for the table. He bequeathed to posterity the "Lucullan feast," any meal of great magnificence, and is also said to have introduced cherries from Asia to Italy, and thus to all of western Europe.

After the spendthrift procurement of such morsels as the brains and tongues of birds, the principal achievement of the Roman table was decoration and disguise in the presentation of foods. At Trimalchio's feast, fattened dormice were "strewed over with honey and poppy [seeds]," a hog was artfully fashioned into a "fat goose, with fishes and all kind of fowl round it," and a roast boar was discovered to have its belly full of live blackbirds which, when released by the

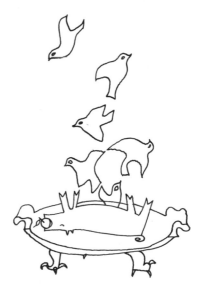

stroke of a knife, flew about the room. These same birds were then caught, "baked in a good pie crust with raisins and chestnuts," and served up later in the meal.

The opening course at the Roman banquet was the *gustus* or *gustatio*. Here were presented the hors d'oeuvres or, more properly, the *antipasti* of ancient Rome—oysters, mussels, caviar, fried snails, pickled vegetables, sausages, eggs, and other appetizers designed to whet the appetite (although these probably amounted to a meal by any but Roman standards). With the *gustus,* wine mixed with honey and spices was served.

The ancient Romans appeared to like their wine sweet or, at the very least, diluted with water. It was seldom taken unmixed. A very good reason for this was that Roman wines, like those of ancient Greece, had a strong flavor from the pitch or resin that was smeared inside the earthenware wine jars to act as a sealer.

The courses that followed the *gustatio* were known as the *mensae primae.* They might include eels, lamprey, mullet, lobster, and other fish and shellfish; birds ranging from songbirds to peacocks, ducks, and other fowl; roast pig, venison, and wild boar. Most of these were accompanied by vegetables in intricate presentations.

The dessert courses, or *mensae secundae,* included pastries, tarts, and "cheesecakes" (which were probably sweet custards of milk and eggs), as well as figs, dates, nuts, apples, grapes, and other fruits. Wine was served throughout the meal. In winter it was often served warm; in summer it was chilled in snow brought down from the Apennines.

A really gala banquet did not end at this point, for now came the *epidipnis,* an aftercourse of savories such as cheeses, pâtés, and hot shellfish. With these savories, for which the guests were often ushered into another dining room, the drinking of wine took on a more intensive aspect known as the rites of the *commissatio.* This was a drinking match at which the amount, the manner, and the order of drinking were prescribed by a master of ceremonies especially appointed for the occasion.

Such a bout often continued until cockcrow—and as the guests reached the end of their endurance and made ready to depart, they called for their sandals, the sign that they were leaving the table, or rather the couches upon which they now heavily reclined. Taking their leave, they wended their way home through the already livening streets, escorted in most cases by their own servants who had arrived with them and remained to attend them throughout the banquet.

FESTIVALS OF THE ROMAN POPULACE

While the wealthy indulged in every known luxury of the day, the common folk of Rome were treated to public spectacles at government expense. The offering of free entertainment along with the free bread and grain supplies, the dried fish and oil that were doled out to the poor in the tens of thousands, led the satirical poet Juvenal to coin the phrase *"panem et circenses."* Bread and circuses were, indeed, deemed by the rulers of Rome to fulfill the needs of the mob.

In the huge oblong arena called the *circus*, thrilling chariot races were held, while in the great amphitheater that was the Colosseum, gladiators were pitted against wild beasts or against other gladiators, and Christians and condemned criminals were thrown to the lions and other man-eaters. The crowd seems thoroughly to have enjoyed these cruel and vicious practices, its thirst for blood increasing with each new savagery.

The Colosseum itself was a marvel of engineering. Beneath the level of the sand-covered arena the animals were kept in cages that were elevated to the surface by slave-operated machinery, and the arena itself could be flooded for the mock naval battles known as *naumachia*. The theater, too, was popular with the Roman populace, particularly low farce, masked dancing, acrobats, and the feats of magicians.

While there was no prescribed day of rest in the Roman calendar, such as the ancient Hebrew Sabbath or the later Christian Sabbath, the Roman people at the time of Claudius (A.D. 41–54) are said to have had 159 holidays in a year, 93 of which were devoted to government-sponsored diversions.

A gay Roman festival was the Saturnalia in honor of Saturn, the Roman harvest god. Beginning on December 17 and lasting seven days, the Saturnalia included religious sacrifices of young hogs, family banqueting, pranks and merrymaking, and the exchange of small terra-cotta images, many in the shape of sweetmeats and other foods.

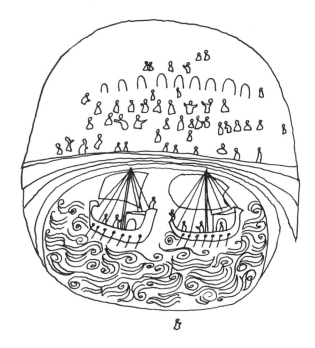

New Year's was a more solemn occasion. The first day of the Roman year honored Janus, the god of gates and doors, of beginnings and endings. It was after this god that the month of January was named. Janus had two faces, one for looking backward and one for looking ahead. On this day people exchanged gifts of some value, and many were careful to ingratiate themselves with the emperor and senators by presenting them with impressive tokens of their esteem.

On New Year's Day, too, Romans came to the circular temple of Vesta, which stood in the center of the city, carrying torches with which to rekindle the fires in their homes. Vesta, the goddess of hearth fires, was the daughter of Saturn. In her temple the sacred fire burned eternally, guarded by the vestal virgins whose duty it was to see that this flame was never extinguished. Although fire making was not a great chore in sophisticated, thickly populated Rome, the keeping of the sacred fire was a symbol, a reminder perhaps of more primitive times when the gift of fire meant life itself to man.

**DINING IN
MEDIEVAL AND
RENAISSANCE
ITALY**

The phrase "fall of the Roman Empire" suggests a single thunderous crash followed by a long and deathly silence. Devastation wrought by man (at least in the pre-atomic age) was not as sudden or overwhelming as this. The Roman demise came about gradually, as the oversized empire, weakly controlled, became the target of the vigorous Germanic tribes that pressed at its frontiers.

By the fourth century A.D. it had become evident that a strong centralized rule of the sprawling Roman domain was no longer possible. In 395 the split became final, with the Eastern Roman Empire being ruled from Constantinople and the dying Western Empire from Italy. The Greek-speaking Eastern or Byzantine half was to flourish until the turks took Constantinople in 1453.

In Italy, however, the Dark Ages were a thundercloud that grew steadily more ominous. Successive invasions of the entire peninsula, and of Rome itself, by the Goths, the Huns, and the brutal, highly destructive Vandals led to the abdication in 476 of the last of the Western Roman emperors. This was a pathetic youth who ironically bore the name of Romulus Augustulus. Italy, now fragmented into small fortified cities, poor, stagnant, and distrustful of one another, was not to know political unity again until the nineteenth century.

During the half-dozen centuries that followed the invasions, the principal centers of civilization in Italy were the surviving towns, the great feudal estates, and the monasteries established by the newborn Christian church. The feudal lords patterned their estates on the *latifundia*, the slave-operated plantations of Roman times, now manned by serfs whose lot was little better than that of the Roman slaves and often even bleaker.

More democratic and beneficial to society were the undertakings of the monks who worked the church lands (which often served as model farms for the community), cooked

and preserved food, and helped to feed the poor and care for
the sick. The monasteries also doubled as inns, the only safe
stopping places for the traveler in a ravaged and danger-
infested countryside, now bereft of Roman road mainte-
nance and Roman military policing.

The age was a dark one, but wheat, barley, and legumes
needed to be planted and harvested, the vines tended, and
the oil pressed from the olive. Diets were simple—coarse
bread, vegetables, cheese, wine, local game, and fish where
available. Even in the crude stone castles of the feudal lords
and in the towns, the cuisine was limited and unimaginative, for trade was at a standstill.

Only in the south, in Sicily, which was invaded by the
Moslems in the ninth century, was there a vital element
added to the cuisine of the day. To Sicily, long under Greek
and then under Roman influence, the Moslems brought (as
they had to Iberia) the lemon and the orange, sugar cane
and rice, the date palm, and the sweetmeats of the Middle
East. Even today this Eastern flavor is evident in Sicilian
cuisine, particularly in the marzipan and almond nougat
(*torrone*), and in the extensive use of candied citrus rinds
and grated orange peel in Sicilian and southern Italian
desserts.

During the 1200s the long-muted cities of the north—
Venice, Genoa, Milan, and Florence—began to emerge as
active centers of trade. The Crusades to liberate Jerusalem
from the Moslems had begun a century earlier and had
stirred European interest in the East. Venetian and Genoese
fleets were engaged to transport fighting men, horses, and
provisions to the Holy Land. Soon these rival port cities were
plying a heavy trade in cargoes of cane sugar, spices, and
silks which their galleys received from Moslem traders at
eastern Mediterranean ports and delivered to ports throughout Europe. Now, too, the cuisines of these and other Italian
cities took on the exotic flavors of faraway places, as the
herb and spice seasonings of the East established themselves
permanently in Italian cookery.

Genoa had been an important port in Roman times and
her seagoing prowess was renewed and strengthened in the

tenth century, during which time she fought the Moslems. Later, of course, Genoa was to produce Christopher Columbus. Venice, on the other hand, was not founded until the fifth century A.D. when the residents of northern Italy fled to the mud islands of the Adriatic coastal lagoons. Hot on their heels were the barbarian hordes ravaging their way south to Rome. In the new city, outlying and inaccessible due to its watery surroundings, the onetime farmers and northern shepherds became seafarers and merchants. Unlike almost every other Italian city and town, Venice was never taken by the Germanic tribes.

With her fine port on the Adriatic Sea, Venice from her inception looked toward Constantinople and the East. It was not surprising, therefore, that the two Polo brothers, Nicolo and Maffeo, being Venetian merchants, should have journeyed all the way to Peking in search of trade goods. In 1275, the Polos made a second trip to China, taking along this time Marco, the seventeen-year-old son of Nicolo. They returned in 1295, so changed in appearance and speaking their native dialect with such an odd inflection that they were barely recognizable and are said to have been denied admission to their own house.

The treasures of the Far East that the Polos brought back were more flamboyant but less important than the record of their travels and of Oriental culture that Marco wrote a few years later in a Genoese prison. The two cities had been warring again and Marco Polo as commander of a Venetian galley had been taken prisoner. He was, however, treated

with courtesy and comfort and released about a year later, returning to Venice with his valuable memoirs which he might not otherwise have found time to put to paper.

Although Marco Polo is generally credited with having brought macaroni back to Italy from China, there is evidence that *pasta* (paste or dough as for spaghetti, ravioli, noodles —or the dried product itself) was already known in Italy. In Roman times a type of noodle called *laganum* was served, usually with a fish sauce (possibly a form of *garum*) or with a mixture of herbs, garlic, grated cheese, and olive oil (the traditional Genoese sauce called *pesto* is such a mixture). It is certainly not difficult to imagine that the Roman slave-cooks and pastry chefs (who explored the possibilities of every known food to meet the demands of their masters) might have mixed a dough of flour, salt, and water or eggs, rolled it thin, and sliced it into various shapes. Dried noodle products had the advantage of keeping indefinitely, and when boiled could be served in any number of guises and flavors depending on the shape of the *pasta* and the kind of sauce.

If *pasta* did derive from ancient Roman cuisine, we still cannot fully discredit its introduction by Marco Polo. For this useful food which was known in China as early as 3000 B.C. and in Japan even earlier (although the Japanese *pasta* was usually prepared from rice flour rather than wheat flour) was doubtless presented to Marco Polo in a very different form from that known in Italy. Spaghetti, the *pasta* most often attributed to Marco Polo, may well be derived directly from the strandlike fried noodles of China, and these in turn from the threadlike noodle forms of Japan. The word spaghetti comes, in fact, from *spago* (string) and means "little strings." Thus it is possible to give credit to both the Italians and the Chinese. As often happens in history, it is entirely plausible that similar kinds of *pasta* could have been independently developed in these two unrelated societies.

Milan, although not a seaport, was the center of a rich farming and grazing area in the Po valley. This city had replaced Rome as capital in the declining years of the West-

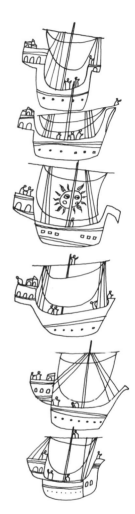

ern Roman Empire. In its position in the direct line of fire of marauders from the north, it had been sacked repeatedly during the Dark Ages, but under the leadership of the powerful Visconti family in the thirteenth and fourteenth centuries, Milan became prosperous. The glories of the ancient Roman banquets appear not to have been forgotten in the Milan of late medieval times.

At the marriage of one of the Viscontis in 1368, sixteen courses were served at dinner, each course announced by a flourish of trumpets. All was elegance and rich display. Even the meats were gilded, a throwback to Roman imperial times when powdered pearls were "dissolved" in the wine as part of the depraved desire to eat and drink money. As an act of even greater ostentation, the Viscontis presented highly valuable gifts to their wedding guests—suits of armor, bolts of silk and brocade, and hounds whose necks were encircled by solid-gold collars.

Of all the Renaissance city-states of Italy, Florence was perhaps the most dazzling. This ancient city, located on the Arno River, dates back to Etruscan times. Despite recurrent flooding, the Arno is now a mild stream. But in Renaissance times this river was a mighty waterway easily navigable to the sea. The richly forested region in which Florence lies is today known as Tuscany, after its onetime Etruscan civilization. Florence went into decline along with the rest of the Western Roman Empire, and slept the long sleep of the Dark Ages. Since she was an inland city, her awakening came a little later than that of the port cities.

During the late Middle Ages, Florentines excelled in the refining, weaving, and dyeing of wool. Their product, immeasurably finer than the coarse woolen cloth hitherto imported from northern Europe, soon made Florence a world textile capital and led to the accumulation of great wealth. From this emerged the city's position as a great banking and financial center.

Prosperity in turn nurtured the arts. Florence became the home of such incomparable painters and sculptors as Raphael, Botticelli, Donatello, da Vinci, and Michelangelo.

The literary works of the Florentines Dante, Petrarch, and Boccaccio were set down, in the 1300s, in the Tuscan language. This language, which we know today as Italian, had been evolving over the centuries from Latin. Through the writings of these giants, it became the established tongue of Italy, reducing all other Italian tongues to the status of dialects.

The rulers of Florence during most of its golden age were the Medici family—bankers, patrons and practitioners of the arts, and highly effective politicians. Their dominance was at its peak in the 1400s, a time when carnivals and public festivals featuring gorgeous floats and gay masked and costumed participants provided entertainment for the masses. For, as in imperial Rome, not all the populace lived in palaces. The poor dwelt in wooden hovels with no water or sanitary facilities. Slop was heaved from the windows and ran down the center of the street to be eaten by wandering hogs, or eventually to be washed away by the rains. It is easy to understand the Hebrew, early Egyptian, and later the Moslem prohibition against eating the flesh of hogs, for these were the scavengers of the early centers of civilization.

Disease spread with alarming rapidity, and it is not surprising that the terrible bubonic plague of 1347–1350, known as the Black Death, should have occurred quite soon after the development of medieval town life. The plague, which began in Constantinople and traveled westward, carried off some twenty-five million people in western Europe alone. Some towns completely disappeared, and it is estimated that more than one-third of the population of Florence died of this disease.

The first symptoms of the disease were egg-size swellings in the groin and armpit. This was followed by the appearance of great black blotches on the skin. Death occurred within a few days. "To cure these maladies no doctors nor any kinds of medicine appeared to be of any avail," Boccaccio wrote in his *Decameron*. Like the others of his day, Bocccaccio believed that the pestilence was evidence of the wrath of God. None thought to look to the filth and poverty of the rat-infested cities.

Fortunately, Florence renewed herself after the plague and her contributions to world culture increased. The art of cookery, along with the crafts and the major arts, was greatly advanced in the Florence of the 1400s and 1500s. When in 1533 Catherine de' Medici married into the royal family of France, later to become queen (when her husband became Henry II), she brought her Florentine chefs with her to court. For the next hundred years the French aristocracy would have it no other way but to import their chefs from Italy.

France had much to learn from the Italians—and she learned her lesson well. Few people realize that modern French *haute cuisine* is largely in the debt of northern Italy. The reasons for Italian eminence in cookery were many: the natural excellence of the fruits, vegetables, dairy products, and meats of the rich northern valleys; the influence of Eastern and other cuisines that reached Italian shores through trade; the subtle refinements applied to cookery through innate good taste and discrimination, just as exhibited in the major arts; and last, the Roman heritage of grandeur, inventiveness, and elegant presentation of dishes at table.

At the French court in the early 1500s, unimaginative coarse and gluttonous feasting went on as in the Middle Ages, featuring great joints of roasted meat, and vegetables that seldom exceeded turnips, cabbage, and beans in variety. Among Catherine's introductions were tender little charcoal-broiled steaks, which the French called *tournedos*, and thick boneless loin slices that were dubbed *filet mignon* (dainty filet). Delicate forcemeats (very finely ground mixtures) of poultry or fish (which the French named *quenelles*) and grilled, wrapped turnovers of sausage or liver (in French, *crépinettes*) pointed the way to finer, more complex dishes. Artichokes, asparagus, cauliflower, broccoli, melons, and even truffles (which today are so strongly associated with France) came into the French cuisine from Italy.

Italian confections that delighted the court were macaroons, sweet biscuits known as Milan cakes, and frangipani tarts (pastry tarts filled with almond-flavored cream or custard). *Zabaglione,* the Italian wine custard, was quickly taken over by the French and became *sabayon.* Ice from the mountains had long been used in Italy to chill beverages. In the 1500s a freezing method using ice and salt was discovered. Now ices, prepared with pulverized ice and fruit flavorings, and an "iced cream," which included milk or cream and any desired flavoring, became the great favorites of the Italian gentry. These, too, Catherine de' Medici introduced to the French court.

As to that great instrument of civilized dining, the fork, Catherine's son, Henry III, is said to have observed the fork being used in Venice. He brought it back to the French court where he ridiculed the ineptness of the first of the fork-using nobility who "let as much fall on their plates, or on the floor, as they managed to put in their mouths." The *first* fork used in Europe had been brought to Venice by the doge's wife who was the daughter of Constantine X of the Byzantine Empire. It was a two-pronged instrument of gold. By the time the fork came to France, it had been known for over a hundred years in Italy.

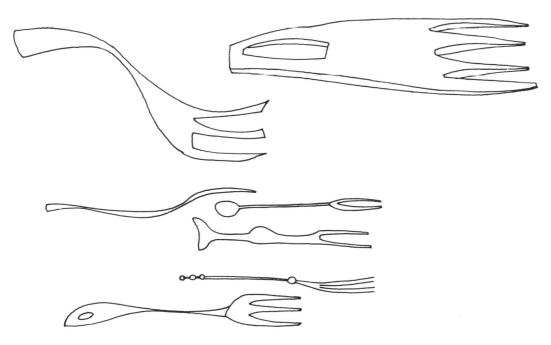

**THE REGIONAL
CUISINES OF A
UNITED ITALY:
THE NORTH**

The Renaissance had been a period of rebirth after the Dark Ages. It was inspired by the classical cultures of Greece and Rome, and it expressed itself in a great flowering of human genius. But the cultural and material riches of the city-states of Renaissance Italy were too alluring to be overlooked by the monarchs of Europe. Their own countries—France, Spain, Austria—were unified and comparatively strong nations. The city-states were divided and easy to conquer.

From the sixteenth century on, the Renaissance paled and, at the same time, Italy became a grab bag for foreign powers. Napoleon's attempt (1796–1815) to rule Italy as a nation failed, but it served to awaken Italians to the concept of nationalism, as well as to stimulate the drive for independence. Unification—an Italy that was an independent political entity for the first time since the fall of the Roman Empire—finally became a reality in the latter half of the nineteenth century.

The quality of regionalism, however, still permeates many aspects of Italian life. Even the iron dictates of a Mussolini could not eradicate it. In modern Italy, for example, the industrial, relatively prosperous north is so different from the rural primitive south that the two might be separate countries. Within these areas there are the regionalisms of the former city-states, as well as regionalisms due to natural geographic boundaries. All of this is strongly expressed in Italian cookery. There is Florentine cooking and there is Venetian cooking. Genoa has its special dishes, and the food of Naples is distinctly different from that of Milan. Sicily and Sardinia are each unique in cuisine, and the daily fare of the grizzled farmer of Apulia (at the heel of the Italian boot) would be quite foreign to the northern Italian auto-worker in Turin.

One reason that regional cookery persists, even in present-day motorized Italy, is that foods are not readily shipped from one part of the country to another. Unlike the United

States, where a Pennsylvania housewife has Florida oranges, Colorado lamb, and Maine lobsters shipped almost to her doorstep, the Italian woman relies chiefly on local products. She must make do with what is at hand, which accounts for variations even *within* a given regional cookery. For example, fresh asparagus in season may be plentiful in one locality but not obtainable in a village thirty miles away. In addition, the Italian housewife may go to market as often as twice a day, never less than once a day, for all the foods she uses must be fresh and most homes have no refrigeration.

Americans seldom think of Italian food as being regional. *Pasta* and tomato sauce, olive oil and garlic, *minestrone*, *spumone*, and, of course, pizza—these are assumed to be the national foods of Italy, consumed daily from the Alps to the Calabrian toe. Americans are not to be blamed for this misconception. It is derived chiefly from those Italian restaurants that have sprung up in every city in the United States ever since the heavy waves of Italian immigration at the turn of the century.

These immigrants were from Naples and the highly impoverished south. The fare offered in the restaurants they opened represented the most translatable elements of the southern Italian menu. Other southern Italian dishes—the roast kid, the highly flavored sausages, the stewed and fried Mediterranean fish dishes—were all either too indigenous to Italy or too specialized for American tastes to be placed on the restaurant menu. The mold for the Italian-American restaurant was thus cast.

Had the Milanese rather than the Neapolitans emigrated to the United States in great numbers, Americans would probably think of Italians as eaters of buttery rice dishes flavored with saffron rather than as lovers of spaghetti and tomato sauce. Milan, the largest city in Italy after Rome, is a banking and commercial center that despite its long art history and its great Gothic cathedral has a surprisingly modern look. The region of Lombardy, in which the city lies, combines industrial development with extensive agriculture. In the Po valley, Italy's principal lowland, cattle are pastured and wheat, corn, and rice are grown. These products directly influence the cuisine. Thus rice and corn meal rather than *pasta,* butter rather than olive oil, fine rich cheeses and tender young veal characterize the cookery of Lombardy.

The rice fields lend an Oriental tinge to the countryside, particularly as one watches the riceworkers—women in large coolie-like straw hats—weed the inundated fields, inching forward in an unbroken line. The rice dishes of northern Italy are sometimes erroneously attributed to Marco Polo because of his visit to the Orient. Rice, however, first appeared in Sicily in the ninth century along with the Moslems and probably traveled north, or made its appearance at northern ports directly from the East, about the time of the Crusades. It is interesting that Italy, although always thought of as a nation of *pasta* eaters, consumes more rice per capita than any other Western country.

Risotto alla Milanese is the classic rice dish of Milan, cooked in butter and chicken stock and flavored with grated Parmesan cheese and saffron, which imparts its pale golden hue to the dish. The use of saffron very likely derives from the Spanish, who in the sixteenth century under Charles V made Milan a dependency of the Spanish crown for a time. In Italy saffron is grown in rugged, mountainous Abruzzi and on the island of Sardinia.

A *risotto* must be creamy, never sticky or dry. It is eaten plain or may include chicken livers, shellfish, mushrooms, or other ingredients. Rice serves, too, as a sometime dessert in northern Italy, sweetened in a mold or pudding. Another mainstay of Lombardy and the north is *polenta,* which translates for Americans into corn-meal mush.

Before the discovery of the New World and its Indian corn or maize, the Italians prepared a *polenta* of semolina (a granular by-product of flour milling). Maize, which the Italians called *granturco* (Turkey wheat), believing it came from the East, was accepted with enthusiasm in Italy, as it had been in Spain and Portugal. (The potato, oddly enough, met with less interest.)

Polenta is prepared by boiling yellow or white corn meal in salted water. It is cooked in a large copper pot and stirred with a long wooden stick or spoon. No northern Italian family is without a *polenta* pot. Eaten boiled, *polenta* is a rather dull but rib-sticking porridge. It is often served with butter and cheese or with a meat or tomato sauce. When roasted quails or other small birds are served on top of the *polenta*, the dish is known as *polenta e osei*. The *polenta* itself is perhaps tastier cooled, sliced, and fried—or baked in a pie layered with mushrooms and a creamy cheese sauce.

Although not a pleasant one, the ancient Roman tradition of eating thrushes, larks, sparrows, and nightingales continues into modern times, causing one writer to refer to Italy as that land "where songbirds are regarded as delicatessen."

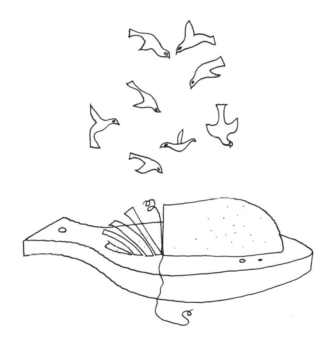

Nevertheless, thrushes fattened on juniper berries (*gineproni*) are sold by the dozen in Italian street markets, and small birds are eaten with *polenta*, or simply grilled or roasted, in Milan, Venice, and elsewhere. Human want, of course, has played its part in perpetuating this practice.

The pigeons of Saint Mark's Square in Venice are a notable exception to the decimation of the Italian bird population. Here overpopulation seems to be the problem. One legend has it that a flight of pigeons warned the villages of northern Italy of the impending onslaught of the Huns in the fifth century. Taking the birds' example, the villagers fled to the lagoons and founded Venice. Hence the flocks today strut and swarm about the famous piazza with the lasting assurance that not a feather will be touched.

Alla Milanese (in the style of Milan) describes one of the numerous Italian ways with veal—sliced thin, breaded, and fried crisp in butter, often with a slice of *stracchino* (a Lombardy cow's-milk cheese something like *mozzarella*) melted on top. Another famous veal dish is *ossi buchi alla Milanese*, veal shanks stewed with herbs, vegetables, lemon, and white wine, and almost always served with *risotto*. Italian veal, and particularly that of Lombardy, is always young and tender, for according to law the animal must be exclusively milk-fed. *Vitello*, true young veal, must not have eaten grass. Since grazing land is limited in Italy, cattlemen can seldom afford to allow the calf to grow to the much larger size slaughtered for veal in the United States. American veal is frequently too mature to show up well in recipes for Italian veal dishes.

Gorgonzola and *bel paese* are the reigning cheeses of Lombardy and are held in high esteem throughout the world. Gorgonzola, a pale creamy cheese, thinly veined with blue and delightfully sharp in flavor, is made in the town of Gorgonzola about ten miles from Milan. It is sometimes compared to the French Roquefort, but the two are different, for Roquefort is made from sheep's milk and Gorgonzola from the milk of cows that have been fed on special pasture grasses. To bring about the formation of the blue veins, the cheeses were at one time matured in cold mountain caves. Nowadays refrigeration is used, and the blue mold is produced by inducing air into the curd with copper wires. Gorgonzola that is exported tends to be harder and stronger-flavored than that eaten in Italy, which is almost creamy-soft and just tangy. Italians proudly call Gorgonzola "*Il Re de Formaggio*" (the king of cheeses). The soft, mild-flavored, adaptable *bel paese* probably qualifies best as the queen of cheeses.

Panettone, a raised cake flecked with raisins and candied fruit, is a well-known specialty of Milan, popular for gift giving at Christmas time. At Easter, the *colomba Pasquale*, an Easter bread shaped like a dove, makes its appearance in Lombardy. Cremona, city of the great violinmakers, is responsible for an unusual relish of candied fruits in a syrup flavored with mustard oil and garlic—*mostarda di frutta*. Probably of ancient origin, this makes a delightful sweet-and-sour to go with cold meat or poultry. Milan grocers sell *mostarda* in bulk from small wooden barrels.

Venice is surely the most romantic and the most startling city in Italy. Arriving by train, one finds oneself in a railroad station like any other. Outside the station, however, lies no boulevard or bustling city street, but rather the Grand Canal. A gondola or waterbus takes you to your destination, for you cannot drive a car in Venice. Those streets that are not water are narrow lanes that constantly ascend and descend the four hundred or so humpbacked bridges that cross the canals. A motorist arrives in Venice by causeway from the mainland and parks his car in a huge public parking lot before entering the city. Consequently, Venice is the only city that does not suffer from the continual harassment of unmuffled motor vehicle noises that plague the visitor elsewhere in Italy.

Because Venice is a seagirt city—it is actually made up of about 120 mud islands—the cuisine is quite naturally oriented toward fish. The canal-side Venetian markets are a veritable menagerie of the sea, shimmering in the watery light with all the shapes and colors of the deep. Rosy mullet, cream-and-gray sole, and fat pink *scampi* are especially good taken from Adriatic waters. Venetian *scampi*, a large variety of shrimp, are delectable grilled, fried, stewed, or boiled, seasoned with oil and garlic, parsley and lemon juice. Another specialty of Venice, as well as other Italian seaside cities, is the *fritto misto di mare* (mixed fish fry) of mullet, squid, shrimp, and possibly other fish, all lightly dusted with flour and fried crisp in very hot olive oil.

A traditional Venetian dish that is not fish is *risi e bisi*

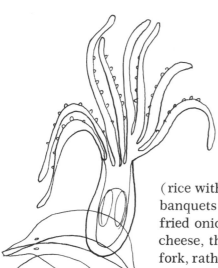

(rice with green peas), which was once served at all official banquets in the Republic of Venice. Flavored with minced fried onion, bits of ham or salt pork, and grated Parmesan cheese, this dish, although somewhat soupy, is eaten with a fork, rather like a stew.

To the north of Venice, not far from the Austrian border, lie the Dolomites. In this mountainous Alpine region noted for both its winter sports and as a summer resort area, the cooking as might be expected shows a strong Austrian influence. One is still in Italy, but here one feasts on smoked pork with sauerkraut and on *leberknödel* (dumplings filled with chopped liver).

Another Alpine region is the Piedmont in northwestern Italy, bordering on Switzerland and France. Here the Swiss and French influence is seen in dishes like *fonduta*, a fondue prepared with eggs, butter, and a rich Piedmontese cheese called *fontina*. A fondue may be used as a hot dip for crusty bread or toast, but the Italian *fonduta* is notable for the raw sliced white truffles which are sprinkled on top. These large truffles which grow in Piedmont (also in Tuscany and Emilia-Romagna) are hunted out by specially trained dogs, for like the black truffles they grow underground. They are actually a beige-brown rather than white and are more flavorful than the black truffles. White truffles may be cooked lightly in butter but are often served raw, very finely sliced, on top of cooked dishes or in a salad.

La bagna cauda ("the hot bath" in Piedmontese dialect) is the traditional sauce of Piedmont. The ingredients are olive oil, butter, anchovies, garlic, and occasionally cream. Into the "bath," which is kept hot, are dipped raw *cardi* (cardoons; edible thistles) or raw cabbage, celery, or peppers. The Piedmontese are fond of this dish as a pick-me-up at any time of day or evening. Good with a robust red wine, *la bagna cauda* is mainly for garlic lovers.

The capital of the Piedmont (which means "foot of the mountains") is Turin, which lies in the level area of the Po valley and is the center of the Italian auto industry. *Grissini*, the slender bread sticks that are popular all over Italy, are said to have originated in Turin. The city is also famous for its caramels and chocolates.

Curving from the French border eastward along the Mediterranean is the province of Liguria. Its coastal strip forms the Italian Riviera with its mild year-round climate, for the mountains to the north are a protection from cold winds and the sea tempers the summer heat. Orange and lemon trees grow here just as they do much farther south in Naples and Sicily.

Genoa, capital of Liguria, is the chief Italian port, noisy and active, its *grattacieli* (skyscrapers) and the luxurious hillside villas of its shipping magnates looking down uneasily upon some of Italy's most appalling slums.

The famous fish stew of Genoa is called *burridà* and always includes a generous sampling of those strange Mediterranean sea beasts that one can visit any day in the raucous Genoese fish markets. Octopus, squid, and cuttlefish (also called inkfish) are eaten throughout Italy and are especially in evidence along the Genoese and Adriatic coasts. They are served boiled, stewed, or fried, and if properly prepared they are not rubbery but are tender and delicate in flavor.

Native to Genoa is the herb-and-cheese paste known as *pesto*. Traditionally, the ingredients for *pesto* are pounded smooth and creamy in a mortar with a pestle. They include basil or parsley, garlic, pine nuts, *sardo* or Parmesan cheese, and olive oil. *Sardo* is a sharp white sheep's-milk cheese made on the island of Sardinia and not too widely distributed. Pine nuts, or *pignoli*, are extracted from the cones of the stone pine. They have been used in the Italian kitchen since classical times, often in meat and game dishes as well as in cakes and confections. The husks of the nuts are saved and burned in braziers for winter warmth.

Pesto, which is neither cooked nor heated, is tossed with hot *pasta* or *gnocchi* (little dumplings made of potato, farina, or other flour). The Genoese also give a delightful flavor to their *minestrone* by adding a tablespoon or so of *pesto* to the soup just before serving. *Pesto* and the other green sauces of Italy, as well as the tuna, anchovy, and sweet-sour (*agrodolce*) sauces of that country, all predate the tomato. Many had their origin in Roman times, when they were frequently used to disguise the flavors of overripe meats and other deteriorating foods.

Of all the rich gastronomic regions of northern Italy, Emilia-Romagna, just south of Lombardy, may well be the undisputed capital. The ancient Romans, for military and political reasons, built one of their remarkable arrow-straight roads through this region. This road, known as the Via Emilia (Emilian Way), ran and still runs from Rimini on the Adriatic coast to Piacenza on the Po. Dotting the realm in a straight line along the road are such citadels of art and gastronomy as Parma, Modena, and Bologna— nicknamed *la Grossa* (the fat), and proud of it.

As in most of northern Italy, the tomato is little in evidence. The famous Bolognese *ragù* (ragout sauce) for *pasta* is composed chiefly of minced beef, pork, and other meats, and of finely chopped vegetables. Just a tablespoon or two of

tomato paste is used in the sauce, but some Bolognese cooks add a cupful of cream. This is quite unusual in Italy, for, unlike the French, the Italians seldom use cream in their meat, fish, or sauce cookery. In Bologna, *ragù* is often served on *tagliatelle* (long egg noodles, about one quarter of an inch wide). Butter and freshly grated cheese are tossed with the *pasta* and sauce.

The baked *pasta* specialty of Bologna is *lasagne verdi al forno* (baked green *lasagne*), but this dish is very different from the *mozzarella*-and-tomato-sauced *lasagne* of the south. In the Bolognese version, the strips of *lasagne* (colored green by the addition of puréed spinach to the noodle dough) are layered with *ragù* and a creamy white sauce to which nutmeg (much used in Bolognese cooking) has been added. The dish is thickly sprinkled with Parmesan cheese and baked.

Very appealing and delicate are the Bolognese *tortellini*, little coils of egg *pasta* dough stuffed with a mixture of pork, veal, chicken, sausage, brains, Parmesan cheese, eggs, and seasonings. Fillings of this type are also used in ravioli and in *cappelleti* ("little hats"; really circular ravioli). Filled *pasta* are a great convenience to the Italian housewife for she may have only scraps of meat, a small piece of cooked chicken, bits of leftover vegetables, none of which would otherwise make a meal. Tastily blending these, or using the popular spinach-and-cheese filling, she can prepare a very substantial dish.

Filled *pasta* are either served *in brodo* (in broth, usually chicken or veal) or are poached in water, drained, and dressed with grated cheese and butter. The use of the over-powering tomato sauce is generally frowned upon by northern Italian cooks, for they feel it masks both the delicacy of the homemade *pasta* and the subtlety of the filling. The Bolognese sometimes serve their *tortellini* in cream. This makes an exceedingly rich dish. No matter how they are served, *tortellini* are traditional in Bologna on Christmas Eve.

Just as Lombardy is highly regarded for its veal, Emilia-Romagna is praised for its pork, particularly Bologna's *mortadella* sausage, Modena's *zampone* (pig's trotter stuffed with pork sausage), and Parma's ham, better known perhaps as *prosciutto*. The excellence of genuine Parma ham is said to be due to the diet of the pigs (which are fed the whey from Parmesan cheese making), to the local climate, and to the special salting and curing methods employed. *Prosciutto*, sliced as thin as pink tissue paper makes a very elegant appetizer with melon or with fresh figs, either green, black, or white. It is also used to great advantage with veal, chicken, and many other cooked dishes.

Parmesan, the cheese of Parma, needs little introduction. Like Parma ham, it is made in other places as well, but the citizens of Parma consider their own far superior. Parmesan, known as *grana* in Italy because of its finely grained texture, is made from cow's milk. It takes at least two years to mature and is more costly the older it is. Known since very early times in Italy, Parmesan cheese has the advantages of not becoming stringy when heated and of keeping for a long time. Its smoky sharp flavor makes it the ideal companion to soups, *pastas*, fresh meats, poultry, and vegetables.

THE FOOD OF CENTRAL AND SOUTHERN ITALY

Tuscany, for the traveler going south, is the region where olive oil begins to play a prominent role in Italian cookery. Excellent oil, good beef, truffles, chestnuts, and spinach are local products that strongly characterize the cuisine of Tuscany and its capital city, Florence. Tuscany is also the home of that best known and most traveled of Italian wines, Chianti.

Bistecca alla Fiorentina is the charcoal-broiled beefsteak (generally from an animal not older than two years) that is served with pride in a country where the beef is otherwise not notable. Usually, however, the term *alla Fiorentina* refers to dishes containing or garnished with finely chopped or puréed spinach. Green spinach noodles dressed with butter and grated Parmesan cheese are a Florentine favorite.

Tuscany's chestnuts show up in soups, in desserts, and in

castagnaccio alla Fiorentina, a cake eaten at Lent that is made with chestnut flour and is studded with pine nuts and candied fruit peels. The *panforte* of Siena is another traditional sweetmeat of Tuscany. *Panforte* is a flat round cake made with cocoa, spices, honey, candied fruit, almonds, and filberts. It is of medieval origin, rather like a plum pudding or a rich fruit cake, and is sold at the *palio,* or banner race, that is held twice yearly at Siena.

In the neighboring inland region of Umbria, Perugia is the city for gourmets. Roast loin of pork, seasoned with fennel, and roast suckling pig are specialties of Perugia. *Pinocatte,* tiny macaroon-like cakes containing pine nuts, appear in Perugia, especially at Christmas. In the regions of the Marches and of Abruzzi e Molise on the Adriatic coast of central Italy, a fish soup called *brodetto,* made with a dozen varieties of fish, is popular. Baked *pasta* dishes, lamb and kid stews, and local cheeses are the staples of the mountainous inland areas of these two regions.

Rome is still the hub of Italy, that place to which all roads lead. Consequently, as in most foreign capitals, the cuisines of other nations are well represented. Among these are American-style quick-lunch bars and restaurants that feature hamburgers, club sandwiches, fried chicken, and apple pie. But Rome has her own specialties, of which *fettucine Alfredo* is probably the best known. Today there are at least three restaurants in Rome called Alfredo's, but the original Alfredo made his name with the simple but excellent dish of *fettucine al burro*—long egg noodles, about half an inch wide, mixed with butter and grated cheese. Alfredo himself was something of a showman, tossing the rich yellow strands in a darkened room with a single spotlight trained on him. After Mary Pickford and Douglas Fairbanks presented him with a fork and spoon of solid gold to be used in his performance, Alfredo became a legend in his own time.

Other Roman favorites are *stracciatelle,* a chicken broth to which the addition of beaten eggs and grated cheese gives a ragged or shredded appearance; fried artichokes, so tender at Easter time in Rome that the entire vegetable can be

eaten; and *saltimbocca,* which translates as "jumps in the mouth." This last—thinly sliced veal rolled with ham and sage leaf and cooked gently in butter and Marsala wine—is well named, for eating it takes no effort at all. *Pecorino romano* is the hard sheep's-milk cheese of Rome, not too unlike Parmesan. It is popular for grating, both in the capital and in the surrounding countryside of Latium. *Abbacchio al forno* (roast baby lamb) and *capretto al forno* (roast kid) are meat specialties of Rome, delicately seasoned with garlic and rosemary and cooked to a peak of succulent crispness.

The southbound traveler from Rome is soon in Campania, the beginning of southern Italy and the region of which Naples is capital. From here to the toe and throughout Sicily, the cookery and the folkways are more vividly colored than in the north. Naples and the south bedazzle with the scarlet of tomato sauce and the crimson of pimento, the flower-garden gaiety of the pizza and the creamy pastels of the *gelati.*

As one travels southward, however, the land yields less. The spiny ridge of the Apennines, which runs the six-hundred-mile length of the Italian peninsula, seems to take up more and more of the narrow boot. Good farmlands such as those of the Po valley are not seen here. In fact, much southern Italian farming is practiced on sloping land broken up into steplike terraces, each one supported by a stone wall. Farm machinery, aside from its cost, is not usable on these patchy hillside farms.

Thus the south remains a region of primitive farming and rural poverty. Many families live in huts with dirt floors, without water, electricity, or sanitary facilities. The land, too poor to graze cattle, supports mainly goats, sheep, and donkeys, but there is little milk or meat. Even spaghetti may prove a luxury for the numerous poor of the south, many of whom live chiefly on bread, olive oil, raw garlic, and tomatoes. In winter they subsist on dried beans—*ceci* (chick-peas), *fava* (broad beans), and lentils. The migration of the impoverished southerner to the cities of the industrial north

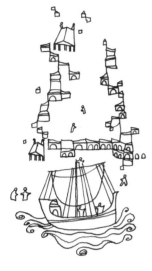

is a continuing trend. It was during the period of 1880 to 1920 that there was heavy emigration from this region to the United States.

Naples is an ancient center of civilization, founded by Greek colonists hundreds of years before the birth of Christ and later taken over by the Romans. At nearby Pompeii and Herculaneum, which lay in the shadow of Mount Vesuvius, the Roman elite, attracted by the mild sunny climate, built villas and country estates. Fine craftsmen practiced in these small prosperous cities, and a lively trade in wine, oil, grains, and *garum* was carried on by the merchants of Pompeii.

Then, as stated in the remarkable eyewitness account of the younger Pliny, "On August 24th about one in the afternoon," there was seen "a cloud of unusual size and aspect . . . later it was found to be Vesuvius. Its shape might best be represented by a pine tree; it rose to a great height, like a trunk, and then spread into branches. . . . At one moment it was white, and then murky and spotted, as if it had carried up earth or cinders."

The year was A.D. 79. The cataclysmic eruption showered volcanic ashes, cinders, and noxious gasses upon the two living cities. Those who could not flee at once were the victims of asphyxiation. In a matter of days, the debris of the eruption had so completely buried the cities that their very sites were soon forgotten. Time had stopped for Pompeii and Herculaneum but the moment was indelibly preserved. The details of daily life revealed by the excavations that have been undertaken in modern times are remarkable. In a Pompeii bakery, for example, eighty-one loaves of bread had been placed in the ovens a few minutes before the eruption. They are still there today, blackened coal-like masses but recognizable loaves nevertheless.

Vesuvius is still active—the only active volcano on the European mainland. Its eruption of 1944 was of major proportions, but Italian farmers still live on the mountain's lower slopes, for the lava-rich soil produces good crops and excellent wines. Lacrima Cristi (tear of Christ), the most famous wine of the Naples region, comes from grapes grown on these slopes.

Modern Naples, third largest city in Italy, provides startling contrasts. Located on the indescribably blue Bay of Naples, one of the most magnificent scenic areas in the world, the city itself teems with overcrowded living quarters and with unattractive tenement and factory districts.

Pasta is the staple food of the south. A favorite way of serving spaghetti in this region is simply with oil and garlic, for Parmesan cheese is relatively expensive and even the ingredients for meatless sauces may be beyond the family's means. Another economy dish is the combination of *pasta* (often the broken pieces, of various shapes and sizes, which are sold at reduced prices) and beans. This is known as *pasta e fagiole* (*pasta* and beans), and variations of it may be found throughout Italy.

Naples is reputed to make the best commercial *pasta* in Italy owing to the quality of its water. Many Italian women still make their own *pasta* at home, particularly noodle and filled varieties. But the consumption of factory-made products increases yearly. Tubular *pastas* such as spaghetti and macaroni require special machinery and are almost always factory-made.

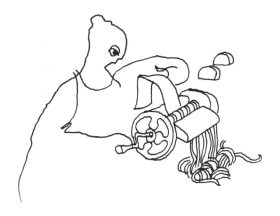

An important distinction is that between *pastas* made without eggs—such as spaghetti (thin or regular) and macaroni (in straight tube shapes, as elbows, seashells, *lasagne*, etc.)—and those made with eggs. The latter are called *pasta all' uovo*. Fettucine, tagliatelle, ravioli, *capelletti*, *tortellini*, and *cannelloni* (squares of *pasta* stuffed and

rolled up, pancake fashion) are examples of *pastas* made with eggs. Within these two categories are numerous varieties not mentioned, many with charming and whimsical names such as *mostaccioli* (little mustaches), *farfalle* (butterflies), *occhi di lupo* (wolf's eyes), and *manicotti* (little muffs). It has been estimated that there are about a hundred different varieties of *pasta,* and additional confusion results from the various provinces having different names for the same variety.

A diversity of *pasta* shapes and sizes, however, has the advantage of offering different-looking and different-tasting dishes to a people who eat basically the same food every single day, and often twice a day. Many Italian families have a *pasta* dish at lunch and again at the evening meal, but a choice may be made from among boiled *pastas* with sauce, baked *pastas,* filled *pastas,* and *pastas* served either in broths or in very thick vegetable soups or stews.

Nor are the various *pasta* shapes designed from pure whimsey. The thin delicate strands are best served directly from the cooking pot, drained and tossed with a fragrant sauce; the thicker macaronis are most satisfactory in hearty baked dishes; and the smaller *pasta* do well in soups. The question of why *pasta* should find such overwhelming acceptance in Italy and not in other Mediterranean countries has never been satisfactorily answered.

While Italy grows a large amount of durum wheat (the special hard wheat required for *pasta* making), other countries, notably Spain, do so too. Yet the Spanish show almost no interest in *pasta*. Italy, on the other hand, does not grow enough durum wheat for her own needs and must import some from other countries. In fact, much Italian olive oil is traded for the cheaper American peanut oil or cottonseed oil so that Italy can use the surplus money to buy wheat. Perhaps the Spanish preference for the *cocido* against the Italian preference for *pasta* is simply a matter of taste. Even national taste, it would seem, can be a very personal thing.

Pizza is, of course, native to Naples. This rough pie of bread dough, tomatoes, and cheese was not known in many parts of Italy until quite recently, even though the first pizzeria is said to have opened in Naples in the sixteenth century when the city was under French rule. Garnished

with anchovies, bits of sausage, ham, black olives, mushrooms, or what have you, the pizza is as appetizing as it is gaudy. It originated, however, as the coarse, simple food of the poor and is never served in the more formal type of Italian restaurant.

Another form of the Neapolitan pizza is the *calzone*, a turnover of thin pizza dough enclosing cheese, ham, or salami, and baked or fried. Its plump half-moon shape accounts for its name, which means "breeches."

The cheeses of the Campania are among the best known in Italy. *Mozzarella* is an elastic white cheese that forms deliciously endless strands when heated. It was originally made from the milk of the *bufali*, white buffaloes with curving horns that were once very familiar to the Italian countryside. But as these become scarcer each year, *mozzarella* is now made largely from cow's milk. *Mozzarella*, which is often eaten in Italy while it is still very fresh, sweet and dripping, makes a fine cheese for many cooked dishes in addition to pizza. *Mozzarella in carrozza*, for example, is a simple nourishing everyday dish from Naples southward. The name means *"mozzarella* in a carriage," for the cheese is sandwiched between slices of bread, dipped in beaten egg, fried quickly in oil, and eaten crisp and hot.

Provolone, a firm smoked cheese that comes in a number of shapes and sizes and varies from mild to sharp, also originated as a buffalo cheese of Campania. It, too, is now usually made from cow's milk.

Although most Italian families, north or south, end their meals with fruit and cheese, Italy is lavish in her outlay of cakes, sweets, and frozen desserts, all of which appear on the Italian table in profusion on saints' days and other special occasions. Naples is surely the confectionery capital of Italy, for its cakes and pastries are the plumpest, the richest, and the creamiest. *Zeppole* are doughnuts, known throughout the south, generally orange-flavored in Naples. Naples is considered the home of the *zuppa Inglese*, the Italian adaptation of English trifle that translates into the rather unattractive "English soup." Hardly a soup is this glamorous dessert of spongecake soaked with rum, layered with custard, bits of fruit, and grated bitter chocolate, and masked with whipped cream or with a swirling golden meringue.

Even more luxurious are the Neapolitan *sfogliatelle*, flaky cone-shaped pastries filled with a mixture of sweetened *ricotta* cheese and candied fruit. These are so time-consuming to prepare that, like the confectionery of Iberia, they were originally made mainly in the convents. *Ricotta* is a very soft white unsalted cheese made from sheep's milk. It adapts beautifully to sweets or savories, may be used in a *torta di ricotta* (a cheese dessert pie) or with *pasta* dishes, as for a ravioli filling. *Ricotta* is especially popular in Rome but is eaten all over Italy.

Although Tuscany is credited with developing the first ice cream in Europe, Naples and Sicily are today the foremost purveyors of *gelato* (ice cream), *granita* (ices of fine crystals, often flavored with coffee or lemon), and the marvelous *coppa*, a tasteful and imaginative sundae usually combining the two. The Neapolitan brick made up of ribbons of chocolate, vanilla, and strawberry ice creams is known the world over. More elegant is the *spumone,* generally molded of chocolate and vanilla ice creams, with a layer of rum-flavored whipped cream containing finely chopped nuts and fruits.

The regions of Apulia (the heel), Basilicata (the instep), and Calabria (the toe) make up the southern extremity of the Italian mainland. Kid and lamb are the principal meats in these regions, but these play a much smaller part in the diet here than do fish and vegetable dishes. In Apulia, *calzone* is often stuffed with a mixture of anchovies, mackerel, and vegetables. Fresh fish is fried in olive oil, or combined in a soup or stew. *Baccalà* (salt cod), common all over Italy as a fast-day dish, makes a cheap and convenient standby in these regions. It is also known as *stoccofisso* (stockfish).

Of vegetables, eggplant is much used, layered with cheese and tomato sauce and baked. Often it is stewed with green peppers, celery, onions, olives, and tomato sauce into a kind of vegetable relish known as *caponata*. Stuffed eggplants, stuffed peppers, and stuffed zucchini make good meatless dishes, as does the ever-popular *fritto misto*, the mixed fry of vegetables, possibly including some meat parts such as liver or brains and small chunks of cheese, all dipped in batter and fried crisp in oil.

Just off the toe of Italy lies the largest island in the Mediterranean—Sicily. Although now separated from the mainland by the narrow Strait of Messina, Sicily was part of the boot in prehistoric times. The long chain of the Apennines curves down through Calabria into Sicily, rendering much of the island quite mountainous. Earthquakes and volcanic eruptions have been frequent. Due to the latter, the soil in the eastern portion is very fertile, but irrigation is necessary throughout.

Sicilian history is colored by Carthaginian, Greek, Roman, Byzantine, Moslem, Norman, French, and Spanish rule. It is interesting to stop and examine the languages of Sicily at the time of Scandinavian Norman rule in the twelfth century. Greek and Arabic were spoken by the people, Latin was used in church services, Norman-French was the language of the royal court, and recent immigrants from the mainland spoke a strange new tongue that was still in the process of development and could best be described as medieval Italian. Today, Sicilians have their own dialect.

The Greeks left Sicily their temples, magnificent ruins that are every bit as splendid as those of Greece itself, if not more so. The Moslems made Palermo, now the capital of Sicily, a center of civilization along with the three great Moslem cities of medieval Spain. The Eastern flavor is undeniable in Sicily. There is, too, a strong feeling of North Africa here—in the cubelike white houses, in the heavily draped clothing of the women, and particularly when the sirocco, the hot, dust-laden wind of the Libyan desert, howls for days along Sicily's southern coast.

The cuisine, too, shows the North African influence in the use of *couscous*, a coarse cereal milled from wheat and cooked somewhat like rice. The Sicilians call it *cuscusu* and serve it with their fish stews. Meat does not appear often on the Sicilian menu. Tuna and sardines from local waters, *baccalà*, fish-and-*pasta* combinations, and vegetable or cereal dishes make up the general diet. Olive oil is used extensively, as elsewhere in the south, while butter is seldom seen.

One of the rare Sicilian meat specialties is *farsumagru alla Messinese* (meat roll, Messina style). This is a larger version of the well-known Italian *braciole* or *braciolette* (individual slices of beef spread with a stuffing, rolled up, and braised). The hearty *farsumagru* stuffing consists of dried salami, hard-cooked eggs, grated cheese, bread crumbs, garlic, and parsley. Tied up, browned in oil, and simmered in tomato sauce, the hefty roll is then cut in thick slices and served. This is definitely a special-occasion dish, as are the rich cream cakes of Sicily and the *gelato* and *granita* for which Sicily is as famous as Naples.

Cannoli alla Siciliana (Sicilian cream rolls) are crisp, deep-fried pastry tubes filled with a mixture of sweetened *ricotta* cheese, shaved bitter chocolate, and citron or orange peel. They are not as elegant as the flaky-pasty *sfogliatelle* of Naples, but they are much easier to make since the dough need only be shaped around wooden or aluminum forms and dropped into the frying kettle. Many Italian housewives make their *cannoli* forms from broomsticks cut into five- or six-inch lengths.

Cassata (Sicilian cream cake) is composed of spongecake layers with a *ricotta* filling similar to that used for *cannoli* and a decorative almond-flavored sugar frosting. Rose water is often used to flavor the *ricotta* in Sicilian desserts. This is a distinctly Eastern touch. There are many kinds of Italian ice-cream cakes that also go by the name of *cassata*.

Over a hundred miles west of the Italian mainland lies the second largest island in the Mediteranean, which is another sizable chunk of Italian offshore territory. This is the island of Sardinia, a very mountainous region where many ancient folkways persist due to isolation. Sardinia, like Sicily, has a history of foreign overlords. Long years of Spanish rule are reflected in the Sardinian dialect, as well as in the culinary use of saffron which is cultivated on the island.

A typical Sardinian dish is *succutundu*, a rich meat broth

containing tiny semolina dumplings flavored with saffron. Myrtle grows in profusion on the Sardinian hillsides and is used for flavoring meats such as *porceddù* (roast suckling pig) and birds such as *tàccula*. The latter is a dish of roast thrushes or blackbirds stuffed while hot into bags of myrtle leaves and left to steep until they absorb the flavor of the myrtle. The leaves are then discarded and the birds are served on a bed of saffron rice.

Pungent cheeses such as *sardo*, from sheep's milk, and Greek-style *feta*, from goat's milk, characterize the Sardinian cuisine, as does the *pasta di sarda*, a macaroni made from flour derived from crushed dried sardines. Sardinian tuna is of excellent quality, but a rather unusual fish product is *buttàriga*. This Sardinian delicacy is prepared from mullet roe, dried and pressed. It is served as an *antipasto*, thinly sliced and drizzled with olive oil and lemon juice.

ITALIAN FEAST DAYS

In a country as old as Italy, yet so recently unified, it is not surprising that there are so few national holidays and so many local ones. Between May and August, almost every town and village has a *festa* in honor of its patron saint. In Sicily, the day of Saint Joseph (March 19), patron saint of the family, is an occasion for village feasting. Tables are set up in the public square, laden with food including the special *sfinge di San Giuseppe* (doughnut-like cakes). The food is blessed by the priest, and all the poor are invited to attend. Each year's grape harvest is also a time for local merrymaking and for drinking up last year's wine.

Music is such a natural form of expression for the Italian people that it bursts forth even without the excuse of a gay occasion. The street song "Funiculi, Funicula" came out of the building of the cable railway (funicular) ascending Mount Vesuvius.

Weddings are particularly exuberant. The Italian custom of giving away sugar-coated Jordan almonds in gay and pastel colors at weddings is also prevalent in Lebanon and appears to have originated in the Middle East. The Italians call these sweetmeats *confetti* (little candies).

Many festivals are associated with the former city-states. Venice has its regatta, Siena its *palio*. The *palio*, or banner race, take its name from the *palio* itself which is a silken flag bearing an image of the Virgin. It is the reward given to the winner of an exciting horse race held twice yearly (in early July and mid-August) in the medieval Tuscan city of Siena. Each of the city's districts sends its jockeys and horses to compete in the brief, no-holds-barred race, which takes place in the Piazza del Campo. The race is preceded by a parade in medieval costume with drummers, intricate flag twirling, and skilled flag throwers who can toss a banner thirty feet in the air. Each district, called a *contrada*, has its own vividly designed flag, the colors of which are repeated in the parade costumes of its members.

The *palio* of Siena is not to be confused with a Sicilian game of the same name. In the Sicilian *palio*, young men attempt to climb a greased pole in order to secure the prize that awaits the winner at the top. This game can be seen at the Feast of San Gennaro held each autumn in the Italian community in New York City.

Parades in costumes and masks are held in some Italian cities during the pre-Lenten period of carnival. But Holy Week in Italy does not call forth the great public lamentation and communal mourning that it does in the cities of Spain. Private pilgrimages, however, are made to the churches, for Easter is a most important religious observance. In Rome, *capretto* (milk-fed kid) is the traditional Easter meat.

Christmas in Italy is a time for setting up the *presepio* (manger scene) in homes and churches, and for bagpipe players in the streets, dressed in sheepskins to represent the shepherds who first came to see the Christ Child. Christmas trees are not traditional in Italy, nor is the exchange of gifts on Christmas Day. This ceremony is reserved for Epiphany, the twelfth day after Christmas (January 6) when the Wise Men brought their gifts to the Child.

Christmas is also a time for serving the traditional *panet-*

tone of Milan and rich sweets ranging from the huge Neapolitan cream puffs to tiny *amaretti* (macaroons) and exquisitely wrapped *torrone* (nougats). Preserved and crystallized whole fruits—figs, oranges, plums, pears, apricots— make handsome displays in confectionery shop windows. A heritage of the East, they add glitter and color to the Italian holiday table.

ITALIAN DINING CUSTOMS, MENU, AND RECIPES

Dining hours in Italy tend to be earlier than in Spain, but the meals themselves follow a similar pattern. Breakfasts are light, continental style, consisting of *caffè latte* (coffee with milk), *tè*, or *cioccolato,* accompanied by a roll or chunk of crisp bread with jam or marmalade. Lunch, at about one, is followed by a siesta in Rome and southward. It is often the main meal of the day, beginning with an *antipasto* and followed by a *minestra* (wet course) or an *asciutta* (dry course), but not both.

Minestre are soups, of which there are several types. *Minestrone*, a soup that is well known outside Italy, is a thick stewlike mixture containing fresh and dried vegetables including dried beans, and usually some form of small *pasta*. A *brodo* (broth) is a consommé derived from meat or chicken. It may be served plain or with *pasta*, rice, or eggs in it. The Roman *stracciatelle* is a broth containing beaten eggs. *Zuppa Pavese*, a soup of Pavia in Lombardy, is a broth that floats a whole poached egg plus rounds of fried bread sprinkled with grated cheese. Fish soups, since they are really stews, are not usually served in the *minestra* course.

As to the *asciutta*, these would include *risotto*, *gnocchi*, or any of the many varieties of *pasta* served with a sauce or other dressing.

The main course of fish, meat, or poultry is usually served with potato or green vegetables and a green salad. Many vegetables, particularly stuffed and fried varieties, appear at Italian meals as *antipasto* rather than as a main-course accompaniment. The meal concludes with *frutta* and usually *formaggio* (cheese). On special occasions there may be a *dolce* (sweet).

Dinner is served at about seven-thirty, somewhat later in Rome, and is similar to the midday meal but may be lighter or even abbreviated to a single dish. The pace of life in the brisk commercial cities of the north, however, has reversed the tradition of the heavy midday meal, so that lunch is frequently the lighter of the two. *Caffè* in small cups, rich and dark, is served after dinner or may be taken later at a coffeehouse.

The family meal often omits the *antipasto* and begins with the soup or *pasta* course. *Antipasto* translates as "before the meal" and is synonymous with the French hors d'oeuvre ("out of the work"—aside from the meal itself). This opening course, however, derives from the *gustatio* of the banquets of ancient Rome and hence is of Italian origin.

Antipasti are delightfully varied—sausages such as salami and *mortadella;* mushrooms, peppers, artichoke hearts, *cannellini* (white kidney beans), or *ceci* in dressings of vinegar, oil, herbs and spices; olives, anchovies, *caponata;* raw vegetables such as *finocchi* (fennel) and tomatoes; *prosciutto* with melon or fresh figs; *tonno* (tuna, usually in olive oil), squid, and all sorts of shellfish; as well as cheeses, hard-cooked eggs, and other imaginative tidbits.

Italy is the world's largest producer of wines, so it is quite natural that wine should be taken with meals. Many table wines are strictly local products, drunk while they are still very young and not even shipped out of the province, much less the country. However, the Tuscan Chianti in the familiar straw-covered flask, Bardolino and Valpolicella and the excellent white Soave (these last three from northern Italy) are among Italy's well-known exported wines.

Before dinner, many Italians enjoy an apéritif of vermouth with a twist of lemon or orange peel. Vermouth is a fortified wine flavored with aromatic herbs. Italian vermouth is a little less light and less dry than French vermouth. The most famous Italian dessert wine is Marsala, which is produced in Sicily. It has many cooking uses as well, and is an ingredient of *zabaglione*, a wine custard prepared by whisk-

ing together egg yolks, sugar, and Marsala. This dessert cooks in a very few minutes and is served warm, although it is also very good chilled.

The *bottiglieria* or wineshop is a picturesque establishment lined with barrels, which dispenses wine by the carafe in quantities from a beaker to a liter. It is noisy and familiar, usually patronized by men only. Like most Mediterranean people, however, the Italians are moderate drinkers and seldom go beyond the limits of propriety.

The *caffè* is the central social institution in Italian life. After the family, it ranks high in the affections of Italian men. The *caffè* is the leisurely club-office where newspapers (on long wooden rods) are perused, where business is transacted, where politics are discussed and where, almost incidentally, one also drinks coffee. Small cream-filled cakes and rich pastries are often devoured by Italian *caffè* patrons along with their coffee.

Most popular is *caffè espresso*, the Italian demitasse made with pulverized coffee that has been roasted very black. It is served in small cups with sugar or, if desired, with a twist of lemon or orange peel. *Espresso* means "made expressly for you" in a kind of inverted drip pot in which the water is forced upward by steam pressure. The pot is called a *caffeteria* or a *machinetta*. *Cappuccino* is *espresso* topped with warm milk or, in a more luxurious version, topped with whipped cream and dusted with cinnamon or grated orange rind. Other *espresso* variations include brandy, rum, or liqueurs and may be spiced with cinnamon or cloves.

The simplest type of Italian restaurant is the *osteria*, where seats are not provided and snacks may be eaten on the run. The *osteria* is reminiscent of the cookshops of ancient Rome. The *pizzerie* of Naples are of this type. A notch above is the *rosticceria* where a selection of inexpensive cooked dishes is offered. Some tables may be provided, but it is possible that here, too, one may have to stand at the counter to eat.

The *trattoria* is a simple family-style restaurant with tables, and a fairly wide selection of dishes permitting snacks to full meals. It is open at almost all hours. Most formal is the *ristorante,* where full meals are served and where prices range from modest to very expensive.

Here is a typical Italian menu, which attempts to incorporate dishes from the various regions of Italy:

Antipasto

*

Minestrone alla Genovese   or   *Tagliatelle alla Bolognese*
(Genoese Minestrone)   (Noodles with Ragout Sauce)

*

Scampi all' Griglia alla Veneziana
(Grilled Prawns, Venetian Style)
or
Scaloppine alla Milanese
(Veal Scallops, Milan Style)
or
Abbacchio al Forno alla Romana
(Roast Baby Lamb, Roman Style)

*

Formaggio con Frutta Fresca   or   *Zabaglione*
(Cheese with Fresh Fruit)   (Wine Custard)

*

Caffè Espresso
(Italian Demitasse)

Italian Recipes

PESTO GENOVESE

(*Genoese Herb-and-cheese Sauce*)

½   cup minced fresh basil or parsley (or half each)
1   clove garlic, put through garlic press
    Pinch salt
⅓   cup pine nuts or walnuts, ground fine
¾   cup freshly grated Parmesan cheese
1   tablespoon butter
¼   cup olive oil

With the back of a wooden spoon, mash all the ingredients in a bowl in the order given, adding the olive oil a little at a time. The *pesto* should have the consistency of creamed butter. If necessary, add a little more olive oil.

To serve, toss the *pesto* rapidly with about ⅔ pound of freshly cooked, very hot, thin spaghetti. Add a lump of butter and toss with the spaghetti and sauce. Serve at once. Makes 4 servings.

RISOTTO ALLA MILANESE

(*Rice, Milan Style*)

2   tablespoons butter
1   small onion, cut fine
1   cup long-grain rice
3   cups chicken broth (or 4 chicken bouillon cubes dissolved in 3 cups boiling water)
⅛   teaspoon saffron
2   tablespoons butter
¼   cup freshly grated Parmesan cheese

In a deep skillet that has a lid melt the 2 tablespoons of butter. Add the onion and fry it just to a pale gold; do not brown it. Add the rice and stir it with a wooden spoon so that it becomes buttery. Add 1 cup of the chicken broth, cover the pan, and cook over low heat about 15 minutes or until the broth is absorbed by the rice.

Add the saffron to a little of the hot broth and set this aside to steep for at least 5 minutes. As the rice in the skillet absorbs the broth, add more broth about 1 cup at a time. Finally add the saffron broth.

The *risotto* is done when the rice is tender, but the individual grains should have a slight firmness to the bite. The mixture should be creamy. If too dry, add a little more broth. Toss the *risotto* lightly with the remaining butter and the Parmesan cheese, and serve at once in a heated bowl.

In Italian meals *risotto*, whether plain or combined with giblets, mushrooms, or chicken livers, is served as a separate course (*asciutta*). It is only served as a side dish with *ossi buchi*. Makes 6 to 8 servings.

MOZZARELLA IN CARROZZA

(Mozzarella *in a Carriage; Naples and the South*)

    18 slices white bread
     1 pound *mozzarella* cheese
        Flour
     3 eggs
    ¼   cup milk
        Olive oil, or salad oil and olive oil combined

Trim crusts from white bread and make up 6 3-decker sandwiches, covering bread slices with ⅛-inch-thick slices of cheese. Cut each sandwich into four triangles and secure each portion with a toothpick.

Coat cut sides of each wedge lightly with flour. Beat eggs and milk together. Dip each wedge into this mixture covering it completely as for French toast. Pour olive oil into a large skillet to a depth of ½ inch. When oil is very hot, fry wedges quickly until crisp and golden on all sides.

Drain wedges, remove toothpicks, and serve at once, or keep them warm on a baking sheet in a 250-degree oven until all are fried. Serve *mozzarella in carrozza* plain or with the following hot anchovy sauce, which is to be poured over the sandwiches just before they are eaten. Makes 6 servings.

Hot Anchovy Sauce:

     4 tablespoons butter
     2 cloves garlic, put through garlic press
     2 tablespoons minced anchovies or anchovy paste
     2 tablespoons crushed capers
     2 tablespoons minced fresh parsley
  2½ tablespoons flour
  1½ cups beef bouillon
     2 teaspoons lemon juice
     2 tablespoons dry sherry

Melt the butter in a saucepan. Add the garlic, anchovies, capers, and parsley. Cook over a low flame for 5 minutes. Blend in the flour. Add the beef bouillon a little at a time, and cook stirring constantly until mixture thickens slightly. Add the lemon juice and the sherry. Serve very hot.

CAPONATA ALLA COSENZA

(*Eggplant-and-vegetable Relish; southern Italy and Sicily*)

         1 eggplant (1¼ to 1½ pounds)
        ½ cup olive oil or salad oil (or half each)
         3 tablespoons olive oil or salad oil
         1 onion, cut fine
         1 clove garlic, minced
         1 large green pepper, cut in 1-inch-long slivers
         1 cup celery, cut in slivers across the rib
  3 to 4 fresh ripe tomatoes, peeled and cut in medium dice
         3 tablespoons sliced pimento-stuffed green olives
         1 tablespoon capers
         2 teaspoons salt
        ¼ teaspoon freshly ground black pepper
         2 tablespoons wine vinegar
         1 tablespoon sugar
         1 teaspoon oregano

Pare eggplant and cut in ½-inch cubes. Heat the ½ cup oil in a large deep skillet. Brown the eggplant lightly, cover the skillet, and continue cooking over low heat until the eggplant is very soft. Remove eggplant and set aside.

Add the additional 3 tablespoons of oil. Add the onion, garlic, green pepper, and celery. Fry lightly, cover skillet, and continue cooking over low heat until very tender.

To peel the tomatoes, immerse them for a few minutes in boiling water. This will loosen the skin. Add the diced, peeled tomatoes to the skillet and cook 5 minutes more or until soft.

Add the eggplant and the remaining ingredients to the skillet. Simmer 5 minutes more. Mixture should be quite thick. Adjust seasoning. *Caponata* may be served hot as a vegetable, but it is usually served chilled as an appetizer or a relish. It will keep well in the refrigerator in a tightly closed jar. Makes 1 quart.

ZABAGLIONE

(*Wine Custard—northern Italy*)

4 egg yolks
.4 tablespoons finely granulated sugar
4 tablespoons Marsala wine or sweet sherry

With a wire whisk beat the egg yolks and the sugar in a double-boiler top until frothy and lemon-colored. Stir in the wine and set into a double-boiler bottom containing very hot but not boiling water.

As mixture cooks over moderate heat, continue beating with whisk until custard is thickened and of a creamy consistency throughout. Pour into sherbet glasses and serve warm. *Zabaglione* may also be served chilled. Makes 2 servings.

Greece

GREECE, with its rocky soil and garlanded hillsides, its craggy shores overhanging a sapphire sea, is surely the most typical of Mediterranean countries. The olive tree sprang from Grecian earth very early in the days of gods and heroes. It is said to have been the gift of the goddess Athene, after whom Athens was named. The grapevine, too, derives from antiquity and was attributed to Dionysus, the god of wine and good living. On Mount Hymettus, rising within sight of Athens, the wild bees, thick among the tight clusters of tiny flowers and aromatic herbs, produced the sweetest honey in all of the ancient world.

The landscape of Greece is little changed today. In true Mediterranean tradition, Greece has remained primarily an agricultural country, limited by thinning soil and rugged terrain to small-scale farming and the pasturing of sheep and goats. The coastline of the Greek mainland is as jagged as that of New England. Together with its hundreds of islands, which make up about one-fifth of its territory,

Greece has an untold number of gulfs, inlets, and bays, although only a few are deep-water harbors. Fishing boats and other light boats known as caïques have no trouble making port. Nor did the smaller seagoing vessels of ancient times, thus making colonization and commerce possible among the isolated seagirt communities.

The Greek mainland, surrounded on three sides by water, was the perfect natural setting for a Mediterranean civilization. Beginning about 1600 B.C., the rich Minoan civilization of Crete gradually succumbed to the vigorous although less cultivated mainland peoples. By 500 B.C., when the early Romans were still repelling their Etruscan rulers in Italy, the Greeks had already colonized Asia Minor, the Black Sea ports, Sicily, southern Italy, and the coasts of France, Spain, and Portugal. Later (in the 300s B.C.) the Greeks were to take Egypt. Although the soil of ancient Greece was more fertile, the wooded regions thicker, than they are today, overpopulation was a recurring problem and colonies, to absorb the excess and to provide trade, were essential.

The Greek city-states, of which the best known are Athens, Corinth, and Sparta, were pockets of civilization separated by untamed and often impassable mountain country. In 500 B.C. Athens, the first (albeit limited) democracy, a citadel of art, architecture, drama, and philosophy, was about to enter its Golden Age under the distinguished statesman Pericles.

THE ATHENIAN MARKETPLACE

Daily life in ancient Athens centered around the large market plaza known as the *agora*. Here portable booths were set up each morning, usually in the *stoas* (long, covered promenades supported by rows of columns). Meeting places and government buildings were all conveniently located here. The open barber shops of the *agora* served as clubs and social centers and also did a thriving business in the cutting, curling, dyeing, and perfuming of men's locks—and in the trimming of beards. Most men were bearded in Greece until the time of Alexander the Great (who ruled from 336 to 323 B.C.). Alexander insisted that his army be clean-shaven; one reason advanced was that the enemy could grasp a beard in hand-to-hand combat!

In the booths, wares ranging from sandals and charcoal to flowers and wine were displayed for sale. No fixed prices were asked. All goods were bargained for. The poor went about with their coins in their mouths (for they carried no purses, only the basket in which to take home their purchases), selecting garlic and onions, dried lentils and peas, barley, salt fish, and bread in large round loaves. Slowly, the shoppers of the *agora* would remove the necessary bit of change from between their lips to pay for each of their purchases.

Informal cookshops sold a hot porridge of barley meal or a dish of cooked legumes. *Fava*, which is commonly eaten today in Greece, is a thick stew of dried split peas seasoned with onion and garlic, parsley and oregano (a favorite Greek herb), and olive oil. This 2500-year-old recipe, possibly prepared with lentils or chick-peas in ancient times, has changed little.

At home, the poor lived frugally in simple single-story dwellings, many of them mere heaps of stones. There were no multistoried tenement buildings in Athens such as the crowded *insulae* that were to be built in Rome. But the lanes outside the Greek houses were narrow and strewn with refuse, and there was no public sewer system such as Rome was to know. Even wealthy homes in Athens had no sanitary facilities or house water supply.

Olive oil was essential to many aspects of daily living. It was a dip for bread, in place of butter; it was a fat and a seasoning agent in cooking; it was used to rub down the body in place of soap; and it often served as lamp fuel. Of all the ravages of war during ancient times, the ones the Greeks feared most was the destruction of their olive groves. Since the trees took more than a decade to bear fruit, a burned-away grove of olive trees was an almost irreplaceable loss.

In very early times, Greek wines were stored in goatskins. These had to be smeared with pitch or resin to prevent leakage and spoilage. Later, resin was also used as a sealer for earthenware wine jugs. This substance imparted to the wine a turpentine-like flavor which the Greeks came to like, and continued to add to their wine long after casks and bottles came into use. *Retsina* wine is an acquired taste. The visitor to Greece who prefers unresinated wine must ask for *aretsinoto*. The ancient Greeks drank their wines diluted, generally three parts of water to two of wine. Whether this was due to the strong resinous flavor or to high alcoholic content is uncertain.

Bread in ancient Greece was sometimes of wheat flour but often of barley flour, for wheat did not grow well in the rocky soil. Barley cakes, as these loaves were called, were stodgy and rather flavorless. They were often dipped in honey, and sometimes even in vinegar, to make them more palatable. Grain, particularly wheat, was Athens' most needed import. For this she traded her Hymettus honey and her prized olive oil.

Most Athenian diets included little meat except after one of the great public religious festivals at which one hundred or more oxen might be slaughtered and distributed to the worshipers. Otherwise goats, hogs, and sheep provided the principal domestic meats, although sheep were raised chiefly for their wool from which most Athenian garments were woven. Goat's flesh, however, and goat's cheese were always for sale in the *agora*.

Beef was a rarity, as most of the land was totally unsuited to cattle grazing. Milk, regardless of its source, was quickly converted into cheese because of its perishability in the hot climate. Figs were plentiful and were eaten at most meals. Many fruits were cultivated, including apples, quinces, and pears, but of course the ancient Greeks had no citrus fruits. The lemons that were later to come into Greek cookery and that play such a vital role in it today—and the rice—were not yet known. The Greeks are believed to have learned of rice first in 326 B.C. when Alexander the Great invaded India, but quite some time was to elapse before rice entered the cuisine.

The slaughter of animals in public sacrifices and the study

of omens resulting therefrom were performed by a priest or seer who took the best joint as a fee for professional services. These services consisted of studying the shape and size of the entrails, liver, spleen, bladder, and lungs, observing the manner in which the sacrifice smoke curled, and interpreting these "signs" for the maker of the sacrifice. New undertakings, from a marriage to a military campaign, required that the gods be consulted and, hopefully, appeased.

The sacrifice of animals to the ancient gods persists today in many parts of Greece, despite the disapproval of the church. It is still customary to kill a cock when the foundation of a new house is laid. For larger buildings, a ram may be slaughtered. Another lingering pagan superstition is the setting out of sweetmeats for the Fates after the birth of a child, for the ancients believed that during the first three days of life these powers hovered over the newborn and had to be appeased if the child was to have a happy future. Also from Greek antiquity comes the custom of placing a coin on the forehead of the deceased to pay his fare to Charon, the ferryman of the Underworld. In ancient times an *obol* (a Greek coin) was placed in the mouth of the deceased for this purpose.

The public festivals of Athens numbered about thirty a year, many lasting more than a day. These centered around athletic contests, dances, processions, and all-day performances at the outdoor theaters that lasted from sunup to sunset with a brief recess for lunch. There was, however, no fixed day of the week set aside for rest or religious observance, for in the pre-Christian era none but the Hebrews observed the ritual of the weekly Sabbath.

Greek homes, particularly those of the more prosperous, were built around an open rectangular court onto which the various rooms opened. The court provided light and air, for in typical southern fashion the walls of the house were windowless. Just behind the open court, which served as a

ATHENIAN HOMES AND DINNER PARTIES

living room in good weather, was the *andron* or dining hall. The family hearth was here, and even if the cooking was done in other quarters (as it was in larger houses), it was customary to cast a little food upon the flames at every meal as an offering to Hestia, the hearth goddess.

Beyond the *andron* were the women's quarters, secluded from the rest of the house just as the Greek woman was secluded from the rest of the world. The women of the East were to continue to be restrained in their activities later under Islam. The Greek girl was usually married at fifteen to a man about twice her age. Except for religious and family occasions, such as the birth of a child, a wedding, or a funeral, the Athenian woman seldom left her home. She did attend the theater occasionally, but only to see tragedies, never comedies. Women usually dined in their own quarters, they did not go to the *agora* to shop (men did the shopping, either alone or accompanied by servants), and they did not attend their husbands' dinner parties.

The Athenians were criticized in their own times for being greater talkers than eaters, for indeed philosophical discussions, storytelling, and versifying seemed much more important at the dinner party than did the food. This balance was to be sharply reversed by the Romans. Through the day the Greeks ate very lightly. They rose at dawn and had at most a few pieces of bread dipped in undiluted wine. This meal, if it was taken at all, was called the *akratisma* (first breakfast). *Ariston* (second breakfast or lunch) was usually at mid-morning, a meal consisting of a dish of legumes eaten perhaps with a raw onion, or of leftovers from the previous day's dinner.

The *deipnon* was the main meal of the day, eaten toward sunset. If there were no invited guests, it was a very simple dinner of fish or meat, bread, cheese, olives, and some fresh figs or other fruit for dessert. If guests were invited, a special cook might be hired for the occasion. The cook was held in high esteem in ancient Greece. He was a skilled artisan, often an intellectual as well, and the regular house staff bowed to his demands from the moment he entered the premises.

It was customary for the guests, particularly the guest of honor, to bring along a friend or two, as well as some servants to attend them at dinner. Parasites, hangers-on who came uninvited but were willing to serve as buffoons for the sake of food and drink, were also commonly accepted at Athenian dinner parties. The guests removed their outer cloaks (this garment was called the *himation*) and their sandals. Wearing only the *chiton* (a tunic, usually sleeveless, that fell from the neck to the knees), they dined from small tables, reclining two to a couch. Fingers were the principal dining utensils, and since napkins were not generally used, large pieces of soft bread served to clean off the hands and face. The bread was then dropped to the floor.

A really lavish dinner was composed of separate fish and meat courses at which several dishes of each were presented —eels, mullet, and cuttlefish followed by boar's head, roast kid, roast lamb, hares, and poultry. With these were provided vegetables such as radishes, turnips, and lettuces, as well as barley cakes, wheaten buns, sweet buns prepared with dried figs, and of course wine.

The second and final part of the meal consisted of honey, fruits, and cheesecakes. These were not made with cheese, but were custardy desserts of a soft curdlike consistency. The *galatopeta* (custard cake) of modern Greece is a puddinglike mixture of milk, eggs, sugar, and farina that may well be a direct descendant of the ancient Grecian cheesecakes.

The party might end at this point, or it might continue with the *symposium*, a period of wine drinking and conversation. At less lofty gatherings, the wine drinking was accompanied by entertainment provided by hired flute girls and dancers. At the true *symposium*, however, music was only a background and, under the direction of the *symposiarch* (master of ceremonies), formal discussion, poetry recitations, and other verbal exercises continued into the midnight hours. At last the guests rose and, calling for sandals and *himation*, took their leave.

THE BYZANTINE
INFLUENCE IN
GREEK COOKERY

One of the many Mediterranean trade centers established by the colonizing Greeks was Byzantium in Asia Minor. In this city (which is today called Istanbul and was long the capital of Turkey), East and West were destined to meet.

By 146 B.C. Rome had overcome Greece politically but Greek culture and learning continued to thrive in Byzantium, as in many other Greek colonies, and even in Rome itself. In A.D. 330, the Roman emperor Constantine established a new capital at Byzantium, calling it New Rome. The city was later named Constantinople in his honor and, after the Empire was divided, served as the seat of the Eastern Roman Empire.

The Byzantine (or Eastern Roman) Empire saw its golden age in the sixth century under the emperor Justinian I. The empress Theodora, although not of noble birth, was a woman of great charm, wit, and influence. Her skilled chefs brought to the Byzantine court cuisines from India, Persia, and Greece, as well as from Syria and Theodora's own home, Cyprus. These were to fuse and to set the pattern for present-day Greek, Turkish, and Middle Eastern gastronomy. Rice, lemons, and eggplant from India, and a flaky tissue-thin pastry that was of Persian origin, were among the foods of the Byzantine world that became prominent in later-day Greece.

No flavor is more typical of modern Greece than *avgolemono*, the egg-and-lemon-juice sauce that gives a tart creaminess to soups, meat-ball dishes, and *dolmades* or *dolmadakia* (stuffed grapevine leaves). It is believed that *dolmadakia* stuffed with chopped meat and spices were prepared in ancient Greece. But today's popular rice-and-meat stuffing, as well as the rice-and-herb stuffing used in the cold appetizer-type *dolmadakia*, date from the Byzantine era.

Rice (or very small *pasta*) is an ingredient of *avgolemono* soup, the base of which is usually a chicken broth. Rice cooked in butter and chicken stock makes a flavorful *pilaf* to accompany a main dish of grilled lamb. Rice mixed with pine nuts, currants, and cinnamon stuffs a chicken; rice combined with chestnuts, raisins, and chopped meat stuffs a turkey. Rice in the company of mint and dill, parsley and onions, pine nuts and chopped meats, stuffs vegetables from tomatoes and eggplants to zucchini and peppers. Rice, sweetened and enriched with milk and eggs, flavored with lemon or cinnamon, makes a creamy dessert, *rizogalo*. Indeed, it is difficult to imagine the Greek cuisine without rice.

The shiny purple eggplant—fried, braised, stuffed, mashed into a dip, or chopped for a salad or relish—is a boon to a people whose land supplies a limited meat diet. The generous green-white flesh of this versatile vegetable is perhaps at its best in the renowned Greek *moussaka*, a baked dish of Turkish origin made up of layers of fried eggplant and ground lamb seasoned with tomato, oregano, and a dash of cinnamon. Topped with an egg-enriched white sauce and grated cheese, the *moussaka* is baked to a golden puffiness and served warm, cut in squares. *Moussaka* may also be prepared with potatoes or zucchini squash instead of eggplant. It is the ancient Greeks, incidentally, who are believed to have invented the basic white sauce. Adaptations of this sauce were much used in northern Italian cuisine in Renaissance times and hence carried over into French cookery, which is so renowned for its sauces, many of which are of borrowed origin.

Ancient Persia was in a sense the sweetmeat kitchen of antiquity. In this richly endowed Middle Eastern empire (of which present-day Iran was the heart), there originated luscious glazed and preserved fruits, concentrated fruit syrups that were the basis of cooling drinks called sherbets, and sugar-and-honey-drenched pastries stuffed with layers of crushed nuts.

The paper-thin pastry sheets used for *baklava* and other delectable sweets (as well as a number of savories) crept into Greek cuisine from the Persian by way of the Byzantine Empire. This pastry is known in Greece as *phyllo* (pronounced fee'-lo). Its large leaves of stretched dough are difficult to prepare at home but may be purchased by the pound in specialty and foreign-food shops. *Phyllo* could only have originated in the East in ancient times, for nowhere else was the flour so finely milled.

The strudel leaves of Austria and Hungary are of the same origin as the Greek *phyllo*, this pastry having been brought to central Europe by the Turks in their sixteenth-century onslaughts on the West. Hungarian cooks pride themselves on their homemade strudel dough, insisting that the test of a properly stretched dough is that it be so thin that the fine print of a newspaper can be read through it. Strudel leaves and *phyllo* may be used interchangeably.

Baklava, so popular in Greek and Middle Eastern cuisine, consists of buttered *phyllo* leaves layered with sugar, cinnamon, and finely chopped nuts. Cut into diamond shapes, baked, and then saturated with a lemon-tinged sugar syrup, *baklava* is but one of numerous similar pastries varying in shape from coiled rounds to long, slender "fingers." A little different is *galatoboureko*, which consists of top and bottom layers of buttered *phyllo* pastry filled with a rich vanilla- or orange-flavored custard.

Copenhagen seems an odd name for a Greek pastry. It is a luxurious sweet consisting of a rich cooky-like pastry crust filled with a mixture of eggs, sugar, and ground walnuts or almonds, and topped with layers of buttered *phyllo*. After baking, *Copenhagen* is drenched in a sugar-and-honey syrup. This ultimate in pastries was devised in honor of King George I of Greece, who was a prince of Denmark before being chosen for the Greek throne in 1863. Unhappily, this honor seems reversed when we learn that George I, after a fifty-year reign, was assassinated at Salonika in 1913.

It must not be supposed that the average Greek concludes his daily meals with these fabulous confections. Fruit is the customary dessert, while the delights of the *zaharoplastia* (sweet or pastry shop) are indulged in chiefly at name-day celebrations, weddings, and on other feast days. *Phyllo* pastries are popular, however, as the accompaniment to an afternoon coffee at the *kafenion* (coffeehouse) where, as in other Mediterranean cafés, men congregate in the after-

noons and evenings for business and social purposes and (in Greece) to play intense games of backgammon usually for low stakes.

Kafes (coffee) is served in Greece in tiny cups, very black, very full-flavored, and sweetened to the taste in the brewing so that nothing is added to the poured cup. At the *kafenion,* coffee is brought to the table with a large glass of water, for water is a prized beverage in the semi-arid lands of Greece and the Middle East and is the first sign of hospitality and well-being.

"Greek" coffee is really Turkish coffee, adopted by the Greeks during the four long centuries (1400s to 1800s) of Turkish domination. "Turkish" coffee, it should be added, is really Arabian in origin, for it was in Arabia in the ninth or tenth century that the coffee bean was first roasted and pulverized for brewing. The coffee of the Middle Eastern, Turkish, and Greek world is brewed, with water and the desired amount of sugar, in a long-handled brass pot. The mixture is brought to a boil and the froth is then poured off into demitasse cups. The pot is then reboiled and the additional coffee poured over the froth to fill the cups. This is important, for the coffee must have the foamy *kaïmak* ("cream") on top, which is formed only by the first boil.

The drinker must wait a few seconds for the grounds to settle. He then sips his coffee carefully so as not to stir up the muddy sediment that forms in the bottom of the cup.

This method of brewing and drinking may seem like much trouble to the American coffee drinker, but the rich concentrated coffee flavor of this brew is unmatched anywhere in the world.

The Greeks are the most hospitable of people; in fact, the word for both foreigner and guest is the same, *xenos*. Remote villages, poor and vegetarian by necessity, will often slaughter a kid or a lamb in honor of the visitor. In the Greek home, *glyko* (syrupy jam or preserved fruit) served with a glass of water is the hallmark of hospitality. These sweet preserves of black or red cherries, of strawberries, of orange, grapefruit, or watermelon rind, all follow in the ancient Persian tradition. In the Greek ritual, the newly arrived guest is presented with a tray containing a small bowl of *glyko*, a spoon, and a glass of cold water. The guest takes a spoonful of preserves, puts the spoon in the glass of water, wishes his host good health, and downs the sweetened water.

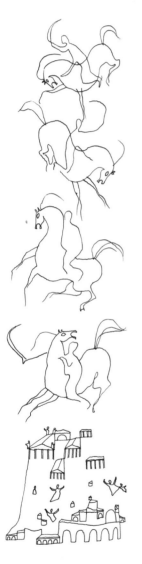

This procedure is more elaborate when the traditional Greek spirit *ouzo* (distilled from grapes and flavored with anise) is offered in addition. Now the guest takes a spoonful of *glyko*, drops the spoon into the glass of water, makes a toast to his host, and downs the small glass of *ouzo*. He follows this by taking a long sip from the water glass, firmly pressing the teaspoon against the side of the glass with his finger in order to prevent injury to his eye.

Ouzo is a clear aromatic liquid that becomes cloudy the moment it is mixed with water. It is popular in Greece as an apéritif, accompanied by *mezes* or *mezethakia* (Greek hors d'oeuvres), and many Greeks sip *ouzo* mixed with water as a table beverage in place of wine. *Ouzo* undiluted is fiery and potent, but the Greek seldom drinks without eating. *Mezes* to accompany an apéritif of *ouzo* or of *retsina* wine run the gamut from olives, salty white *feta* cheese (made from goat's milk), Greek sausages, *keftaidakia* (tiny meat balls), stuffed mussels, pickled squid, and broiled baby octopus to *dolmadakia* and *taramasalata* (a dip of carp roe pounded with onion, olive oil, bread, and lemon juice).

Tiny cheese-filled triangles of *phyllo* pastry called *tiropetes* make delectable hot appetizers, as do those filled with a spinach-and-cheese mixture. *Phyllo* pastry may also be prepared in the form of a main-dish pie, filled with cheese or spinach and served cut in squares. *Phyllo* pastry savories also come under the general term *bourekia*.

Wherever one ventures in the Greek cuisine, one seems always to return to the culinary heritage of the ancient Middle East, transported westward by way of the Byzantine capital. But still a stronger tide was to come from Constantinople, for in 1453 that city fell to the Ottoman Turks, a people who had swept out of central Asia. The Byzantine or Eastern Roman Empire expired, and the Ottoman Empire began to expand. By 1460 the Turks had taken Greece, and it was not until 1821 that the Greeks began the long struggle to wrench themselves free.

Despite the animosity between conquered and conqueror, the Greeks and the Turks came to have many things in common—the wailing airs of their folk music, the male habit of fingering a string of "worry beads" when the hands are restless, the ritual of breaking the siesta with a sip of Turkish coffee and a large glass of ice water, and above all their cuisines which contain elements so similar it is sometimes difficult to distinguish between them.

Visitors are sometimes dismayed at the temperature of foods served in Greece. The emphasis in the United States and other countries on serving hot foods hot and cold foods cold does not exist in native Greek cookery.

Since few Greek homes have ovens, oven-baked dishes such as *moussaka*, cheese or spinach pies, and the popular macaroni, meat, and white-sauce dish called *pastichio* must be sent to the baker's. Consequently these are never quite hot at serving time. By the same token, foods meant to be served chilled or very cold may be served at room temperature due to lack of refrigeration. It must be remembered that in ancient civilizations it was only the very wealthy, the slave-endowed, who could afford to have their dishes presented at

COOKING AND EATING IN MODERN GREECE

other than room temperature. This is still true in many Mediterranean lands today.

Most Greek cooking is done atop a kerosene stove or over an open charcoal fire, thus accounting for the large number of soups, stews, and spit-roasted meats in the Greek cuisine. Soup is usually a main course in Greece, eaten with chunks of bread and the typical Greek salad of raw vegetables (greens, cucumbers, peppers, scallions, tomatoes, radishes, parsley) torn or cut to bite-size pieces, dressed with olive oil and vinegar or lemon juice, and mixed or garnished with anchovies, black olives, and *feta* cheese.

Bean, pea, and lentil soups, a heritage of ancient times, are almost daily fare in the Greek village, and if fresh vegetables for a salad are out of season, pickled vegetables or even a sliced raw onion will do as a side dish. *Trahana*, a homemade noodle dough prepared with flour and either milk or yogurt, is crumbled into tiny morsels and served in soups as a change from rice.

Fish with wonderful Greek names translate into red mullet, mackerel, sea bass, squid, octopus, shrimp, and mussels, for Greek shorelines are extensive and are dotted with fishing villages. Fish and shellfish are boiled and broiled, braised and baked, fried in sizzling olive oil, or combined into a *kakavia*, a fish chowder or stew that represents the entire day's catch.

The staple meat dish of Greece is the lamb stew cooked with a vegetable, *any* vegetable from artichokes to zucchini, or even with quince. The *tourlou* is a lamb stew to which *many* vegetables are added—eggplant, peppers, string beans, and several more. *Giouvetsi* is a baked lamb dish flavored with tomatoes, onions, and garlic, and to which *pasta* is added.

Neither beef nor veal is plentiful or of particularly high quality in Greece. But beef, veal, or hare is cooked with small white onions in a tomato-seasoned sauce to make a *stefado*, a stew to which walnut halves and cubes of *feta* cheese are sometimes added. A dash of cinnamon, too, adds subtle but distinctive flavor to Grecian meat dishes.

Pork is not widely used in the Greek cuisine. Perhaps this

is due to the centuries of Moslem-Turkish influence, for the religion of Islam prohibits the eating of pork. The Greek Orthodox religion, however, to which more than 95 per cent of the Greek people belong (and which prevailed throughout the Turkish occupation), makes no such restriction. Suckling pig, spit-roasted over charcoal, is a festive dish although spit-roasted baby lamb rubbed with lemon and garlic surely rates first as a special-occasion dish.

Superb, too, is *souvlakia*, the Greek *shishkebab*. It consists of chunks of tender lamb marinated in olive oil, lemon juice, and wine, dusted with oregano, and grilled on skewers over hot coals. *Shishkebab* is a Turkish word that translates as "sword meat," for this dish is said to have originated with Turkish horsemen who impaled the meat of slaughtered lambs on their swords and roasted it over outdoor fires.

Almost as prominent as *avgolemono* sauce, especially in the country regions, is the potent Greek *skordalia* sauce. This heavy-on-the-garlic mixture includes olive oil and lemon juice or vinegar. It is thickened with potatoes, walnuts, or bread crumbs and is pounded to a smooth paste to be served on boiled or fried fish and on vegetables such as squash and eggplant. *Skordalia*, like many other garlicky Mediterranean sauces, was very likely known in ancient times, prepared with vinegar instead of lemon juice and thickened with crushed nuts.

In modern Greece the day begins with a breakfast of hot milk, usually with a thick skin on top, into which sugar is stirred. Chunks of bread are dipped into the milk to complete the meal. Occasionally tea is substituted. Lunch is served any time from one o'clock on (sometimes as late as three in private homes) and is often the principal meal of the day. As such, it consists of a lamb, chicken, or fish dish, generally in the form of a stew or *pilaf* (cooked with rice), a salad, crusty white or dark brown bread, and a simple dessert of fruit, yogurt, rice pudding, or custard. The meal concludes with Greek coffee.

Before dinner, a stop at the *taverna* for a glass of *ouzo* or *retsina* accompanied by *mezes* is almost obligatory. There

are many kinds of *tavernes*. They may be tiny candlelit rooms tucked away in basements, or outdoor summer gardens; they may be relatively peaceful with the hum of convivial conversation, or dizzying with laughter and song and the music of a radio, a phonograph, or an itinerant *bouzoukia* (mandolin) player. The *taverna*, too, may be the setting for one of the informal yet ritualistic Greek dances performed only by men, bending and leaping, hissing and finger-snapping, with intense grace and agility.

Another late-afternoon pastime is the *peripato*, the leisurely strolling of families and groups of young people, akin to the Spanish *paseo*. Dinner is served from eight o'clock on, but in many Greek homes where lunch has been the main meal, the family may have an informal snack of leftovers or a simple one-dish supper.

The religion of modern Greece was created as a result of the schism of 1054. In that year the Eastern Orthodox church, its power centered in Constantinople, threw off the jurisdiction of the Roman Catholic church. The Eastern Orthodox church with which the Greek Orthodox is affiliated has no pope nor his equivalent, permits its priests to marry, but prohibits marriage for bishops and other higher clergy. The long black robes and flat-topped brimless stovepipe hat of the Greek priest are a distinctive feature of the Greek scene. The priest's headgear was designed to accommodate the hair, which according to the religion is not supposed to be cut and hence must be rolled up into a bulky bun and worn inside the hat.

It is not by accident that the tall white chef's hat so closely resembles that of the Eastern Orthodox priest. The story goes that a white hat patterned after the priest's black one was originally worn by the cooks in Byzantine monasteries. Later this hat became the symbol of chefdom around the world.

The Greek Orthodox calendar is studded with feast days and holy days. Most important of these is Easter, the apex of the Greek festival year. Easter is preceded by the pre-Lenten week of *Apokreos*, a period of carnival during which parties and masquerades are held and meats and rich foods are disposed of. Lent, which lasts for seven weeks in the Eastern Orthodox church, is strictly observed with fasting and prayer.

On the eve of Easter Sunday, the entire village troops to the church, each person bearing an unlit candle. This most solemn ceremony is attended even by those who are not customarily churchgoers. Exactly at midnight in the darkened church, the first candle, the Resurrection light, is lit by the priest from the eternal vigil light at the holy altar. "*Christos Anesti*," he pronounces—"Christ is risen."

The flame is transmitted to the candles of the altar boys

THE GREEK FESTIVAL YEAR

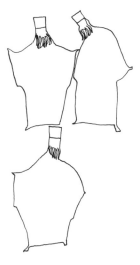

and one by one to the entire congregation. It is said that when a girl lights her candle from one held by a man, she will marry him within the year. As the church grows from dark to dim and from dim to dazzling, all of the possible noises of the village or town assert themselves. Rockets and firecrackers spurt and crackle, factory whistles blow, air-raid sirens scream, and fire engines clang. The candles twinkle through the midnight lanes as the worshipers stroll home-ward to partake of the traditional supper of Easter morn.

The Resurrection candles are set on the table and *mageritsa*, the meat soup that breaks the Lenten fast, is set forth. Baby lamb parts—liver, heart, tripe, lung, entrails, and even the head tied together with string—are the princi-pal ingredients of this soup, which includes dill and green onions and is always flavored with *avgolemono* sauce. An-other food of the Easter morn repast is *lambropsomo*, the yeast-raised Easter bread sprinkled with sesame seeds and studded with five red-dyed Easter eggs in the design of the Greek cross—one for the center and four for each of the equal-length arms.

Members of the family tap the eggs against each other to crack them. One says *"Christos Anesti,"* and the other replies *"Alithos Anesti"*—"Truly, He is risen." Greek Easter eggs are dyed red to symbolize the blood of Christ. The egg, of course, is the sign of resurrection, for it holds life.

The Easter Sunday dinner is one of the great feasts of the year. It is sure to feature spit-roasted baby lamb preceded by elaborate *mezes*, more *mageritsa*, and *kokoretsi* (highly sea-soned baby lamb parts, baked or grilled over charcoal like *souvlakia*). The meal will close with *koulourakia* (rich, varishaped butter cookies sprinkled with sesame seeds; tradi-tional for Easter), *baklava*, and Greek coffee.

The Greek Christmas consists of twelve days of festivity commencing on December 25 and ending on Epiphany (January 6), which in the Eastern church commemorates the baptism of Christ. The Christmas dinner stars spit-roasted suckling pig, roast leg of lamb, or roast turkey stuffed with mixtures of overwhelming richness—chestnuts, pine nuts, walnuts, rice, ground meat, onions, tomatoes, raisins, cinnamon, and cloves, in a variety of combinations. *Mezes*, *sarmades* (Macedonian cabbage rolls stuffed with pork and cooked with sauerkraut), and Greek salads precede or accompany the main dish. *Christopsomo*, the rich yeast-raised Christmas bread, decorated with a cross outlined in walnuts, graces the holiday table.

Dried figs, dates, roasted chestnuts, quince preserves, honey-dipped cookies, *baklava* and other *phyllo* pastries, bring the meal to a glorious climax. Always present, too, at Christmas are *kourambiedes*, the favorite Greek cooky. Shaped in crescents or balls, these very rich, brandy-flavored, clove-studded morsels rolled in confectioner's sugar appear at all gay occasions.

Gifts are exchanged on the first of January, which is the feast day of the philanthropic Saint Basil. New Year's Eve in Greece is a family holiday when even small children stay up to see the New Year in. Traditional is *vasilopeta*, the New Year cake of raised yeast dough, flavored with lemon or *mahlepi*, a unique Syrian spice derived from black-cherry kernels.

Baked inside the *vasilopeta* is a gold or silver coin wrapped in moistened paper. As the New Year chimes ring, the cake is cut by the head of the family and he who gets the piece with the coin will have exceptionally good luck in the year to come. Other signs of the future are sought through the breaking of a pomegranate on the doorstep of the house. If the pomegranate casts a great many seeds, the year will be prosperous and happy. There is little chance of bad news here, for what pomegranate is *not* full of seeds!

On Epiphany, the baptism of Christ in the River Jordan is recalled through the immersion of the cross. In Piraeus, the harbor city near Athens, and in other waterside towns and villages, a cross is cast into the water and youths dive into the chilly depths for the honor of retrieving it.

Koufeta (sugared almonds, also called Jordan almonds) are distributed at baptisms and weddings, for these predict sweetness in life. Funerals call for *kolyva*, a mixture of boiled wheat, browned flour, and raisins flavored with sugar, cumin, and cinnamon and sprinkled with chopped walnuts and parsley. This dish is prepared by the family forty days after the death has taken place, wheat being the symbol of everlasting life. The *kolyva* is spread on a tray and decorated with a cross flanked by the initials of the deceased formed in almonds. It is brought to the church to be blessed and distributed to the congregation.

Most Greek children are named after saints and hence do not celebrate a birthday but rather a name day—the commemorative day of the saint after whom they have been named. Thus all the Johns will celebrate on Saint John's Day. The names of popular saints—John, George, Peter, Michael, Maria, Anna, Catherine, Helena—are recurrent among the Greek people. Those who bear the names of the more obscure saints, who have no special day, celebrate on All Saints' Day. The name day celebration is gay and generous, with open house and an offering of sweetmeats, especially *baklava* and *kourambiedes*.

A festive sight, not on any special day but all year round, are the *evzones*, the honor guards of the Royal Palace and the Tomb of the Unknown Soldier in Athens. Their striking costume of short white ballet skirt, long white stockings, pompommed shoes, and tasseled caps is of Macedonian origin. Tall and vigorous, the *evzones* are permitted to wear their costumes on their days off, and there is hardly a tourist who can resist the opportunity of photographing a pair of *evzones* leaning casually and rather incongruously against the crumbling pillars of the Acropolis.

A GREEK MENU AND SOME GREEK RECIPES

Ouzo

Taramasalata
(Carp Roe Dip)

Keftaidakia
(Small Meat Balls)

Tiropetes
(Cheese-filled Phyllo Pastries)

*

Moussaka
(Baked Meat and Eggplant)

or

Tourlou
(Lamb and Vegetable Stew)

or

Dolmadakia me Avgolemono
(Stuffed Vine Leaves with
Egg-and-lemon Sauce)

Salata
(Greek Salad)

*

Fresh Fruit   or   *Rizogalo*   or   *Baklava*
(Rice Pudding)

*

Kafes
(Greek Coffee)

DOLMADAKIA ME AVGOLEMONO

(*Stuffed Vine Leaves with Egg-and-lemon Sauce*)

½   pound vine leaves, bottled in brine
¾   pound ground lamb or beef
½   cup raw rice
½   small onion, minced
 1   teaspoon oregano
¼   teaspoon cinnamon
½   teaspoon salt
¼   teaspoon freshly ground black pepper
¼   cup water
 2   teaspoons olive oil
 2   cups chicken bouillon (3 chicken bouillon cubes dis-
     solved in 2 cups boiling water)
 1   tablespoon butter
 2   eggs
 3   tablespoons lemon juice

Rinse leaves one by one and cover with cold water while preparing filling. Combine ground meat, rice, onion, oregano, cinnamon, salt, pepper, water, and 1 teaspoon of the olive oil. Form this mixture into small oblongs and place each on a vine leaf near the base. Fold leaf over once, fold in edges, and roll up tightly toward the point. There should be 25 to 30 *dolmadakia*.

Pour the remaining teaspoon of olive oil into a large, heavy saucepan or a deep skillet that has a tight-fitting lid. Line the bottom with any leftover torn vine leaves. Arrange *dolmadakia* in pan close together, in layers if necessary. Pour 1¼ cups of the chicken bouillon over the *dolmadakia*. Dot with the butter. Cover with a heavy plate to prevent *dolmadakia* from opening as rice swells. Cover pan and simmer over low heat 45 minutes or until rice is tender.

Add remaining ¾ cup bouillon to pan and heat through. In a bowl, beat eggs with lemon juice. Add ½ cup of the hot liquid from the pan, beating vigorously with a wire whisk. Pour entire mixture over *dolmadakia* and let stand for 5 minutes in pan which has been removed from heat. Sauce will thicken. Serve at once.

Dolmadakia me avgolemono should not be reheated as the sauce will curdle. If it must be reheated, warm it *very* slowly in an uncovered pan. Makes 6 servings.

MOUSSAKA

(*Baked Meat and Eggplant*)

1	1½-pound eggplant
	Salt
	Olive oil or salad oil for frying
2	small onions, cut fine
1	clove garlic, put through garlic press
1	pound finely ground lamb or beef
1	cup thick tomato sauce
½	teaspoon cinnamon
½	teaspoon oregano

     1   teaspoon parsley, cut fine
3 to 4   tablespoons dried bread crumbs
         Salt to taste
     2   tablespoons butter
     2   tablespoons flour
  1½   cups milk
    ½   teaspoon salt
    ¼   teaspoon nutmeg
     2   egg yolks
    ½   cup grated *kefalotiri* or Parmesan cheese

Pare the eggplant, cut it into ¼-inch-thick rounds, salt it well, and layer the slices in a colander with a heavy plate or other weight on top. Drain for one hour, dry well, and fry in oil just until tender. Drain on absorbent paper.

Heat one tablespoon of oil in a skillet and cook the onions and the garlic in the oil just until soft, not brown. Add the meat, well crumbled, to the skillet and cook just until it loses its redness. Add the tomato sauce, the cinnamon, oregano, parsley, bread crumbs, and salt to taste. Mixture should not be too moist.

Butter or otherwise grease a 9 x 13-inch baking dish. Arrange a layer of eggplant on the bottom, half of the meat mixture, and repeat. To prepare the white sauce, melt the butter in a saucepan, blend in the flour to a smooth paste, and add the milk a little at a time, beating with a wire whisk to keep the mixture smooth. Cook until thickened. Add salt and nutmeg to sauce. Beat the 2 egg yolks in a bowl, add a little of the hot sauce, beating well, return the entire mixture to the saucepan, and cook 1 minute longer over very moderate heat.

Pour the sauce over the eggplant and meat mixture in the baking dish. Sprinkle with the grated cheese and bake 30 minutes at 350 degrees. Mixture should be puffy and golden-brown on top. To serve *moussaka,* cut in squares. This dish is very good accompanied by a Greek salad. Makes 6 to 8 servings.

KOURAMBIEDES

(*Greek Clove Cookies*)

½ pound sweet butter
½ cup confectioner's sugar
½ yolk of an egg
1½ tablespoons brandy or whisky
2½ cups sifted all-purpose flour
Whole cloves
Confectioner's sugar for coating

Soften the butter at room temperature. Cream it well, gradually add the ½ cup of confectioner's sugar, and beat light and fluffy. This may be done in an electric mixer. Add the ½ egg yolk and the brandy or whisky and beat at medium high speed until the mixture is very pale in color.

Add the flour gradually, blending it into the mixture on very low speed or with a wooden spoon. Chill the dough about 20 minutes to facilitate handling, and shape it into 1½-inch crescents or half-moons or into small balls. Stud each cooky with a whole clove inserted up to the bud end.

Bake on ungreased cooky sheets at 325 degrees for 25 to 30 minutes, or until light brown.

Sift confectioner's sugar onto waxed paper. Place the warm *kourambiedes* on the sugar and sift more sugar over the cookies. Toss lightly until well coated. Cool on wire racks. Makes 65 to 70 cookies.

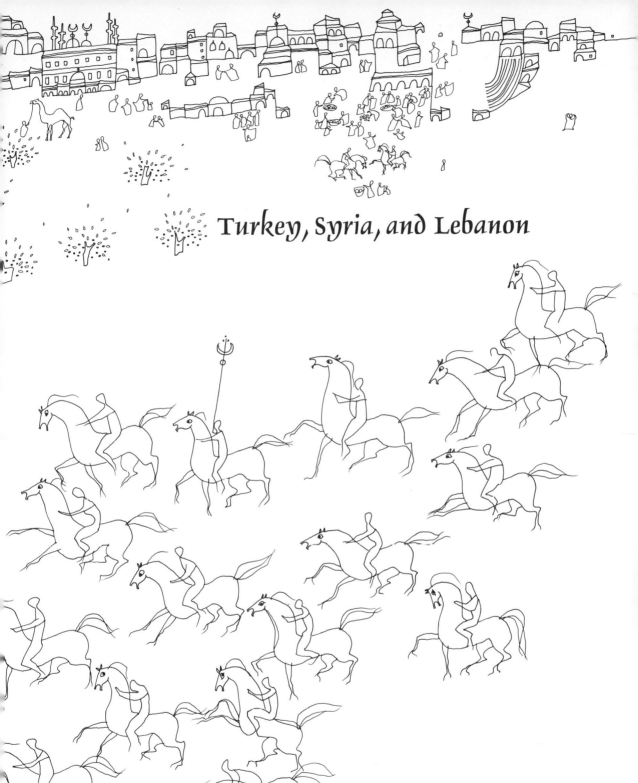

Turkey, Syria, and Lebanon

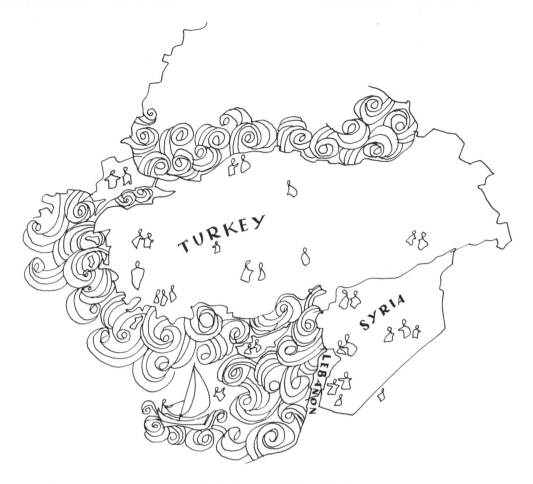

A CLOCKWISE tour of the lands of the Mediterranean brings one at last to the domes and minarets of Istanbul. This is Turkey, a principal gateway to the Moslem world and, for the clockwise Mediterranean traveler, a world that will embrace him until he reaches the shores of the Atlantic at Morocco. There are two exceptions along this predominantly Mohammedan coastline: one is half-Christian Lebanon, the other is the Hebrew state of Israel.

Mohammedanism or, as its followers prefer to call it, Islam (meaning submission to the will of God), is the newest of the world's major religions. It dates from A.D. 622, the year the prophet Mohammed fled from his native city of Mecca, in Arabia, to nearby Medina to escape the death plot of his enemies. Born in 570, Mohammed, the orphaned son of a camel driver, did not begin to receive his divine revelations until he had reached the age of forty. In Arabia the worship of idols and nature gods was very quickly

177

replaced by the doctrine preached by Mohammed, the simple belief in one God, Allah.

Earliest of the new Moslems, or Islamites, were the desert Arabs or Bedouins. Through their nomadic life and the militancy of their horse- or camel-mounted warrior-leaders, they carried the banner of Islam out of Arabia and into the surrounding lands. The impetus of the new religion was such that in less than one hundred years after Mohammed's death Islam had overcome a huge domain reaching westward to North Africa and Iberia and eastward to India. Arabic became the language of many of these lands, including Syria and Lebanon. It is to the credit of the pioneering Moslems, however, that except in a very few cases they permitted the non-believer to follow his own religion without undue pressure or strain.

THE MOSLEM CREED: FASTS AND FESTIVALS

Daily prayer, fasting, almsgiving, and the pilgrimage to Mecca are the four basic requirements of the Islamic faith— in addition of course to the belief in one God. Thus the Moslem, be he in India or Algeria, in sophisticated city, humble village, or surrounded by desert sands, must fall to his knees facing in the direction of the city of Mecca five times a day. At dawn, at noon, at midafternoon, at sunset, and at dusk, the believer recites the fixed passages in praise of Allah. The town Moslem is summoned to prayer from the minaret, the slender tower that soars high above the handsome domed crown of the mosque. The call is traditionally chanted by a trained crier called a muezzin, for Mohammed is said to have disliked the sound of bells. Nowadays in larger Moslem cities a recording played through a loudspeaker is often used in place of the live crier.

Friday is the Moslem holy day. Although it is not as strict a day of rest and devotion as the orthodox Hebrew Saturday or Christian Sunday, the Moslem is expected to attend congregational noon prayers at the mosque. As always before prayer, the ceremonial ablutions are performed. Face, hands, and feet are washed at the mosque's courtyard fountains. The faithful remove their shoes before entering the mosque, and are hatted in a brimless fez, turban, or head shawl, for the forehead must be touched to the floor at specified times during the devotions.

Islam has no organized priesthood. The imam (prayer leader) is the chief officer of the mosque. His qualifications are piety, virtue, and scholarship in Moslem theology. The mosque itself, although it may be richly carpeted, its walls glazed with colorful tilework and its ceilings exquisitely carved and honeycombed, is decorated only with the geometrics of Arabic writing and design, for Islam prohibits the representation of human or animal forms in its art. Nor does the mosque have pews or other seating facilities. The act of praying is performed on the floor, with many Moslems bringing along their own small prayer rugs. Instead of an altar, the mosque contains the *mihrab* or prayer niche pointing toward Mecca, with a pulpit beside the niche.

The eating of pork and the drinking of alcoholic beverages are forbidden by the Koran, the holy book of Islam. The first of these commands is carefully obeyed, probably due to the scavenger-like habits of the hog and the unsanitary conditions that still prevail in many Moslem countries. The Turkish *raki*, however, and the Syrian-Lebanese *arak*, aromatic anise-flavored liquors distilled from grapes or dates, are widely consumed. But wine drinking is limited as compared to the non-Moslem Mediterranean countries.

Smoking is also frowned upon by Islam, but the hookah or narghile (also called the hubble-bubble or Turkish water pipe) is popular in coffeehouses and in homes, where host and guests take turns enjoying the fragrant tobacco smoke that is drawn through water to cool it and to reduce the nicotine content. The constant fingering of the "worry beads" occupies the restless Moslem man who might otherwise be smoking forbidden cigarettes. This Moslem-Arab habit has been adopted by many Christian Arabs, as well as by the men of Greece through contact with the Turkish Moslem world. For the Moslem, the thirty-three beads represent the names of Allah; for the Christian, the thirty-three years of Christ's life.

The great fast of Islam is that of Ramadan, the ninth

month of the Moslem year. Each day of Ramadan, from that moment at dawn when a white thread becomes distinguishable from a black thread, until evening when the darkness is such that the two appear identical, the believer may not eat, drink, or smoke. Since the Moslems use the 354-day lunar calendar, Ramadan does not occur at the same season every year, but comes eleven days earlier each time. When the twenty-nine day fast takes place during the intense heat of summer with its sixteen hours of daylight, the prohibition against drinking water causes extreme hardship, particularly among laborers, field hands, and others engaged in outdoor physical work. Even the swallowing of saliva is forbidden.

As soon as it is dark enough for the day's fast to end, a cannon booms and families fall to feasting and drinking. Wealthy families often skirt the difficulties of Ramadan by turning day into night—sleeping by day and eating two or three hearty meals between nightfall and dawn. But the poor go with little food and less sleep for, as early as one-thirty in the morning in summer, men with drums and cymbals go through the streets reminding working people to rise and partake of nourishment before dawn appears and the long day begins.

Young children, pregnant women, the old, and the ailing are exempt from the rigors of Ramadan, but others if they are of the faithful must make up every day's infraction with two days of fasting. This fast, which is much harsher than the Lenten fast of the Christian world, causes frayed tempers and often brings about public as well as private unrest, so that riots occasionally result. The end of Ramadan is joyfully celebrated, usually for three days, with unrestrained feasting, the exchange of presents, new clothes for all the family, and open house for a constant stream of callers—a sort of combined Christmas, Easter, and New Year.

Another joyful occasion in Moslem life is the return of a family member from Mecca. The outside of the proud family's house is decorated, often strung with lights, and a great feast featuring a whole roast lamb is prepared. The pilgrimage to Mecca, which every Moslem strives to make at least once during his lifetime, entails much planning and the careful saving-up of money, for the Moslem world is far-flung and no pilgrim is admitted to Mecca unless he possesses a return ticket. The pilgrimage is held during the twelfth calendar month of the Moslem year, and journeys must be timed for arrival by the sixth day of the month. The four-day ritual that follows includes ceremonial dress, the sacrifice of a sheep, and prayers and processions centered around the Ka'baa, the ancient pre-Moslem religious building that held the idols destroyed by Mohammed.

Islam came very simply and naturally to the lands of the Middle East. It was a religion that grew out of the dry soil, the desert wastes, and the crowded misery-filled cities. Among other things long related to Middle Eastern life, Islam maintained the reverence for water by making it a part of the religious ritual. (Even today in Turkey, water for drinking is so highly regarded that the Turk prides himself as much on being a connoisseur of waters as is the Frenchman of wines.) It is difficult to imagine an Istanbul or a Damascus without its skyline of graceful needle-like minarets. Yet for centuries before the birth of Mohammed there were powerful civilizations—among them Phoenician, Greek, and Roman—in the lands of the eastern Mediterranean.

Turkey, long the meeting place for East and West, is itself torn between Europe and Asia. Istanbul straddles the two segments divided by the Bosporus, but sits mostly in the one thirty-third of Turkish territory that is geographically a part of Europe. European Turkey is called Thrace. The massive body of Turkey lies in Asia. It is often referred to as Anatolia and was known by the ancients as Asia Minor.

The Minoans of Crete, the Greeks, the Etruscans, and other ancient peoples are believed originally to have pushed their way westward out of Asia Minor looking for favorable

THE TURKS

ARRIVE

IN TURKEY

places to settle, for most of this land is a vast steppe without navigable rivers and with a harsh inland climate of hot summers and severely cold winters. The mild moist coastal areas are another matter—and it was here, on the western edge of Asia Minor, that the ancient city of Troy was built.

Archaeologists digging on this site in modern times have found not one city of Troy, but nine such cities built one on top of the other, a witness to the repeated destruction wrought by wars and by marauding tribes. Later the Persians coming from the East and the Greeks from the West made a centuries-long battlefield of Asia Minor. A thousand years of relative peace came when the Romans took the ancient city of Byzantium, renamed it Constantinople, and made it the heart of the Eastern Roman Empire.

The city, however, was never really Roman. It was Greek-speaking, Greek and Persian in culture, and the center of the Eastern Orthodox church which had evolved out of the Christian religion. This blend was referred to as Byzantine. And all this time there was not a single Turk in Turkey, nor was this region even called by that name.

Little is known of the origin of the Turkish people except that they came riding out of the East from somewhere in central Asia, possibly Turkestan. Legend says that they were led by a gray wolf. The eleventh century saw the first of these nomadic tribes in Asia Minor, an army of fierce and vigorous horsemen, already converted to Islam, their women and children trailing behind them with their livestock and the conical black felt tents in which they lived.

Their harassment of the Byzantines was unabated, and in 1453 the powerful Turkish clan led by Othman (and hence called the Ottomans) took the Byzantine capital. Constantinople was renamed Istanbul, and its great Byzantine cathedral, Santa Sophia, became a mosque of Islam. Today 98 per cent of the people living in Turkey are Moslems, but minority groups have freedom of religion.

The Turks who came galloping out of central Asia were a milk-and-meat people. Yogurt, derived from fermented mare's milk, was a mainstay in their diet. They did not attempt to keep milk fresh, but soured it as quickly as possible since fermented milk keeps longer. Cheese was made by pouring milk into animal skins and tying them to the saddlebags of hard-riding horsemen of the Asian steppes. After a day of such vigorous churning, the milk was transformed into curds.

Meats were cut into chunks, strung onto swords, and roasted over an open fire. This, of course, was *shishkebab*, "sword meat." Less tender cuts were stewed. Wheat and barley were cultivated by some of the seminomadic groups, and a rich yellow fat that was used like butter was skimmed from sheep's milk. But fish, eggs, fruits, and vegetables were largely absent from the diet of the Turkish tribes when they first entered Asia Minor.

Yogurt dishes and grilled meats still hold a vital place in Turkish cuisine. Especially refreshing in the hot, dry Anatolian summer, or in humid Istanbul, is a cold, tangy yogurt soup prepared with cucumbers, dill, and fresh mint. Yogurt is also an ingredient of hot soups prepared with meat or chicken stock. Lamb is still the favorite meat, broiled or stewed with dried beans or fresh vegetables such as squash, okra, and eggplant. The long skewer or spit, a modern substitute for the horseman's sword, is much in evidence in Turkish cookery. Even meat balls, strung onto the skewer like giant beads, are broiled *shishkebab* fashion—and in

THE TURKISH TABLE TODAY

Istanbul, where it is said the tenderest fish in the world come to market, swordfish cut into chunks and marinated in herbs, olive oil, and lemon juice is grilled to perfection on the spit.

Modern Turkish food is wondrous in its variety. This is partially due to the natural resources of the soil and the sea: wheat and other cereals from the Anatolian steppes; rich-meated fish from the mixed waters of the Mediterranean and the Black Sea; remarkable peaches, pears, apples, cherries, figs, melons, and grapes from both coastal and inland regions. The delights of the Turkish table are also due to the fact that the Turkish people have been the great borrowers and adapters of the culinary world.

When the Ottoman Turks took Constantinople, they found a food heritage ready-made. Employing Byzantine cooks and pastry chefs, they at once took this cuisine for their very own. The tissue-thin pastry of the Persians became the Turkish *boerek*, either filled with cheese, meat, or other savory mixture and served as an appetizer, or layered with nuts, sugar, and cinnamon for *baklava* and other delectable sweets. The stuffed vegetables of the ancient Persians and the rolled grape leaves of the ancient Greeks became the Turkish *dolmas*. This name comes from the Turkish word *doldurmak*—to stuff.

Lamb and rice flavored with mint and dill is the favorite Turkish filling for green peppers, tomatoes, squash, and small whole eggplants. These are often cooked and served in assortment. Grape-leaf *dolmas* are frequently eaten in Turkey with yogurt, which makes a tangy substitute for the egg-and-lemon sauce of Greece. Even mussels are stuffed in Turkish cookery, a mixture of rice, onions, parsley, pine nuts, and currants tucked inside the shells, which are then closed down, tied securely with string, and cooked in water. Stuffed mussels are served cold as a *meze* or appetizer.

A dish reputed to have been the favorite of the great twentieth-century Turkish political reformer and westernizer, Kemal Atatürk, is Circassian chicken. This dish was adopted from the Circassians, a handsome Caucasian people whose women were once prized as slaves in Turkey. Circassian chicken is a cold dish of chopped cooked chicken mixed with a paste of finely ground walnuts, bread, paprika, and chicken broth. It is garnished with more of this paste and decorated with paprika-red walnut oil. The paprika used so extensively in Turkish cuisine is a variety originally grown in India.

The cooling Persian beverage called sherbet is a popular refreshment in Turkey, particularly in wild-cherry flavor, and Arabian coffee was so wholeheartedly accepted by the early Turkish tribes that few people think of coffee as being other than Turkish in origin. But the Turks were not only borrowers of cuisine. They were lenders, too, although their motive was usually one of conquest rather than benevolence.

In the 1500s under Suleiman the Magnificent, the Ottoman Empire controlled Syria, Lebanon, part of Arabia, Egypt, North Africa—and in Europe, the Balkans, much of Hungary, and the very gates of Vienna. Modern Hungarian cuisine owes its intriguing flavors largely to the Turks who during their 150-year occupation introduced into Hungarian cooking the use of both paprika and sour cream, a combination that produced those notable meat and poultry dishes designated as *paprikash*. The Turks introduced, too, the flaky *boerek* pastry which, rolled around apples, cherries, nuts, cheese, and even cabbage, was to become famous as *strudel*.

The Turkish attempt to take Vienna failed in 1529 and again in 1683. It is said that on this latter occasion the retreating Turks left behind a bag of green coffee beans. With these an enterprising young Austrian soldier opened the first Viennese coffeehouse, thereby establishing the tradition of coffee drinking and of elegant rich pastries that was to bring world renown to the city of waltzes.

The Ottoman Empire began to contract during the 1700's, and by the next century was losing territories so rapidly it was known as "the sick man of Europe." But during the period of Ottoman expansion, Turkey had scattered so many gifts from the East that Europe came to regard any new food as being unquestionably of Turkish introduction. This explains why maize, the corn of the American Indian, was at

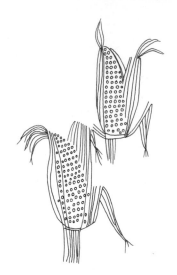

first labeled "Turkey wheat" by Europeans, and why the large, plumaged, edible fowl of the New World was—and still is—called turkey.

Many Turkish dishes have imaginative and colorful names. *Imam bayildi* ("the imam fainted") is slashed egg-plant stuffed with an herb-seasoned meat or vegetable mixture. It is said that when a Turkish imam had this dish served to him at the end of the fast of Ramadan, its aroma and flavor so overwhelmed him that he swooned with delight.

"The emir's pearls" is a salad of sliced oranges, pale sweet onion, and glistening black olives drizzled with olive oil and lemon juice. The rare-pearl colors of the ingredients are considered worthy of an emir, a Turkish potentate or other very wealthy dignitary. Loveliest of all is "lips of the beauty," a pastry fashioned into lip-shaped rolls, fried golden, and immersed in a syrup sweeter than a kiss.

Rahat lakoum (Turkish delight) is, of course, the world-famous chewy candy made of fruit juice and gelatin, studded with pistachios or almonds, cut into cubes, and rolled in confectioner's sugar. Even more delightful is Turkish *halva*, a molded confection of sugar syrup, honey, sesame seeds, and almonds. This sweetmeat is believed to have originated in India. For confections such as these, or for pastries like *baklava*, one visits the *pastahane* (pastry shop) in Turkish cities and towns.

Peasant families of the great Anatolian plateau eat a monotonous winter diet of cereals, dried white kidney beans, lentils, and chick-peas, goat's-milk cheese, and mutton stews. Even in Ankara, the inland Turkish city that replaced Istanbul as capital in 1923, fresh fish is seldom seen at market due to lack of refrigerated transport. But summer brings to the inland regions locally grown fresh vegetables and fruits including the much-favored and versatile eggplant and the superior Turkish watermelon. The coastal regions are better supplied with fish and year-round fresh produce, but otherwise there are no marked regional differences in Turkish cuisine.

Although rice and rice dishes are popular in Turkey, the cereal mainstay is *burghul* (cracked wheat, also called *bulgur*). This excellent product is derived from wheat by a rather complicated process, but its nutty flavor and slightly crunchy texture make it a more interesting staple than rice. It is popular throughout the Middle East.

The Turkish family meal usually consists of a mutton-and-dried-bean dish, or in summer a lamb-and-fresh-vegetable stew. With this main dish a *pilav* is served—rice or *burghul* cooked in water or broth, alone or with other ingredients. Dessert in winter may be a compote of stewed raisins or a simple pudding of milk and sugar thickened with farina or rice flour and flavored with cinnamon or rose water. In summer, peaches, fresh figs, or melon are served.

A more formal Turkish dinner begins with glasses of *raki* (like the Greek *ouzo*), accompanied by as many as thirty different kinds of appetizers. *Raki* is referred to in Turkey as "lion's milk." Because of its potency, it is always taken with food.

TURKISH FAMILY MEALS AND A TURKISH MENU

Here is a typical Turkish menu:

Raki

Stuffed Mussels   Cheese *Boerek*   Assorted *Dolmas*

*

Shishkebab

Burghul Pilav   Green Bean Salad with Olive Oil

*

Turkish Rice-flour Pudding   or   *Baklava*

*

Turkish Coffee

SYRIA
AND LEBANON:
FROM THE
PHOENICIANS
TO THE FRENCH

In ancient times Syria was a vast domain that reached from the Mediterranean shores to the Fertile Crescent, that birthplace of civilization between the Tigris and Euphrates rivers. Egypt was Syria's immediate neighbor to the west. Like Asia Minor, Syria served as an East-West battleground, first for the Egyptians and the Babylonians, later for the Greeks and the Persians. Meantime other civilizations rose and fell within this territory.

One of the most vital civilizations in Syria was that of the Phoenicians, who established themselves on a narrow strip of land between the Lebanon Mountains in western Syria and the sea. This region that is today the land of Lebanon was not formally separated from Syria until 1926.

The Phoenicians took little interest in the well-watered Euphrates valley, or in the then-fertile rolling country of the interior. Their eyes and hearts looked toward the sea—and the excellent shipbuilding timber that grew on the slopes of the Lebanon Mountains enabled them to carry out their extensive trading ventures. Today the cedars of Lebanon are sadly depleted. What wood-using man has not taken over the centuries, the goats have nibbled away at. As elsewhere throughout the Mediterranean world, goats have been permitted to graze on the first tender green shoots of tree saplings; thus, for the sake of pasturelands forests have been sacrificed.

We do not know a great deal about the daily life of the Phoenicians, but we know that they made an excellent purple dye which they extracted from a mollusk found along the Lebanese shore. Phoenician purple-dyed wools and linens were much in demand. Since they were distinctive and fairly expensive, purple was destined to become the color of royalty.

The Phoenicians also made glass, and stone-encrusted jewelry. They exported such foodstuffs as wheat and oil, wine, chick-peas and other legumes, and are believed to have brought the fig, the pomegranate, and the plum to Greece. Their cities—Byblos, Sidon, Tyre—were strung along the coast and were independent of one another. Unlike the Greek, and later the Italian city-states, the Phoenician city-states seem to have had relatively peaceful relations with each other. But within these realms, as in many early civilizations, the Phoenicians practiced human sacrifice.

The Greeks under Alexander the Great conquered Syria in the fourth century B.C. and were followed by the Romans in the first century B.C. Syria was one of the fairest provinces of the Empire. Her fruits especially were prized at the Roman banquet table. Syria became a Christian country and even provided a series of Roman emperors, all of native Syrian birth. A stretch of well-preserved Roman road still lies between the cities of Aleppo and Antioch. A most impressive reminder of Roman splendor is found at Baalbek in Lebanon. The ruins are dominated by the mighty Temple of Jupiter with its six remaining columns, each standing sixty-five feet high and measuring eight feet in diameter.

Islam reached Syria a very few years after the death of Mohammed and converted it to a Moslem Arab land, with the Arabic language gradually replacing both the Syriac and Greek tongues. The region of Lebanon, however, was less saturated with the new faith. The desert tribesmen who had carried Islam out of Arabia were not attracted to the strange snow-capped Lebanese mountains with their rugged slopes, or to the lush coastal areas that lay beyond them. It is probably because the Arab horsemen largely bypassed this segment of Syria that the country of Lebanon is today half Christian while Syria is 85 per cent Moslem.

Damascus, the capital of Syria, was the capital of the Moslem world in the seventh and eighth centuries. This was the period of Islam's most vigorous expansion, a time during which countries as far-flung as Spain and India came under the sign of the crescent. Damascus had long been a caravan center, a crossroads of trade as well as a city renowned for its rich silks and brocades, its wood and metal inlay-work, and its fine steel blades. Now it also became the seat of the caliphate and the gathering place for the great pilgrimage to Mecca.

The eleventh century in Syria, however, saw onslaughts from both the East and the West. The first of the Turkish tribes came riding out of central Asia, while from Europe came the Crusaders, bent on wresting the Holy Land from

the Moslem. Syria, including the region known as the Lebanon, fell under Ottoman rule in the 1500s and remained thus until given to France under a League of Nations mandate after World War I. Not until the 1940s did Syria and Lebanon become fully independent nations.

Syria is much poorer in natural resources today than she was in Roman times. The irrigation canals, drawing from the Euphrates, that once watered her orchards were destroyed by marauding tribes from the East after the fall of the Byzantine Empire. The last of her forests was cut down during the Ottoman regime to provide wood for Turkish railroads, and her eroded uplands have been stripped of their topsoil through centuries of misuse, thus rendering modern Syria two-thirds desert. Most recently Syria has lost coastal territories, through formal partitioning, to Turkey in the north and to Lebanon in the south.

Syria also suffered a severe blow to her commerce after 1500, when Vasco da Gama found the sea route to India and at the same time Columbus' discovery drew much European trade to the New World. In Aleppo alone, eighteen miles of *souks* (little shops) had been constantly active in the great days of the caravan trade. But in the era of the discoveries, the flow of caravans from the East to the Syrian terminal

BEEHIVE VILLAGES AND FAT-TAILED SHEEP

cities diminished to a trickle, and the trade never became fully revitalized.

The *souks* of Aleppo and Damascus are still, however, centers of activity, with pungent smells, vivid colors, and noise. Their profusion of merchandise arranged by trade (so that all cloth merchants are in one section, all goldsmiths in another, and so forth) is eclipsed only by the variety of humanity. Here one finds desert lords in sweeping white robes and *kaffiyah* (Arab head scarf held down by a coil of weighted black cord), Bedouin women decked in gold-coin necklaces, their faces tattooed with blue tribal marks, village women in baggy trousers, men in fezzes and turbans, in long Arab skirts, and in European business suits—as well as camels, goats, and donkeys.

Quite different from timeless Damascus is Beirut, the capital of Lebanon. This modern, highly motorized, international city perched on the Mediterranean shore is surely the most Western metropolis in the East. The French influence is noticeable in Beirut with its trilingual population that switches from Arabic to French to English and back again. Beirut's setting against the rather abrupt snow-capped Lebanese mountains is striking. Visitors bent on recreational sports can snow-ski among the cedars in the morning and water-ski in the Mediterranean in the afternoon, so varied is the terrain within this tiny gemlike country, smaller than the state of Connecticut.

Even more intriguing is the variety of vegetation. Along the humid shore banana trees grow, and on the sandy coastal plain there are orange and lemon groves. At slightly higher elevations one finds grapevines and olive trees, while close to the snow line cornfields and apple orchards are cultivated. Lebanon is the only country of the Middle East that has no desert region and therefore no Bedouin population. Its mountain villages, many of which contain the summer villas of well-to-do Beirut families, are typically Mediterranean in appearance with red-tiled roofs and walled gardens. These villas are in sharp contrast to the dun-colored mud-brick cube houses and beehive dwellings frequently seen in Syria.

Between the Lebanon Mountains and the Anti-Lebanon Mountains (which form the eastern border with Syria) lies the inland plain of the Bekáa, fertile and well irrigated. With its springs and streams supplied by melting mountain snows, with a high coastal rainfall, and with a verdant appearance, Lebanon is much richer in natural resources than the rest of the parched eastern Mediterranean lands. It almost certainly fits the description of the biblical "land of milk and honey."

The most fertile region of Syria nestles against the Anti-Lebanon Mountains, but even this is largely treeless country. Traveling north from Damascus, nearing Aleppo, one comes upon the characteristic Syrian beehive villages dotting the plains. Their picturesque dome-shaped dwellings are built of sun-dried bricks made of clayey mud mixed with chopped straw. The beehive house begins with a square which is then rounded and narrowed to form a pointed dome.

A coating of more mud and straw plasters the bricks, but each year after the heavy winter rains this outer layer must be patched. Generally, however, the one-room beehive house is well suited to its climate for it is warm in winter and can be kept cool in summer by unplugging the ventilating holes that are built into the dome. Away from the plains with their clayey building soil, the Syrian village house is likely to be a square building with a flat roof, constructed of roughly cut stone.

Regardless of the type of house in which he lives, the Syrian or Lebanese villager partakes of the wheat, milk, and mutton diet that prevails in the eastern Mediterranean. Bread and olives appear at every meal, and yogurt is eaten at any time of day, alone or in the company of other dishes. Much of Syria's wheat is grown in the Jezira, a large triangle of land formed by the Euphrates River and the Turkish and Iraqi borders. *Burghul* is the staple cereal food, eaten in winter as a thick porridge. It is scooped up with a wedge of flexible pancake-shaped Arab bread made of water, salt, and coarse wheat flour.

Bread baking is done out-of-doors in small communal cone-shaped ovens, or at the village baker's, for fuel is scarce and individual homes do not as a rule have fireplaces. Most other cooking is done on low, portable charcoal braziers. The thin round of bread dough bakes in a few minutes. In Syria it is slapped against the rounded inside of the oven and caught or peeled off the oven wall when done. Arab pancake bread is slightly puffy and hollow inside, but it flattens as it cools, and dries out quickly. It is brought to the table in stacks that look like a pile of large crudely made saucers, and serves as spoon, fork, dinner plate, *and* napkin. The long, crusty loaf occasionally seen in Beirut and other cities is, of course, not native but French in origin.

The village family, seated cross-legged on the floor, eats from a low table set only with the bowls or platters of food and with bread. A triangle of pancake bread, expertly folded, conveys the food from the common dish to the mouth, whether the food be porridge, stew, salad, or vegetable. Breakfast consists of olives and of pancake bread spread with olive oil and sprinkled with a dash of herbs, or spread with a smooth white curd cheese made from *laban* (yogurt). This cheese is called *labneh* or *labanee* and it is usually sprinkled with *zahtar* (thyme, often blended with powdered sumac).

Burghul has easily as many uses as bread, for this wheat cereal is an ingredient of salads and desserts as well as porridge, and is indispensable to the Syrian and Lebanese national dish, *kibbeh*. *Kibbeh* may be considered the ham-

burger of the eastern Mediterranean world. It is prepared
with finely ground, almost pasty lamb, and *burghul.* The two
are traditionally pounded together in a stone mortar. *Kibbeh*
may be eaten raw; it may be baked in a shallow pan in two
layers with an in-between layer of more chopped lamb,
browned onions, pine nuts, and cinnamon; or it may be
shaped in five-inch-long footballs that are filled with a
stuffing mixture and fried in hot oil.

Kibbeh, in whatever form preferred—and there are further variations—goes well with tangy flavors and is frequently accompanied by a salad of chopped cucumbers and
yogurt seasoned with salt, garlic, and mint. In the villages
kibbeh is not an everyday dish, but is reserved for feast days
and for important family celebrations. Chunks of tender
lamb marinated and broiled on a spit like the Turkish
shishkebab are also very special. More usual in Syria and
Lebanon is the *kefta kebab,* small sausage-shaped spit-
broiled patties of ground lamb mixed with parsley and
flavored with onion.

Sheep are a major source of meat in Syria and Lebanon.
Goats, although raised for their milk, cheese, and wool, are
not considered a meat animal because they are frequently
the garbage collectors of villages and towns, being driven
each evening along a regular route where refuse is set out
for them. Beef and dairy cattle are quite scarce in these
lands due to lack of pasturage. In the absence of the Moslem-
prohibited hog, animal fat is obtained from a special breed of
Asian sheep known as the fat-tailed sheep.

It is customary for Syrian and Lebanese village families to
buy a young sheep in the spring and to force-feed the animal
day and night with mulberry leaves, vine leaves, and bundles
of grass. Often one of the children is assigned to this task by
day. Soon the animal becomes so fat and its tail (where
much of the fat is stored) grows so heavy that the sheep can
scarcely move. A small wooden plank to which runners or
wheels are fastened is then attached to the tail to support it
and to facilitate the sheep's ambling about.

The tail, which may weigh up to fifty pounds, is rendered
at slaughtering time (usually in November) and the fat is

packed in earthenware crocks sealed with clay, to provide a winter's cooking supply. Combined with the fat are small pieces of salt-and-pepper-seasoned lamb. This fat-and-meat mixture is called *qawwrama* and is handy for stews and vegetable stuffings. It may also be used like butter for frying eggs, and is even melted and mixed with lemon juice as a spread for bread.

Another fat, used especially in making pastries and sweetmeats, is *samneh,* a bright yellow butter derived from sheep's milk or sometimes from goat's milk. *Samneh* is clarified (the water and impurities removed) so that it will keep a long time without refrigeration. The Lebanese usually import their *samneh* from Syria where very large flocks of sheep are raised. *Samneh* is the butter used in preparing *baqlawa* (*baklava*) and *knafee,* a shredded-wheat-like pastry stuffed with nuts and sugar and drenched with butter and syrup. It is also used in the dough for *ma'mool,* a rich molded cooky whose hollowed-out center is filled with a mixture of sugar and crushed walnuts flavored with rose water. A design is impressed on the cookies by molding each in the bowl of a specially made carved wooden spoon before baking, or the cookies may be patterned with the tines of a fork. *Samneh* is also melted and spooned over raw *kibbeh* before serving, and it is almost always used in Lebanon in preparing rice.

Somewhat different from the village diet is that of the nomadic, pasture-seeking Bedouins who live chiefly by raising camels and horses, hunting desert gazelles and other animals, and bartering in the town *souks* for the rest of their needs. The camel provides meat and milk for the Bedouin diet (Syrian villagers seldom eat camel meat) and wool for clothing and tents. The desert tribes raise these rather ill-tempered, evil-smelling brutes both as beasts of burden and as racing animals—and look down with some contempt on the fixed and dreary lives of the sheep- and goat-raising villagers.

Spring is heralded with much delight in the villages and towns, for vegetables form an important part of the Syrian and Lebanese diet. It is not uncommon to see people walking through the streets of cities and fairly large towns nibbling on long-leaved lettuce in the early days of the warm season. Soon other fresh vegetables come to market and it is time to prepare *tabbouleh,* the national salad of Syria and Lebanon.

To prepare *tabbouleh,* uncooked *burghul* is soaked in water until it is tender but still firm to the bite. It is combined with chopped vegetables—mint, parsley, tomatoes, and onions or scallions—and dressed with olive oil and lemon juice. Enormously refreshing and with a pleasant nutty flavor and crunchy texture due to the presence of the *burghul, tabbouleh* is traditionally eaten with little scoops fashioned from lettuce, cabbage, or vine leaves in place of forks.

Eggplant and squash are favorite summer vegetables, often stuffed with meat and rice like Turkish *dolmas.* Very popular is *baba ghannouj,* a purée of broiled eggplant combined with *tahini* (sesame oil), seasoned with garlic, lemon juice, and salt, and garnished with chopped parsley and bright red pomegranate seeds that have an irresistible tang. *Baba ghannouj* is eaten like a dip with scoops of Arab bread. Another dish of this type is *hommus bi tahini,* a purée of cooked mashed chick-peas combined with sesame oil and spicy seasonings.

Both *baba ghannouj* and *hommus* are frequently served as *maza* (appetizers) with *arak,* the Syrian and Lebanese anise-flavored grape brandy. Like the Greek *ouzo* and Turkish *raki*, this high-potency beverage is clear and colorless, but becomes cloudy when mixed with water or ice. The Moslem prohibition against alcohol does not seem to apply to *arak*. Other *maza* that often accompany glasses of *arak* are olives, cheese, tiny meat pies, miniature fried *kibbeh,* stuffed vine leaves, and pickled vegetables including mushrooms, inch-long baby eggplants, and pickled turnips glamorous with the hot-pink stain of beet juice.

Fruits, fresh or dried, are the usual dessert at the town or village meal, sweetmeats and pastries being reserved for special occasions. Apricots, pomegranates, melons, grapes, and ripe figs in black, white, and green varieties are plentiful in summer. In winter, dried figs are eaten plain or cooked with lemon and sugar, anise seeds and nuts, to a sticky preserve that makes a dessert sweet or a spread. Rice, farina, and cornstarch are the basis of simple dessert puddings prepared with milk and sugar and delicately flavored with rose or orange-flower water.

COFFEEHOUSES AND WEDDING FEASTS

While Syrian and Lebanese women meet at the well or at the village baker's to gossip, the men congregate at the coffeehouse. As in all Mediterranean countries, this is the business and recreational center for the man outside the home. Here he sips Turkish, or more accurately Arabian, coffee, sweetened to taste in preparation and served black in small cups. Here he plays tric-trac (backgammon) or simply relaxes, puffing contentedly on a narghile.

The separation of the sexes is more marked in the Moslem lands than in other Mediterranean countries, although Turkey prides herself on her degree of westernization since the reforms of Kemal Atatürk. In the traditional Moslem home, the woman still does not join her husband when he is entertaining guests, but remains in her own quarters. When she leaves her home, she is veiled. She may go to a special park set aside for women and children, or she may go to a film matinee for women only. Her husband will go with other men to see the same film in the evening.

In the home or out of it, coffee is the traditional symbol of eastern Mediterranean hospitality. In business offices, as soon as an important caller arrives the office boy slips out to the nearest coffeehouse, returning with a round brass tray holding a pot of freshly brewed coffee, demitasse cups, and glasses of cold water. The same is true at the rug merchant's or the jeweler's. Prices are never fixed but are arrived at indirectly and graciously by proprietor and customer over innumerable cups of coffee or tea.

The visitor to the Syrian or Lebanese home is always offered coffee as well as refreshments of crystallized fruits, sugared almonds, salted watermelon seeds, and pistachio nuts. The Syrians usually add a few cardamom seeds to their coffee while it is brewing, while the Lebanese may prefer the flavor of orange-blossom essence added to the beverage. The thick sediment that remains at the bottom of the cup after the coffee is drunk is frequently read like tea leaves to tell fortunes. The cup is inverted onto the saucer, and the sediment runs down the inside of the cup forming a pattern.

In summer a cooling fruit beverage called *sharab* or *shraab* is served to callers and is also vended in the streets. It is composed of a concentrated syrup—orange, pomegranate, strawberry, lemon, or mulberry—diluted with water and ice and flavored with almond, violet, rose, or banana essence. In Western cuisine a fruit-syrup beverage adapted from *shraab* is called shrub. A street snack that seems to be everywhere in Syria is *ka'ick*, a flat round of bread containing anise seed and dipped, for the purchaser, in a hot milk, butter, and sugar syrup. *Ka'ick* goes especially fast when peddled at the school gates to hungry homeward-bound students. In Lebanon *ka'ick* is sprinkled with sesame seeds before baking and is eaten dry and crisp.

In Syria and Lebanon, particularly in the sweet stalls of Damascus, one sees long, leathery strips of a bright golden color. This is not leather, but a confection made by spreading puréed apricots on trays to be dehydrated by the sun, and then cut into long narrow slices. This sweet can be munched like prunes or raisins, or may be soaked in water to make a sweet, refreshing drink that is especially popular for breaking the fast each evening during Ramadan.

The village wedding in Syria or Lebanon is a gay affair that may be preceded by a week of festive preparation at the home of the bride. The climax is a great family dinner or even a village feast of *kibbeh*, mutton stew with rice and peppers, stuffed whole roast lamb, and stuffed vegetables such as eggplant, squash, and cabbage or vine leaves. If chickens are served, they will be crammed with a mixture of rice, ground lamb, giblets, pine nuts, pistachios, and walnuts, all flavored with cinnamon. Sweetmeats and pastries of every description, fruits, nuts, *arak*, and even wine round out the feast, which may go on for days, until the bridegroom's money gives out.

As in Greece, it is traditional for Syrian or Lebanese wedding guests to be offered sugar-coated (Jordan) almonds as tokens of good luck. These are either passed around on trays or, at more elegant affairs, packed in little boxes of carved wood or cut glass to take home and keep, as one would a slice of wedding cake. The very well-to-do may even distribute the almonds in exquisite wood-mosaic boxes inlaid with mother-of-pearl. Such boxes, usually made in Damascus, are later used for jewelry or cosmetics.

The bride herself is made ready for the wedding by her women friends. In villages where the old customs are followed, her face is powdered with a paste made of pulverized egg shells and water, her eyes are ringed with an ancient black cosmetic called kohl, and her hair is dressed with olive oil. Her fingernails and toenails are stained with henna, and she sits wailing—as tradition requires—at having to take leave of her parents. At last the bridegroom and his friends come to collect her and she is led, often on horseback, to the home of her in-laws where she will henceforth live. At the entrance to the house she steps upon a pomegranate, scattering its seeds far and wide, for here as in other eastern Mediterranean countries this fruit is the symbol of the fertility and abundance that ensure a happy life.

Arak

Black Olives   *Baba Ghannouj*   *Hommus bi Tahini*
(Eggplant Dip)   (Chick-pea Dip)
Pickled Turnips

*

Baked *Kibbeh*

Braised Eggplant   Yogurt-Cucumber Salad

*

Ma'mool   or   *Knafee*

Fig Jam   or   Fresh Fruit

Arabian Coffee

A SYRIAN-
LEBANESE MENU
AND SOME
EASTERN
MEDITERRANEAN
RECIPES

SHISHKEBAB

2½ pounds tender, boneless lamb in 1½- to 2-inch cubes
     (preferably cut from leg)
⅓   cup olive oil or salad oil, or part each
1½ tablespoons red wine vinegar
1½ tablespoons lemon juice
1   clove garlic, put through garlic press
1   small onion, sliced into very thin rings
1   teaspoon salt
¼   teaspoon freshly ground black pepper
¼   teaspoon thyme
1   bay leaf, crumbled
     Green pepper squares, parboiled 5 minutes
     Eggplant cubes, parboiled 10 minutes
     Firm tomato halves or wedges
     Large mushroom caps

Combine oil, vinegar, lemon juice, garlic, onion, salt, pepper, thyme, and bay leaf. Pour over cubes of lamb in shallow bowl. Cover and marinate in refrigerator overnight.

String lamb onto spits alternating with any or all of the prepared vegetables. Spoon a little marinade onto the vegetables. Broil close to the flame, turning once, until lamb is well browned on outside but still pink and juicy within. Serve with lemon wedges and with rice or *burghul*. Makes 6 servings.

YOGURT SOUP

2 medium cucumbers
1 teaspoon salt
1 clove garlic, put through garlic press
2 teaspoons vinegar
2 teaspoons fresh dill, cut fine
1 teaspoon crumbled dried mint, or 1½ tablespoons chopped fresh mint
1 pint yogurt
2 teaspoons olive oil
6 tablespoons cold water

Pare cucumbers, slice each lengthwise into 6 shafts, then slice crosswise ⅛ inch thick. Add remaining ingredients. Chill. Serve garnished with additional chopped mint. Makes 6 servings.

SWORDFISH BROILED ON SPITS

1½ pounds swordfish steaks, cut 1 inch thick
3 tablespoons lemon juice
3 tablespoons olive oil
1 teaspoon minced onion
¾ teaspoon paprika
¼ teaspoon salt
2 tablespoons minced fresh parsley
2 bay leaves, crumbled

Skin the swordfish and cut into 1-inch cubes. Combine all remaining ingredients, pour over swordfish in shallow dish, cover, and marinate in refrigerator for 3 to 4 hours.

Put swordfish cubes on spits, rest spits across shallow drip pan, dust with additional paprika, and broil as close to flame as possible, turning once. Fish may be basted during broiling with pan juices or with leftover marinade. Broil about 8 minutes. Do not overcook. Fish should be golden and sizzling on outside, just tender within. Serve at once with lemon wedges. Makes 4 servings.

TABBOULEH

(*Syrian-Lebanese Mint-and-parsley Salad*)

½ cup *burghul* (cracked wheat) or wheat germ
1 cup coarsely chopped peeled ripe tomatoes
¼ cup finely cut fresh mint, or 2 tablespoons dried mint moistened in hot water ½ hour
¾ cup finely cut fresh parsley
½ cup finely cut scallions (including both white and green parts)
3 tablespoons olive oil
¼ cup lemon juice
   Salt and freshly ground black pepper to taste

Add enough boiling water to the *burghul* to cover. As water is absorbed grains will swell. Add water again until *burghul* is tender but grains are still firm to the bite and crunchy. Allow about 1 hour for soaking. Drain any excess water.

If wheat germ is substituted for the *burghul*, add only enough boiling water to soften it. This will take just a few minutes. *Burghul* (also called *bulgur* wheat) may be obtained packed in cartons at food specialty shops and health-food stores. *Tabbouleh* prepared with wheat germ, however, makes a very good approximation of the authentic Syrian-Lebanese salad.

To peel the tomatoes, immerse them for a few minutes in boiling water. This will loosen the skin. Combine all the ingredients with the prepared *burghul* or wheat germ. Chill. Serve with romaine lettuce or tender green cabbage leaves to be used as scoops. *Tabbouleh* may also be eaten with salad forks. Makes 6 to 8 servings.

Israel

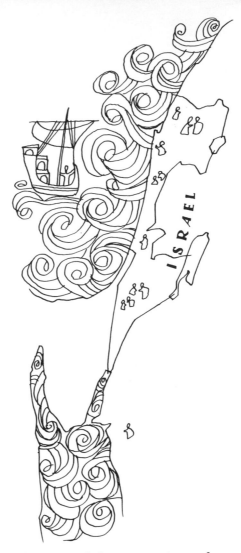

S HALOM, the ancient Hebrew word for peace, is used
in Israel to mean both hello and good-by. "How can
you tell," a bewildered visitor asked a busy young Israeli,
"whether you are coming or going?" "That's just it," the
harried young man replied, "we can't!"

Modern Israel is a melting pot, having received and absorbed people from nearly eighty countries since she pro-
claimed herself an independent nation on May 14, 1948.
Israel is also a boiling cauldron, an ancient land reborn
through an enormous concentration of human energy. The
region that Mark Twain viewed in the nineteenth century
and called "a hopeless, dreary, heartbroken land" is today a
marvel of both industrial and agricultural productivity.

Israel's territory includes most of what was once called Palestine. This land of historical turmoil, source of two of the world's great religions, is actually a little smaller than the state of New Jersey. Its geographical phenomena include the great barren Negev desert or South Country, once considered totally worthless, and the Dead Sea, lowest point on the earth's surface at 1286 feet below sea level. The Dead Sea, which is fed by the River Jordan, is a great evaporation basin, six times saltier than the ocean and heavily laden with minerals. No birds fly over the Dead Sea. In the Middle Ages it was believed that the air emanating from it was poisonous, but today we know that birds avoid it because no fish or other life on which birds feed can live in its waters. Israelis and visitors occasionally take a dip in this buoyant sea but are careful not to swallow any of it.

Israel's chief port, Haifa, is a handsome city set like Beirut against a mountain backdrop. Tel Aviv, to the south along the Mediterranean coast, merged in 1948 with the ancient port of Jaffa to become Israel's largest city. Israel's capital lies inland in the Israeli sector of Jerusalem, for this ancient citadel has been divided and today belongs partly to Israel and partly to the neighboring country of Jordan.

The first Hebrews came to Palestine from Mesopotamia about four thousand years ago, in the 1900s B.C. Some went on to Egypt where they were later enslaved by the Egyptians. They were led back to Palestine by Moses in the 1200s B.C., and soon afterward a great Hebrew civilization, centered in Jerusalem, developed in that land. It did not survive, however, due to both internal strife and attacks from without. From the time of the Assyrian conquest in 721 B.C., a great many of the Jewish people were to know exile and dispersal to other lands. The Roman conquest, in particular, drove great numbers of Jews from Palestine.

The history of Palestine from the fourth century B.C. to World War I closely parallels that of Syria and Lebanon— successive domination by Greeks, Romans, Byzantines, Moslems, and Turks. After World War I, the British were appointed to rule this territory under a League of Nations mandate. Meantime the Zionist movement, with its goal of a

Jewish homeland in Palestine, was gathering force. Centuries of persecution, punctuated by barbarisms like the Spanish Inquisition unleashed by Ferdinand and Isabella, had been stripping masses of Jews of their possessions and driving them from place to place. In the late nineteenth century the first Zionist pioneers began to trickle into Palestine. In the twentieth century perhaps no one person gave greater impetus to the Zionist cause than did Adolf Hitler, though this was certainly inadvertent. His genocidal efforts forced the displaced humanity of Europe into Palestine and thus struck the life spark that created Israel.

The return of people of ancient Hebrew lineage from all parts of the world, including Europe, Asia, Africa, and America, has given Israel its multitude of over two and one-half million. It has given her more than mere numbers, however. It has given her a diversity and enrichment—in her skills and professions, her arts, crafts, languages, folkways, and cuisine. To simplify the language problem, ancient Hebrew has been updated to become a modern living tongue. Free schools teach it to foreign-born adults.

The two principal languages of the early immigrant Jews in Israel were Yiddish, derived from Middle High German, and Ladino, mixed Spanish and Hebrew spoken by the Sephardic (Spanish and Portuguese) Jews. Although these tongues are still heard in Israel, the country's official languages are Hebrew and Arabic. Many Israelis also speak English.

While Israel is essentially a Hebrew state, open to Jews from anywhere in the world, there are Christians and Moslems living in Israel with complete religious, political, and social freedom. It is especially interesting to note that while Israel's Moslem neighbor countries have looked with displeasure and hostility upon the new country, 250,000 Arabs live within Israel's borders and receive the benefits of schooling, medical care, and other social services that are not generally enjoyed by their fellows in the surrounding Arab lands.

COMMUNAL FARM AND BEDOUIN TENT

Almost side by side in Israel, one finds the neat encampment of the *kibbutz* and the black goat's-hair tent of the Bedouin; the newest in farm tractors and the primitive camel-drawn plow.

When the first Zionists came to Palestine, they settled on small tracts of land that had been bought at high prices and with privately raised funds. Because many hands were needed (both men's and women's) to rehabilitate the rocky arid soil or to drain swamps so that crops could be planted, the communal or cooperative farming system worked best. Living in a single large building, eating in a single dining hall, raising young children as a group in a supervised nursery produced greater human efficiency than if each settler had tried to run an isolated family farm. This type of agricultural farm settlement (which also provided protection against the armed assaults of hostile Arab neighbors) is called the *kibbutz*—and the hardy young pioneers who established and worked them became known as *khalutzim*.

The *khalutzim,* the ground-breaking *kibbutzniks,* have been compared to the early American frontiersmen, but with one great exception. The Americans gained their farmlands by cutting down trees; the *khalutzim's* task wherever possible has been to plant trees, for Israel is an ancient forest-stripped land. Life under the assembly-line farming system is often rigorous but has deep rewards in terms of accomplishment. No one is forced to become a *kibbutznik,* and anyone who wishes to may leave at any time. Nor is more than a minor fraction of Israel's agricultural production organized under this system. Today there are many individually owned farms, as well as a number of cooperative farms where families live in their own homes and have their own livestock but work on collectively owned land.

Meals in the *kibbutz* dining hall tend to be simple but nourishing. They are made up of the foods raised on the *kibbutz* itself—wheat, barley, and quite recently corn introduced from America; fresh vegetables and salad greens; poultry, eggs, and dairy products; and a variety of fruits ranging from biblical figs and pomegranates to oranges and grapefruits. In many of the *kibbutzim* fish ponds have been built and stocked with carp, a favorite fish of Jews the world over.

Tomatoes, which along with olives appear on *kibbutz* breakfast tables, were scorned by the early pioneers from Russia and northern Europe who distrusted this unfamiliar fruit, once thought to be poisonous. Today tomatoes are grown and served extensively on the *kibbutz* and are eaten cooked or simply raw like fruit. So bountiful, in fact, is Israel's yield of winter tomatoes that she exports them to England where they are served as a delicacy in London restaurants. Israel's excellent Jaffa oranges, also plentiful, are exported to the United States.

In the black Bedouin tents, dietary habits have changed little over the centuries. The Israeli Bedouin's principal food is Arab pancake bread baked in large thin rounds, one at a time, on a disk of sheet iron. This griddle-like cooking surface rests on low hearthstones and is heated by a fire of desert brush or even of dried camel dung. Other fuel is very scarce in the Negev, that desolate triangle of land dipping southward from Beersheba to the Red Sea. Even the *kibbutzim* of the Negev find progress slowest in this region with its dry treeless plains and stony, rugged mountains— and the Negev covers more than half of Israel's total land area.

Nevertheless the Bedouins manage to grow some wheat,

barley, and lentils during the brief rains that periodically visit the southern Negev. These crops they carefully store against drought years. Bedouin sheep, goats, and camels provide milk which is clabbered or soured (to produce a kind of yogurt) so that it will keep for a long time. Camel milk contains no butterfat, but it can be made into cheese. Both *samneh* and cheese are derived from the milk of the Bedouin's sheep and goats. Mint-flavored sweet tea and Arabian coffee flavored with cardamom seed are the principal beverages. *Dibs*, a sticky sweet made from dates, is used like a honey or preserve.

A sheep or goat is sure to be slaughtered for a Bedouin feast and will be served with rice or *burghul* and a rather fatty gravy. If the feast is prepared for an important visitor, the honored guest is offered the eyeballs of the animal, and it is bad manners to refuse them for they are considered a great delicacy. Aside from special occasions, however, meat is seldom served. Some chickens may be kept, chiefly for their eggs. As for fish, fresh vegetables, and fresh fruits, these do not often appear at Israeli Bedouin meals. Pork, forbidden to Jews and Moslems alike, does not have any importance even in the diet of the Christian Arab in Israel.

Not all of the Arab population of Israel lives a Bedouin life. Many Israeli Arabs dwell in permanent villages of mud-brick houses with flat roofs on which they dry the tomatoes, figs, and raisins grown on their primitively cultivated land. Whether in Bedouin tent or one-room village house, an Arab dinnertime is very different from that in the *kibbutz* dining hall.

As in other Arab communities, the Israeli Arab men usually eat separately from the women of the household. They are served first, the platters of food being set on low tables or directly on the floor. The Arab man sits on the floor with his legs crossed, never stretched out in front of him, for it would be very rude to expose the soles of his feet whether bare or slippered. It is also considered highly uncouth to eat with the left hand. Only the right hand is used for conveying food to the mouth. Utensils consist of the fingers or a piece of Arab bread, but the food is so adroitly managed that it is

thrust into the mouth without touching the fingers to the lips or tongue. Even rice and *burghul* are skillfully rolled into balls and tossed into the mouth with very little spillage. Lip-smacking and other noises indicative of satiety are considered very good form, for they are tokens of appreciation tendered the host for an ample meal.

In firm contrast is the evening meal on the *kibbutz,* with its several hundred workers, most of them young, freshly scrubbed and dressed after the day's toil in the fields or citrus groves, the barns or poultry sheds, the laundry or the nursery. In the dining hall at long tables, men and women eat together discussing matters of the *kibbutz* (a new cow, a new tractor), the latest national or world news received on the radio, or the contents of the daily newspaper or a periodical recently perused in the reading room.

Many of the tanned eager faces at the tables are those of *sabras*, native-born Israeli sons and daughters. The *sabra* is also the name of the prickly pear, fruit of the cactus. Like this fruit, the forthright young Israeli is often thorny on the outside but always sweet within.

Sabra is also the name given to the emerging Israeli cuisine, its many origins both Eastern and Western now beginning to fuse with the new Israeli food resources. This cuisine, less starchy than the European and less oily than the Arabic, is better balanced nutritionally than either. It consists—whether on the *kibbutz*, in the towns, or in the cities of Haifa and Tel Aviv—of fish, eggs, cheese and other dairy products, fresh vegetables and fruits, and poultry. Foods of the eastern Mediterranean such as yogurt, *burghul*, honey, olives, and fresh mint also figure importantly in *sabra* cuisine. Meat, which is relatively expensive, may not appear on the Israeli table more than once a week. A good deal of mutton (mature lamb), however, goes to the Arab markets. *Sabra* poultry stuffings, pot roasts, and stews are tinged with Mediterranean and Middle Eastern flavors— saffron, cinnamon, lemon or orange—and many include dried fruits, nuts, olives, or wine.

Many Israelis are vegetarian by choice. This is a very old tradition among the Jewish people, for according to the dietary restrictions of the Hebrew religion only certain parts of specified animals may be used for food, and these animals must be slaughtered according to ritual law. During their long years of exile in foreign lands, Jews often avoided meat entirely in order to remain true to the tenets of their faith. Queen Esther is said to have lived chiefly on legumes at the court of King Ahasuerus (Xerxes) of Persia so as not to break the dietary laws of her religion.

Mock "chopped liver" and mock "veal cutlets" may be found in vegetarian restaurants in large cities the world over wherever large numbers of Jews have lived. These remarkable imitations of meat are prepared exclusively with vegetables, vegetable oils, and appropriate seasonings. In Israel, the eggplant with its bland, meaty flesh is a great favorite in the preparation of vegetarian dishes.

How astonishing it is that the Jewish people, driven from their homeland and dispersed to distant corners of the earth, should have preserved their dietary laws and customs for over twenty-five hundred years. Proof of this remarkable adherence to the faith, never superimposed by any central, world religious body (since none existed), is seen in the harmonious adjustment of Jews of differing backgrounds brought together in modern times on Israeli soil.

Of course the Jews who have returned to Israel have been deeply influenced by the food customs of their adopted lands. Take, for example, the matter of breads. The ancient bread of Israel was the coarse "barley cake" that is mentioned in the Bible; Israel's most native bread for many centuries has been the disk-shaped Arab pancake bread. Yet in Israel today French *croissants* (crisp, buttery, crescent-shaped rolls) are sold at street-corner kiosks. Israelis also consume German *schnecken* (snail-shaped cinnamon rolls) and Polish *bobke* (a rich yeast-raised bread made with eggs and raisins; the name means "granny" in Polish). Bagels are of Russian origin, but their name comes from the German word *Buegel* meaning stirrup. The shape of these dense, chewy rolls was changed from a stirrup shape to a doughnut-like ring, and they were adopted by Jews in many other parts of the world before making their appearance in Israel. Split (and preferably toasted) the bagel makes a base for the traditional spread of cream cheese and *laks* (Yiddish for smoked salmon), popularly known as lox.

Despite their use of breads of other lands, the Jewish people have always prepared for the Sabbath their traditional festive bread, the *challah*. This golden-brown glazed loaf is made of an egg-rich yeast dough, fancifully braided and sometimes sprinkled with poppy or sesame seeds. No Hebrew Sabbath, in Israel or elsewhere, would be complete without the gleaming white tablecloth, the glow of the Sabbath candles, and the blessed Sabbath loaf, the *challah*.

HEBREW
DIETARY LAWS
AND TRADITIONAL
DISHES

The dietary laws of the Jewish people go back to very ancient times when paganism was discarded by the Hebrew tribes and this people became the first to believe in and worship one God. Although many of the dietary laws seem arbitrary and unreasonable today, each had a valid purpose at its inception. Most of these laws were formally delivered by Moses at the time of the Exodus, the Hebrew flight from Egypt.

"Thou shalt not seethe a kid in its mother's milk." The purpose of this law was probably to prevent the ancient Hebrews from participating in certain pagan customs of the time, relating to the practice of animal sacrifices. As a result of this ancient ruling, traditionalist Jews still do not eat dairy products and meat products at the same meal. In addition, separate cooking and serving utensils must be used for the two types of food. While Mediterranean Jews have always had olive oil, a vegetable oil, to use in their cooking, the Jews of northern and eastern Europe depended largely on butter. Since butter, a dairy product, may not be eaten with meats, and since lard, a pork fat, is forbidden to Jews, chicken and other poultry fats have always figured importantly in a number of European Jewish cuisines.

The prohibition against eating pork and pork products, shrimp, oysters, and other shellfish, is obviously designed for sanitary and health purposes. Hogs and shellfish are scavengers, eating both rotted vegetable matter and decayed animal matter. Many other ancient peoples avoided these animals as food because their unclean habits frequently resulted in disease or even death for those who partook of their flesh. Thus the Jewish people are forbidden to eat any fish but those with scales and fins; any mammals but those that are both cloven-hoofed *and* cud-chewing. This permits the eating of cattle and sheep, but prohibits, in addition to pork, such foods as horsemeat, camel, rabbit or hare, and whale steaks.

The rules for slaughtering animals spring from ethical principles and are also designed to reject the sacrificial practices of paganism. Thus the animal must be killed swiftly and skillfully with a minimum infliction of pain, for the true religionist shows sympathy for all living things and avoids cruelty insofar as possible. Slaughterers are trained in the special methods approved under Hebrew ritual law. In addition, all traces of blood must be removed from the carcass through proper slaughtering followed by washing, soaking, and salting the meat before cooking. The pagan practice of drinking blood was particularly reprehensible to the Hebrews.

Meat killed by hunters, whether mammals or game birds, is strictly forbidden. Most Jews do not eat the hindquarters of sheep and cattle because of the difficulty of removing the large blood vessels. In Israel, however, expert slaughterers are able to render the entire animal kosher. Kosher, or *kasher* as it is often pronounced in Israel, means "proper for use." Thus a Hebrew Israeli village may celebrate Israel's Independence Day by roasting several whole young sheep stuffed with rice or *burghul*, raisins, pine nuts, and cinnamon. Such a communal feast is called a *kumzits*, which translates literally into "come sit." There will be a minimum of sitting, however, for the energetic *hora*, a traditional Israeli folk dance performed in a circle, is sure to be performed on this occasion.

In Israel, as elsewhere throughout the world, contemporary Jews vary in their adherence to these ancient laws, ranging from strict orthodoxy to complete lack of observance. Among Reform Jews, each may follow his own convictions regarding the dietary laws and other ritual observances, but the prophetic teachings, the ethical and moral aspects of the religion, are not subject to variation and remain uppermost in importance. There are many non-kosher restaurants in Israel today, but most of Israel's hotel dining rooms serve kosher food only. This means, among other things, that no butter is served at meat or poultry meals and that if coffee is served after such a meal, cream or milk may not be added to it.

The ancient Hebrews were the first people to decree a weekly day of rest and religious devotion, for they realized the importance of regular physical and spiritual renewal. *Shabbat*, as the Hebrew Sabbath is called, begins at sunset on Friday and lasts until sunset on Saturday. For traditionalist Jews the world over, the pre-Sabbath has always been a time for thorough housecleaning, for personal bathing and grooming, and for preparing the Sabbath meal. This meal is usually shopped for on Thursday, and its preparation begins early on Friday, for once the sun has set the meal must be completed and no further cooking is to be done until after the Sabbath.

Traditionalist Jews do not light fires for cooking or other purposes, do not smoke, do not carry objects, handle money, or ride in vehicles on the Sabbath. They believe in carrying out the command to rest, despite the fact that in modern times heating foods or providing illumination is not necessarily an onerous chore but may be accomplished by the flick of a switch. Since cruelty must not be practiced, the farmer or *kibbutznik* milks his cows on the Sabbath to relieve their suffering, but the very orthodox Hebrew farmer will not use the milk. Unpleasantness is also to be avoided on the Sabbath. Therefore no funerals are held on this day, and the mourning period that follows a funeral is temporarily broken when the Sabbath intervenes.

Tel Aviv has been called a "dead city" on the Sabbath. In this largest Israeli city, shops and offices close on Friday afternoon and just before sunset ancient bearded men ride through the streets blowing trumpets to herald the Sabbath. By sunset the buses have stopped running. On Friday evening after dinner, and again on Saturday morning, the faithful stroll to the synagogue to attend religious services, greeting one another as they meet with the traditional "*Shabbat shalom!*" (Peace to you on the Sabbath.)

The Friday evening meal is always the best meal of the week. Even the very poor have a relatively festive dinner, often with communal assistance. Jewish tradition, both in Israel and elsewhere, dictates that this should be a meal of meat or poultry. It usually features boiled or roast chicken preceded by chicken broth containing dumplings, noodles, rice, barley, or *burghul*.

Gefilte (stuffed or filled) fish is often the appetizer at the Sabbath eve dinner. In Israel it is prepared with local varieties of fish—carp, snapper, mullet, and bream. The fish is skinned and boned and the flesh either chopped by hand or ground. It is then combined with onions, dry bread, eggs, and seasoning. The mixture is shaped into balls or patties and cooked in a fish stock. *Gefilte* fish is served chilled, often garnished with carrot slices and a little of the jellied broth. A sharp relish prepared by grating fresh horseradish root and combining it with vinegar, beets, and spices is the perfect accompaniment. The origin of this very traditional Jewish dish is uncertain, but it is believed to date from the Middle Ages, possibly even earlier.

The *challah*, which is prepared without butter, is eaten with the Sabbath meal. Light airy spongecake or cookies of non-dairy composition may be served as dessert with tea and lemon. The Jews of northern and eastern Europe customarily ended their Sabbath meal with a compote of stewed dried fruits such as prunes, pears, and apricots. But in Israel, stewed fresh fruits or fresh fruits such as oranges, figs, or melon close the meal in true Mediterranean fashion.

Because of the restriction on cooking or even heating foods on the Sabbath, the Jewish people long ago evolved a dish that could be put on the fire the day before and, cooking slowly in the waning heat, still provide a warm cooked dish for the Sabbath day meal. This dish, not unlike Boston baked beans in its design, is known by North African Jews as *hamim* and by eastern European Jews as *cholent*.

The ingredients of a *cholent* vary but may include dried chick-peas or beans, barley or *burghul*, beef, potatoes, and possibly a large dumpling. All of these cooked with fat, seasoning, and a little water in a heavy iron or earthenware pot provide a satisfying although somewhat heavy midday meal that is traditionally served right after morning services have ended on the Sabbath.

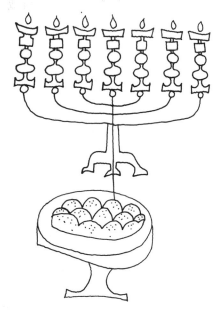

Another slow-cooking dish that may be prepared for this meal is *tzimmes*. Similar to *cholent* but with sweet overtones, the *tzimmes* may include beef, sweet potatoes, turnips, carrots, and dried prunes and apricots. Seasoned with salt and pepper, sweetened with honey or brown sugar, and tangy with lemon juice, the *tzimmes* is a medley of rich, fat mellowness.

On the Sabbath afternoon, bowls of *nahit* or *b'ob* (salted and peppered chick-peas or fava beans) are set out to be nibbled by family and guests. To prepare these snacks, these dried legumes of ancient origin are soaked overnight, boiled tender, drained, and seasoned. They are eaten like salted nuts. Chick-peas and fava beans (also known as broad beans) may also be combined in an oil-and-vinegar dressing for an Israeli salad.

Saturday night after the Sabbath has ended is movie night in Tel Aviv. The buses start running again and crowds throng the streets and cafés. Israeli cafés, like those in other Mediterranean lands, are centers for chess, talk, and newspaper browsing. They are, however, attended by women and by family groups, for ice cream and for soft drinks, as well as by men. Many have national clienteles—former residents of Warsaw, Vienna, or Budapest who frequent them to keep in touch with their countrymen. The coffee served in Israel's cafés is international in variety—Italian *espresso*, Viennese *kaffee mit schlag* (coffee with whipped cream), thick sweet Turkish coffee, and even American instant coffee.

ISRAELI STREET SNACKS AND HOLIDAY FEASTS

Falafel are the Israeli answer to the American hot dog. These little deep-fried tidbits, really vegetable fritters, are sold on street corners in Israel. They are a mixture of mashed chick-peas, *burghul*, and spicy seasonings and are usually stuffed into puffed Arab pancake bread and covered with a bit of salad and a nippy sauce. In this respect they resemble the Mexican *enchilada*. *Falafel* may also be eaten unadorned as crisp, tasty cocktail snacks.

Universal in its appeal is the *knish*, the hot baked pastry snack enclosing a well-seasoned potato, *kasha* (buckwheat), or chopped-liver filling. *Knishes* are members of that vast family of baked or boiled dough pockets, with their range of sweet or savory fillings. Almost every nation has such a food, as evidenced by the Italian ravioli, the Chinese *won ton*, and the Russian *piroshki*. *Kreplach* are the traditional Jewish dough pocket of the boiled (or occasionally fried) variety, usually served in soups. When these soft dough pockets are filled with cherries or other fruit they are called *varenikis*.

Of international popularity are such snacks as pizza, brought to Israel by Italian Jews and prepared in many Tel Aviv cafés, and American "Eskeemo" pies, hawked by vendors on Israeli beaches. Another American favorite sold from pushcarts and street stands is hot, buttered, sweet corn, offered on the cob, Coney Island fashion. This New World plant food is being grown in increasing quantity in Israel. Turkish Delight and other Middle East confections, many prepared with honey, almonds, and sesame or poppy seeds, are consumed in large amounts in Israel, as are a worldwide variety of cakes and pastries.

The holy days of the Hebrew calendar year begin with Rosh Hashanah, the Jewish New Year, which generally falls in September or October. In the Jewish faith, the New Year is not a time of carousing but one of gentle joy, hope, and spiritual stock-taking. Honey, the ancient symbol of sweetness, permeates the festival dishes. Traditional at Rosh Hashanah is *lekach* (honey cake), deep brown and delicately spiced, studded with almonds. In Israel where citrus fruits grow in such abundance, the *lekach* is likely to be flavored with citron peel, and the honey used is generally orange-blossom honey. *Tayglach* are a honeyed confection, very possibly of ancient Greek origin, that are always identified with Rosh Hashanah. They consist of cookylike nuggets of dough, coated with honey, combined with whole nutmeats, and usually formed into golden glazed pyramids studded with candied cherries.

The Rosh Hashanah dinner is an elaborate version of the Sabbath eve meal. The *challah* for this feast is usually baked in a braided round loaf rather than an oblong to symbolize the roundness of the year. It is traditional at Rosh Hashanah to eat pieces of this *challah* or of apple dipped in honey.

Variety meats—lungs, liver, intestines, and brains—are much used by the Jewish people. The intestines or *kishke* are used as casing, as in sausage making. Stuffed with a mixture of flour, suet (beef or mutton fat), onions, and seasonings, and roasted in a slow oven, this *kishke* delicacy is known as stuffed *derma*. On Rosh Hashanah cooked brains, sliced and dressed with olive oil and lemon juice in Israel, are sometimes served as an appetizer. The brain symbolizes wisdom and is a token of esteem when set before the head of the house. The soup served at the Rosh Hashanah dinner often contains *mandlen* (literally, "almonds"), crisp nut-shaped bits of dough prepared with flour, eggs, and oil.

The tenth day of the New Year is Yom Kippur, the Day of Atonement, and the holiest day of the Jewish year. Yom Kippur, a time of seeking God's grace through penitence toward one's fellow man, is observed by a twenty-four-hour sunset-to-sunset fast. The blowing of the *shofar*, the ram's horn, signifies the conclusion of the fast and of the ten-day period of the High Holy Days.

Since both eating and drinking are forbidden on Yom Kippur, the pre-fast meal is made up of bland foods prepared with as little salt or spice as possible. Jews of the eastern Mediterranean often break their fast with a glass of almond milk, a snow-white beverage prepared by pounding blanched almonds and combining them with water. The meal that follows the Yom Kippur fast may be of meat or dairy composition depending on local custom or personal taste. *Kreplach* are popular at this meal.

Sukkoth, coming five days after Yom Kippur, is the Hebrew harvest festival and probably the most ancient of these celebrations that is still regularly observed. The American Thanksgiving, with its expression of gratitude for nature's bounty, follows in this age-old tradition. During Sukkoth, which is celebrated in Israel for eight days, traditionalist Jews live or at least take their meals in leafy-bowered outdoor huts, commemorating the frail shelters in which their ancestors lived during their wanderings between Egypt and Palestine.

In the days of heavy immigration from eastern Europe to the United States, it was not uncommon to see the fire escapes of New York's tenement districts adorned with branches and leaves, and even vegetables and fruit, during the holiday of Sukkoth. These were the leafy shelters of the newly arrived city-dwelling Jew. Among the food plants carried to the Temple in Jerusalem in ancient times was the *etrog* (citron), which was considered a fertility symbol. In Israel today, the abundantly grown citron still appears in these Sukkoth processions.

Hanukkah (also spelled Chanukah), which often parallels Christmas in December, has a delightful candle-lighting ceremony lasting through the eight days of its observance. Hanukkah celebrates the defeat of the Syrians in 165 B.C. and the rededication of the Temple in Jerusalem. After ridding the Temple of the Syrian idols, the Jews sought oil with which to light their holy lamps. They found only a single cruse or small jar of oil which miraculously provided enough light for eight days. Thus each evening of Hanukkah an additional candle is lighted on the *menorah* (candelabra), until on the last evening eight lighted candles stand glowing together.

Latkes (pancakes) are the traditional dish at Hanukkah. Before the potato was brought to the Old World these pancakes were prepared with buckwheat or other flour. In Russia, buckwheat was an important staple, and *kasha* (a porridge of coarse or ground buckwheat groats) was the everyday food of the poor Jews. At Hanukkah, instead of pancakes many Jews ate *kasha varenitchkes*, a combination of noodles (such as bowknots) and buckwheat groats, well-seasoned and flavored with fried onion. After the introduction of the potato, crisp-edged *latkes*, prepared with grated raw potato and sometimes served with applesauce, became favorite Hanukkah fare in Europe, and consequently in the United States.

Purim is the most joyous of the Hebrew festivals. It falls in February or March and commemorates the defeat of Haman, vizier to King Ahasuerus of Persia. According to legend, Haman planned to exterminate all the Jews in the empire. The queen, Esther, pleaded with the king to save her people, thereby risking her life by revealing that she herself was Jewish. Her success is still lustily celebrated on Purim as noisemakers are swung to cheer a victory over anti-Semitism.

Nahit is eaten on Purim in remembrance of Queen Esther's diet of legumes at the Persian court. Traditional, too, are the triangular-shaped Purim cakes known as *hamantaschen,* mocking the tricorne hat (some say the three-cornered purse) of the villainous Haman. *Hamantaschen* are made of yeast or cooky dough and filled with prune butter (prune jam) in the Bohemian tradition, or with a mixture of ground poppy seeds and honey. The poppy seed is another vegetarian food said to have sustained Queen Esther during her endeavor to abide by the dietary laws of her people.

Probably best known of the Jewish holidays is *Pesach* or Passover, which sometimes coincides with Easter in March or April. Passover commemorates the Hebrew exodus from Egypt. *Matzoth,* which is eaten throughout the eight days of Passover (seven days in Israel), is a flat cracker-like baked product that recalls the unleavened loaves the Hebrews baked and took with them at the time of their hasty departure from Egypt. The traditionalist Jew eats no bread during Passover.

The *Seder* is the ritual feast of Passover. Special foods are placed on the holiday table in addition to the rather extensive meal, which is similar to that eaten on the Sabbath eve. These token foods relate to the hardships of the period of Egyptian bondage. Among them are the *matzoth,* known as "the unleavened bread of affliction," bitter herbs for their taste of sorrow and misery, and a pasty mixture called *haroset* which represents the mortar on which the Jews worked as slaves in Egypt.

Haroset, in central Europe and the United States, is generally prepared with chopped apples, nuts, cinnamon, and red wine. In Israel, apples, dates, citrus fruits, and the excellent native-grown peanuts make up the *haroset.* In any case, this mixture seldom *tastes* like mortar, and to eat a token portion of it is not at all a hardship, as it is to partake of the bitter herbs.

A flour or meal ground from *matzoths* is much used in Passover cooking. *Knaidlach* (*matzoth*-meal dumplings) almost always appear in the chicken broth served at the *Seder* meal. The *knaidle* is supposed to represent the round stone thrown by Moses to smash the walls that bound the Jews within Egypt. However, a light, feathery texture is preferred in these *matzoth* balls to the "cannon balls" produced by less successful Jewish cooks. *Matzoth* meal is also used in pancake making during Passover.

Since many foods in addition to bread are prohibited during Passover, special dishes such as *matzoth brie*, a fry of eggs and softened *matzoths*, help greatly in menu making. In former times *matzoths* were round, like the unleavened loaves they represented. But since the era of commercial production, they are most often of rectangular shape for more efficient baking, packing, and shipping.

Shabuoth, coming in May or June, is among the last of the major Jewish festivals for the year. It celebrates the day the Ten Commandments were revealed to Moses on Mount Sinai. Legend says that the Jews awaiting the Commandments were kept so long at the foot of Mount Sinai that by the time they returned to their tents all the milk had soured and had to be made into cheese.

Therefore dairy dishes and especially cheese are traditional on Shabouth. Cheese-filled *blintzes*, delicate crepes enclosing a flavorful cottage-cheese mixture, are fried or baked in butter for this holiday. The *blintz* is of Russian origin and is usually topped with sour cream by the Jews of eastern Europe. It may also be filled with cherries, apples, or other fruit, if desired.

In Israel the Shabouth cheese blintzes are often eaten with a topping of honey. Cottage cheese, incidentally, is so great a favorite in Israel that one of her leading statesmen is said to prefer it for breakfast, combined with grated carrot and drizzled with honey and melted butter.

Chopped Eggplant Appetizer

*

Cold *Borscht*
(Chilled Beet Soup)

*

Palestinian Meat Balls
Burghul or Rice   Carrot Salad

*

Fresh Figs or Melon

AN ISRAELI MENU

AND SOME

ISRAELI RECIPES

FALAFEL

(*Chick-pea Croquettes*)

    2 tablespoons *burghul* (or wheat germ)
    ¼ cup boiling water
    2 cups drained canned chick-peas
    1 beaten egg
    2 tablespoons dried bread crumbs
    ½ teaspoon salt
    ¼ teaspoon thyme
    ¼ teaspoon marjoram
    ⅛ teaspoon white pepper
       Pinch cayenne pepper
       Salad oil for frying

Add the boiling water to the *burghul* and let it stand one hour or until grains are tender (not hard in center, but still crunchy). Add more boiling water if necessary. If wheat germ is substituted for the *burghul*, add only enough boiling water, a tablespoon at a time, to soften it. This will take just a few minutes. Mash chick-peas with a fork.

Combine *burghul* or wheat germ with mashed chick-peas and remaining ingredients except salad oil. Adjust seasoning. Mixture should be quite spicy and sharp. Form *falafel* mixture into about 30 small balls, 1 inch in diameter. Fry in

¼-inch-deep hot oil in a skillet, turning *falafel* to brown on all sides. When golden-brown remove, drain on absorbent paper toweling, and serve hot. *Falafel* are delicious as a snack or appetizer. Makes about 30.

PALESTINIAN MEAT BALLS

    1 pound ground beef
    1 cup pared and coarsely grated tart fresh apples
    1 cup pared and coarsely grated fresh pears
    1 small onion, finely grated
    2 small eggs
    ¾ cup fine dried-bread crumbs
 1½ teaspoons salt
    ½ teaspoon ground nutmeg
    ½ teaspoon ground allspice
    ⅛ teaspoon white pepper
        Flour for dredging
    4 tablespoons margarine (or butter)
    4 tablespoons sliced blanched almonds
    2 cups chicken bouillon (3 chicken bouillon cubes dissolved in 2 cups boiling water)
    4 tablespoons diced dried apricots (¼-inch dice)
    ½ teaspoon lemon juice
 1½ teaspoons cornstarch
    1 tablespoon water

Combine first ten ingredients, shape into 1-inch balls, and coat lightly with flour.

In a large deep skillet that has a lid melt 2 tablespoons of the margarine. Add the almonds, sauté until golden, and set aside. Add the remaining 2 tablespoons of margarine, melt it to sizzling, add the meat balls, and brown well on all sides.

Add the chicken bouillon, the dried apricots, the lemon juice, and the reserved sautéed almonds. Stir to blend, cover skillet, and cook over medium-low heat 10 to 15 minutes.

Combine the cornstarch and the water, add to skillet, and cook a few minutes longer, just until sauce has thickened. (If sauce becomes too thick on standing, thin with additional bouillon.) Serve Palestinian meat balls with rice, *burghul,* noodles, or *kasha.* Makes 6 servings.

ISRAELI NOODLE PUDDING

½   pound broad noodles
⅓   cup chicken fat or margarine (or butter)
 3   eggs, beaten
½   teaspoon salt
¼   cup sugar
¼   teaspoon cinnamon
⅛   teaspoon nutmeg
 2   tablespoons raisins
 1   tablespoon grated orange rind

Cook noodles according to directions on package and drain well. Add chicken fat or margarine, or part each, and toss until melted. (Butter may be used. However, since this dish is usually served as a meat accompaniment, traditionalist Jews prefer a poultry or vegetable fat.)

Cool mixture slightly, add beaten eggs and remaining ingredients. Bake in a lightly greased 8 × 8 × 2-inch pan at 350 to 375 degrees for about 40 minutes, or until the top is lightly browned. Cut noodle pudding in squares and serve hot. It is very good with roast chicken or beef. Makes 6 to 8 servings.

PRUNE-FILLED HAMANTASCHEN

(*Purim Cakes*)

½   cup butter or margarine
¼   cup vegetable shortening
⅓   cup sugar
 1   egg
 1   teaspoon vanilla extract
 2   cups sifted all-purpose flour
½   teaspoon salt
 2   teaspoons grated lemon rind
1½ cups prune butter

Prune butter, also known as "lekvar," may be purchased in jars already prepared in many supermarkets and specialty food shops. To prepare prune butter at home, wash ½ pound prunes and soak overnight. Next day pit prunes, add water to cover and ½ cup sugar. Cook about 1 hour or until mixture is thick. Cool and flavor to taste with lemon juice or rind, cinnamon, and additional sugar if necessary.

Cream butter or margarine with vegetable shortening. Add sugar and beat fluffy. Add egg and vanilla and beat well. Blend in flour and salt, and add lemon rind. Dough should be of rolling consistency, but if it seems too soft or sticky, chill for 30 minutes or add a little additional flour.

Divide dough in half. Roll out first portion about ⅛ inch thick to form a 9 × 12-inch rectangle. Cut into twelve 3-inch squares. Place a generous teaspoonful of prune butter in the center of each square. To form triangular *hamantaschen* shape, bring two of the adjoining corners to the center. Seal their sides by pinching dough into a ridge. Bring up remaining side and seal at corners by pinching each end to the dough at the corner directly opposing it. Leave center open, showing filling. The triangle thus formed will not be equilateral. Repeat with second portion of dough.

Bake *hamantaschen* on greased cooky sheets in 350-degree oven for 20 to 25 minutes, or until lightly browned. Cool on wire racks. If desired, dust with confectioner's sugar. Makes 24.

North Africa:
Egypt to Morocco

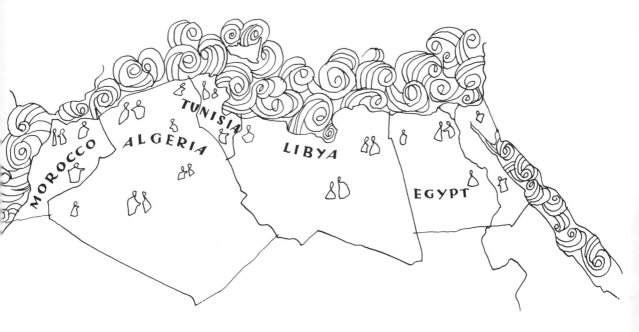

THE SANDS of the Sahara sweep across the face of
North Africa from the Red Sea to the Atlantic. Of the
five African countries that border the Mediterranean, three
—Egypt, Libya, and Algeria—are chiefly desert. Tunisia
and Morocco, which are smaller, predominantly coastal
territories, are nevertheless substantially made up of desert.

It is difficult to realize the vastness of the Sahara until one
recalls that this wasteland is nearly as large as the United
States—and that its east-west distance is even *greater* than
that between New York and San Francisco. Contrary to
popular impression, the Sahara is not all dunes and patterned surfaces of ever-shifting sand. There are areas of bare
plateau like the mesas of the American Southwest, there are
heaps of rocks and boulders that look like a giant stone-
mason's dumping ground, and there are the bleak and
barren cliffs of high mountains.

235

The Sahara sands, however, have the greatest powers of treachery and destruction. A violent sandstorm can "sand down" the paint on a car or truck within hours or even minutes, stripping every vestige of enamel and exposing the bare, bright metal. Desert windstorms are not only blinding and abrasive, but act like a huge automatic drying machine, dehydrating man and beast so rapidly that, without water replenishment, death may occur within a few hours of exposure.

The Sahara sends many of its massive winds beyond the limits of the desert. The *ghibli* rushes up from the south to blast the Libyan coast with hot dust-laden air. Egypt has the similar *khamsin,* which means "fifty" in Arabic and is said to blow at irregular intervals for a total of fifty days in the spring. The sirocco is a Saharan wind of such scope that it crosses the Mediterranean, picking up moisture and afflicting southern Europe with its heat, dust, and high humidity. All of these winds have a most depressing and unsettling effect on man, and are even said to be responsible for suicides and for outbreaks of violence.

In the desert, temperatures go to incredible extremes within a twenty-four-hour period. At a camp in the Algerian Sahara the water cans may hold a thin glaze of ice at dawn, yet to go hatless at noon even for a few minutes is to risk sunstroke. The temperature can soar or drop as much as sixty degrees within a few hours. The lover in the popular song who swore devotion "till the sands of the desert grow cold" was promising very little, for after sunset in the desert the mercury begins to plunge. The Sahara outdoes all other deserts in terms of maximum heat. The world's highest natural temperature of 136.4 degrees *F.* was recorded in Libya in 1922.

If North Africa were all Saharan waste there would be little to say about its people or its way of life, for human existence is of course impossible without water. Three factors have given life to this great stretch of land. They are the comparatively narrow Mediterranean coastal strip, the desert oases, and the world's longest river, the Nile.

It is astonishing that in the midst of a huge desert that even in modern times cannot support life on a reasonable scale one of the world's greatest civilizations sprang into existence nearly six thousand years ago. Egypt was indeed, as the Greek historian Herodotus put it, "the gift of the Nile." This 4,160-mile river, rising in central Africa's highlands and flowing into the Mediterranean, sliced through the Egyptian desert and brought not only planted fields and villages, but great stone tombs and temples filled with magnificent wall paintings and exquisitely wrought jewelry and decorative objects. Where all might have been desolation, as elsewhere in the windswept Sahara, there arose a highly developed culture that was already over two thousand years old in the days when ancient Greece was very young.

One of the places where prehistoric peoples first began to practice agriculture was along the banks of the Nile. Although Egypt was and is a land of extremely low rainfall, the yearly flooding of the Nile valley with its rich deposits of silt washed down from the mountains produced both fertile and well-moistened soil. A simple irrigation system permitted watering well into the growing season. By 3100 B.C. an Egyptian kingdom had been formed. It extended five hundred miles along the Nile but averaged only about twelve miles in width. On either side lay the forbidding desert, so forbidding in fact to possible invaders that the growing Egyptian civilization benefited from its proximity.

The ancient Egyptian year was a twelve-month period divided into three seasons based on the behavior of the Nile. The first season was that of inundation. In late June the Nile began to rise, overflowing its banks, until by late October the waters had receded and the ground was ready for planting. In November, the beginning of the cool season, the seed was sown, often by merely scattering it and allowing sheep or pigs to tread it into the ground. Plowing was seldom necessary. During the early part of the growing season, which

THE FAR-REACHING GIFTS OF THE NILE

lasted until February, the crops were irrigated by a device called a *shadoof*, a rope- or pole-lifted bucket that took up water from a catch basin and poured it into an irrigation trench. The *sakieh* (water wheel) that is so much in evidence in modern Egypt was of Asian origin and probably did not come into use in Egypt until Greco-Roman times.

The last four-month period was the season of harvest and heat. In May the last of the crops were gathered, and by June the Nile had diminished to a mere trickle. The countryside lay parched and withered along its shrunken banks, and the two halves of the desert seemed about to close in and snuff out forever the life of the Nile dwellers. It is no wonder that the Nile god was among the elite of Egyptian deities. Rich offerings were promised to him to renew the river, and in gratitude a human life was cast into the Nile each year as the waters rose and swelled.

Wheat and barley were the principal Egyptian crops, and from the paintings and engravings on tomb walls we learn much about planting, crop harvesting, bread baking, food preparation, and meal service. Stalks of grain were spread on a threshing floor and trampled by oxen. Next the grain and the straw were separated by forking. The grain was winnowed by raising it up in a flat scoop and letting it fall to the ground, while the lighter chaff was carried away by the wind. These ancient methods are still in use in Egypt today.

The sieved grain was stored in silos shaped like sugar loaves. A ladder led to the top of the cone through which the grain was poured in. The grain was extracted as needed through a small door at the base of the cone. The Bible tells how Joseph, the Hebrew slave, interpreted the pharaoh's dream of seven fat kine and seven good ears of grain devoured by seven lean kine and seven thin ears of grain. The vagaries of the Nile, sometimes too violent in its flooding, sometimes too mild, must have been well known by the time of the Hebrew sojourn in Egypt. Nevertheless Joseph's pronouncement that the dream meant Egypt must build up her food reserves against a time of famine was treated as an important revelation, and he was raised up from slavery to become the overseer of the Egyptian granaries.

The bread of Egypt was of barley or wheat flour, laboriously milled by stone grinding. Bread was baked in many shapes but most loaves are depicted as being round and fairly flat. It was in ancient Egypt that the first yeast-raised loaves are believed to have been baked. According to legend, a baker in the royal household forgot about a batch of dough that he had prepared and left it in the palace kitchen overnight. In the morning he discovered his oversight and was appalled to find that the dough had expanded greatly. Hastily he beat it down, only to have it blow up again while he was shaping the loaves. In despair, he baked them anyway. To his surprise, the finished bread was light and porous, far more palatable than the flat, rather hard cakes that were then common.

Whether yeast-raised bread was discovered quite this way or not is unknown. It is perfectly possible, however, that yeast plant spores floating in the air settled on the baker's batch of dough, fed on the sugars and starches in the mixture, and produced the gases that cause leavening, or rising. Raised bread was certainly common in Egypt at the time of the Hebrew Exodus (about 1200 B.C.), for we know that the hastily departing Jews had to bake their loaves unleavened and that these are commemorated in the flat, cracker-like *matzoth*.

Dried legumes and pungent vegetables such as onions, leeks, garlic, and radishes, as well as cucumbers and lettuces, were everyday foods in ancient Egypt. Melons, grapes, figs, and dates were the principal fruits. Beer, the Egyptian national drink, was brewed from barley or wheat. The grain was combined with water to make a mash or paste which was then poured into molds and partially baked. The moist, uncooked centers were crumbled and mixed with a sweet liquid extracted from dates, in order to bring about fermentation. Beer was the drink of the people at outdoor festivals, at taverns, at home, and even at banquets.

The Egyptians produced wines, too, from grapes and from the fermented juice of dates. The latter type was said to be very potent. Until the time of the Hyksos invasion in the 1700s B.C., oils were derived chiefly from the castor plant and from various nuts. The Hyksos, a nomadic Asian people, brought the pomegranate, the apple, and the olive to Egypt, as well as horses, chariots, and body armor.

Honey was the Egyptian sweetener. Sugar cane, which the modern Egyptian *fellah* (peasant) is often seen chewing, was of course unknown. The ancients did chew, however, on the pith of papyrus stalks and the thick roots of various water plants. Cattle, particularly the African ox, were a principal source of meat, as were the desert gazelle and a variety of large birds and waterfowl. Pigs, goats, and sheep were kept but appear not to have been used as food animals. Pigs were raised as beasts of cultivation for they served as harrows, turning up the muddy Nile shores with their snouts. They were, however, considered so unhygienic that even the swineherds were treated as untouchables. The Nile, of course, abounded in fish, and much of the catch was preserved by drying or salting.

But the gifts of the Nile reached far beyond supplying the necessities of peasant life, or even the luxuries of the banquet table. Shipbuilding, navigation, and astronomy grew out of the role played by the Nile in transportation and as a training ground for ventures into the Mediterranean. In addition, the yearly flooding of the Nile washed away all land boundaries and hence required the development of a system of land surveying employing geometry, at which the Egyptians soon became masters. From the cyclical behavior of the Nile came the 365-day Egyptian calendar that is in use today.

The keeping of property records and the enforcement of property laws required offices of government and so led to the creation of a complex and competent political organization. The Nile also served as a floating highway, carrying the monstrous stones used in building the pyramids and colonnaded temples from the quarry lands to their selected settings along the banks of the river. Thus, the science of engineering and the art of architecture at which the Egyptians excelled may be partially attributed to the beneficial Nile. And of course none of the Egyptian arts and sciences could have advanced as they did without a system of writing —and something to write on, other than stones. Again the Nile obliged, and gave the Egyptians a light, flexible writing material—papyrus.

In ancient Egypt the privileged classes not only lived better but died better than the mass of the people. The priests, nobles, and members of the royal family made up the topmost rank of society. The lower classes were made up of artisans and merchants, peasants and laborers, and slaves, in descending order.

The wealthy had handsome homes with columned entryways, lotus pools, and gardens. The poor lived in boxlike huts of sun-dried mud bricks, much like those seen through-

FEASTS AND FUNERALS AMONG THE ANCIENT EGYPTIANS

out North Africa today. An outside staircase led to the flat rooftop where shocks of grain were kept for seasoning and where fruits and other foods could be dried in the sun.

Both rich and poor, however, rose at dawn to take full advantage of the daylight hours. The first meal of the day was an informal one, often eaten while dressing or attending to other morning chores. The man of wealth and social standing was barbered and dressed by servants or slaves as he drank his morning beer and partook of bread and perhaps a thick slice of meat. Most men of high station wore beards that were clipped square and constantly trimmed to retain their contour. Some men, however, kept themselves clean-shaven and wore a false beard attached by a chin strap to the elaborate headdress that was fashionable. Bracelets, rings, and pectoral (a heavy many-stranded jeweled collar) were all part of the daily attire. Feet were shod in sandals of plaited papyrus or leather, or, if one were very affluent, of extremely uncomfortable solid-gold metal.

While the man of the house was being dressed, his wife was having her breakfast while going through the morning ritual of her toilette. This was extensive and required the services of several slave girls, for upper-class Egyptian women appeared with kohl-outlined, almond-shaped eyes, blackened eyebrows, reddened lips, henna-dyed orange fingernails, and long black wigs of sheep's wool or human hair. In addition, beauty lotions, body oils, deodorants, wrinkle removers, and other preparations were in everyday use.

The two main meals of the day in the well-to-do household consisted of beef, birds, or game, with vegetables and fruits, breads and cakes, all washed down with beer. At a lavish banquet an entire ox, spitted and roasted geese, wines, liqueurs, and sweetmeats were presented to the guests. The meal was served at a number of small tables, each accommodating one or two diners, and since most Egyptians, regardless of rank, ate with their fingers, the servants were ever in attendance with water jugs and bowls, scented pomades, perfumes, and lotus blossoms. Male and female singers, dancers, acrobats, and musicians entertained the guests—and as the evening wore on fresh delicacies and wines were brought, so that frequently the assembled company indulged in excesses similar to those of later-day Rome.

The religion of ancient Egypt dictated both the way of life and the way of death of the people, for it was based on the belief that the body remained the dwelling place of the soul after death. This meant that the survival of the soul depended on the physical preservation of the body, and of the presence in the tomb of all those necessities and luxuries that the deceased had enjoyed during life and might possibly make use of after death. Foods, dining utensils, furniture, jewelry, ornaments, and personal effects were placed in the tomb, and the walls of the burial chamber were often inscribed with scenes from daily life that might magically enter into the consciousness of its occupant. The truly great value of these drawings has been in supplying posterity with an artistic and historical record of one of the world's great civilizations.

Ancient Egypt was dominated throughout its long history by a powerful priesthood. At the slaughter of an ox or other food animal, the public worship of one of the many deities, or the burial of a great pharaoh, the presence and leadership of the priests was essential. The failure of King Akhenaton, husband of Queen Nefertiti (who began his reign in 1370 B.C.), to enforce the worship of one God shows how subservient even the rulers of Egypt were to the priesthood. As might be expected, in this highly undemocratic society only the wealthy were able to buy the more important services of the priests.

The preservation of the body, for example, was seldom within the reach of any but the upper classes. It consisted of so lengthy and detailed a process that it took from two to five months to ready the body for interment. First the internal organs were removed. Then the body was soaked in a soda solution known as natron. Later it was filled with aromatic spices, oils, and resins. The resins (which were derived from the famed cedars of Lebanon) gave the mummified body its tarry, blackish appearance. At last the preserved body was dressed, adorned in jewelry, and completely wrapped in linen bands. A mask was placed over the face and the entire body was then wrapped in an outer shroud and laid in the mummy case.

The mass of the people were not accorded such care after death, and thus we can assume that the survival of their souls was not considered very important. Usually they were not embalmed, and their bodies were only partially treated for preservation, with an injection of juniper oil and a pickling in natron. Coffins might contain some jewelry, sandals, and utensils, but they were stacked in a communal tomb. Slaves and paupers were merely buried in a common pit, their bodies wrapped in coarse cloth.

In the case of a prosperous family, the procession of the funeral party to the tomb looked like a deranged house-moving. The mourners, observing the tradition of torn garments and mud-smeared faces, moaned and beat the tops of their heads. Hired mourners enlarged the entourage and added to the commotion. In addition to the mummified body of the deceased, the procession included servants bearing every sort of personal and household item, from drinking cups and figurines to chests and cupboards.

When the party reached the tomb, the contents of the burial room were placed within it and arranged, and the chamber was then sealed. Now all of the mourners withdrew, either to another part of the tomb or to an open space just outside, where they partook with quite good appetites of the funeral feast. The relatives of the deceased generally mourned for at least seventy days.

The ancient Egyptians' lifelong preoccupation with death seems to us a morbid and depressing attitude. However, there may be another aspect to this thinking. Indeed it has been suggested that life on the banks of the Nile was so rich and joyous an experience (at least, for those with wealth and leisure) that the Egyptians were unwilling to part with life and sought its happy extension into the long future.

The greater and lesser pyramids, of which about eighty are still standing, were not the only burial accommodations provided by the ancient Egyptians. From about the 1800s

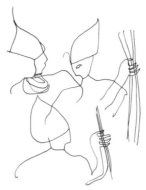

B.C. to the 1200s B.C. the tombs of the Egyptian rulers with their rich contents were cut into huge rock cliffs in the inaccessible Valley of the Kings not far from Thebes. But even these were discovered by the grave robbers who had begun to loot the tombs of their treasures. Only the secret of the valley tomb of King Tutankhamen seems to have been well kept, for it was not until 1922 that Howard Carter, an English archaeologist, opened it and found it intact. Several of its rooms were heaped to their ceilings with objects that had belonged to Tutankhamen, the boy pharaoh who had ruled Egypt for only nine years and died while still in his teens. Most impressive was the exquisite gold mask that covered the face of Tutankhamen's mummy. This and other works of art from his tomb are on exhibit at the Cairo Museum.

By 1100 B.C. the eastern Mediterranean world had entered the Iron Age, and Egypt, having no iron, found it increasingly difficult to compete with enemy armies whose weapons were cast of this cheap and elsewhere-abundant metal. The empire that Egypt had held throughout the earlier Bronze Age began to crumble. In 332 B.C. Alexander the Great, who was a Macedonian Greek, conquered Egypt. The city of Alexandria was founded in his honor, and one of his generals, Ptolemy, set up a final ruling dynasty in Egypt.

The last of the Ptolemys was the ill-fated Cleopatra, more Greek than Egyptian, who played the dangerous game of love and war with the evolving Roman Empire and lost. Her death by suicide in 30 B.C. marked the close of the great Egyptian era, but unlike the deluded kings in their tombs, Egyptian civilization never really died. Its gifts had shaped the evolving Mediterranean world, and hence all of Western civilization.

FROM CARTHAGE TO THE ROMAN GRANARY

Ancient Egypt was not the only pre-Roman civilization of a high order to exist in North Africa. In the 800s B.C. the Phoenicians living in the coastal cities of what is now Lebanon founded a colony near the site of the present-day Tunisian capital of Tunis. Its settlers were mainly from the city of Tyre, which due to its great commercial wealth was being increasingly harassed, pillaged, and taxed by the threatening hordes of Assyrians who arrived yearly from the interior.

The colony on the Tunisian coast was named *Kart-Hadasht*, the Phoenician words for New City. To the world this city came to be known as Carthage. Its peninsula-like site on a hump of North African shoreline was chosen for its productive land and good climate, and of course its access to the Mediterranean which was the life fluid of the Phoenician trading economy.

In addition there were cedars for shipbuilding in the Tunisian mountains, and the murex was to be found along the shore. The murex was the all-important shellfish from which the famous purple dye of the Phoenicians was extracted. It was from the decayed flesh of the murex that the purple stain was obtained, and in modern times piles of discarded shells and huge stone decomposing vats have been found along the North African shore. The vats gave off a hideous odor but were so located that the prevailing winds should not defile the city of Carthage. The mother city of Tyre had long been known in the ancient world for the foul odor that hung about it because of its dye works.

The Carthaginians continued the traditions of their Phoenician forebears. They grew olives, grapes, figs, dates, and pomegranates on North African soil, as well as wheat, barley, and vegetables. They kept sheep, goats, and poultry on their country estates and domesticated the native African gazelle and the ostrich. At Lake Tunis waterfowl were plentiful, as they are even today. The Phoenicians did not eat pork, but they did consume dogs, and there is still evidence of this practice in present-day North Africa.

As with most Mediterranean peoples, meat was eaten chiefly when sacrifices were made. But the coast was well stocked with fish, and much of the varied catch was salted and used in trade by the enterprising Carthaginians. The staple of the poor was a porridge of cereal grains, supplemented with vegetables such as cabbage, chick-peas, artichokes, and garlic.

Wealthy and important Carthaginians followed the practice of giving sumptuous public or semipublic banquets, as a sort of prosperous businessman's display of munificence. These impressive feasts featured whole roasted sheep and oxen, free-flowing wine, and the fanciful pastry-cooks' confections for which the Carthaginians were widely praised. Principally, however, the Carthaginian banquets appear to have been a form of rivalry in which the titans of the trading world showed off to one another.

The Phoenician religion with its tradition of human sacrifice was unfortunately carried forward and expanded in Carthage. Based on the belief that the gods would release their beneficial powers only if offered something of value, dreadful holocausts of infants and young children took place with alarming frequency among the Carthaginians. It was the function of the powerful priesthood to procure the victims from their families and to organize and preside at the sacrificial ceremonies.

Misfortunes of war, crop failures, and natural disasters intensified the need for appeasement of the gods and increased the number of offerings. Fortunately it was decreed that some gods required only animal victims, and thus a bull, a ram, a goat, or even feathered fowl might be sacrificed instead of a human life. As in Egypt and Greece, the priests exacted a share of the animal victim's flesh as partial payment for performing the sacrifice.

Aside from public religious ceremonies and the popular feasts given by social benefactors, the people of Carthage had few recreational or creative outlets. There were no theaters or public games as in Greece, and the arts with the possible exception of music and Greek-influenced architecture were little cultivated. Carthaginian jewelry was, for the most part, crude, while the pottery and glass produced

delighted chiefly those more primitive peoples to whom any manufactured goods were remarkable. As weavers and dyers of cloth, however, the Carthaginians were highly skilled, and they were expert of course in all matters of business and trading. Their principal contribution to Western civilization was the twenty-two-letter Phoenician alphabet which they passed on to the Greeks. This, in turn, evolved into the Latin alphabet that is used in much of the Western world today.

The lands under Carthaginian domination included the entire coast of North Africa (with the exception of Egypt), Sardinia, Corsica, Sicily, and part of Spain. The Spanish city of Cartagena, which was the chief Carthaginian base in Iberia, takes its name from that of its conquering city, just as Barcelona is named after Hamilcar Barca, father of Hannibal and the creator of the Carthaginian military empire in Spain.

On the island of Sicily, Carthage came into growing conflict with Greece, for while Carthage held the western part, the Greeks were established in the east. When Rome came to power and took southern Italy and Sicily from the Greeks, the struggle with the Carthaginians flared into a series of three military contests known as the Punic Wars. The Second Punic War was launched from Carthaginian Spain by Hannibal, and was a courageous attempt to level Rome itself and to avenge the loss of Sicily resulting from the First Punic War.

The Second Punic War saw the strange phenomenon of African elephants crossing the Alps, sliding and tumbling on the narrow paths and over the precipitous ledges in the snow and icy slush of an early Alpine winter. One wonders where Hannibal got both the idea of employing elephants as animals of war and the beasts themselves. Elephants, although smaller and less powerful than those of central Africa, still roamed the grasslands of North Africa in Punic times (the term Punic derives from the word Phoenician). It was Alexander the Great, however, who on his military campaigns in India first encountered the use of elephants in war. Later other Greek generals used them. They were the tanks of antiquity, their thick hides reinforced with plates of armor, and archers perched high upon their backs. They were also useful after the battle as a means of trampling prisoners to death.

Hannibal had used elephants successfully against the Romans in Sicily for a time, and in the conquest of Spain. Their chief drawback was that once wounded they became panic-stricken and enraged, a danger to their masters as well as to the enemy. The only recourse in such cases was to kill the animal instantly by driving an iron wedge into its eyeball. This procedure, invented by Hannibal's brother Hasdrubel, seems immeasurably cruel. But in the days before gunpowder this was a swift and therefore humane way of disposing of so large and impervious an animal as an elephant.

On Hannibal's Alpine route to Italy elephants proved to be a disadvantage. After initial successes, he failed to take Rome, and the Second Punic War ended with his withdrawal to Carthage. In the Third Punic War, concluded in 146 B.C., the Romans captured and completely destroyed Carthage. Its demolition, largely by fire, is said to have taken two weeks. After this had been accomplished, the Roman Senate directed that the land be plowed and sprinkled with salt, to render it incapable of productivity. It was clear that Rome intended to brook no rivals in the Mediterranean. Egypt was next to be brought under Roman rule.

The Roman era saw much of North Africa under cultivation as a granary for the Empire. Wheat, barley, and legumes, as well as olives and fruits, were grown by the native Berber population of what later came to be known as the Barbary States—Libya, Tunisia, Algeria, and Morocco. As in Rome itself, porridges and pulses were the staple foods. It was out of this heavy, enforced grain production that there emerged the very popular North African cereal known as *couscous*.

Couscous (pronounced koos-koos) is produced from wheat middlings which are a by-product of flour milling. Uncooked, the cereal consists of small golden pellets of wheat grain, a trifle larger than the head of a pin. *Couscous* is also known as *semolina*. In any case, the wheat used is of the durum or other hard variety, the same as that from which spaghetti and macaroni are manufactured.

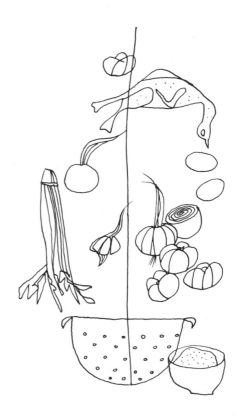

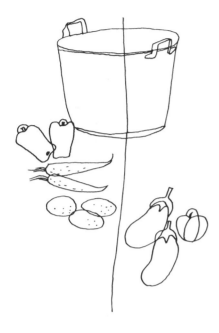

The North African *couscous*, which is cooked through water absorption followed by steaming, is served in the company of a savory stew containing lamb or chicken (or even fish) and many kinds of vegetables including turnips, squash, and the inevitable chick-pea of ancient lineage. The chick-pea was brought to the North African coast, as it was to Spain, by Phoenician traders.

Raisins and nuts are often added to the *couscous* stew, and a garnish of chopped broad-leaf parsley and tangy red pomegranate seeds adds much in flavor and appearance. For greater piquancy, both *couscous* and stew are eaten generously splashed with a "hot sauce" prepared with some of the stew liquid seasoned with coriander (a much-used North African spice) and as much cayenne pepper as the diner can bear. *Couscous* may also be served like rice—in soups, as a side dish with meat or fish, or sweetened for use as a dessert. It is to the North African what rice or *burghul* is to the Middle Easterner and what maize once was to the American Indian.

North African cuisine has changed surprisingly little since
Moslem times. Following the fall of the Roman Empire, the
local Berber overlords and the Vandals who had crossed
from Spain continued to vie for power. Then, in the 600s
A.D., the Moslem crusaders swept westward out of Asia. The
Moslems brought the North Africans citrus fruits, almonds,
sugar cane and rice (grown today largely in Egypt), new
varieties of figs and dates; a new language, Arabic; and a
new religion, Islam. This merger of Arab and Berber stock
created the powerful Moorish force that invaded Iberia in
711 and held on until the last Moslem city, Granada, fell in
1492.

Today all of North Africa, including Egypt, is predominantly Arabic-speaking and Moslem by religion. The laws of
Islam govern the lives of the people. Mosques and minarets
grace and punctuate the cities; traditionalist Moslem
women, discreetly veiled, lead a quiet sequestered life; and
the feast of Ramadan and the pilgrimage to Mecca are
events of marked importance.

There have, however, been other influences in North
Africa. From the 1500s to the 1800s the Barbary States,
deprived of their Iberian empire and under the weak and
corrupt rule of the Ottoman Turks, derived most of their
income from piracy. This activity consisted mainly of attack-
ing and looting ships of other nations in the Mediterranean,
and of exacting tribute from foreign vessels for "protection"
whenever possible.

Irritated by the Barbary demands on their sea traffic, the
European powers finally stepped into North Africa. The
French are said to have gained control of Algeria as the
result of a famous face-slapping incident. At a palace recep-
tion the Turkish ruler of Algiers was piqued by a remark
made by the French consul. Becoming enraged, he lost his
temper and slapped the French dignitary with a silken
flyswatter. The French lost no opportunity to turn the insult

to good account. They demanded much more than a mere verbal apology—and eventually gained control of the entire country of Algeria.

The French colonial administration brought political order, modernization of facilities, and an extensive wine industry to Algeria, but the desire for independence grew rapidly after World War II. Algeria achieved her independence from France in 1962 after a particularly bloody and savage revolution. Morocco and Tunisia, too, had come under French domination, gaining their independence in 1956, while Libya was subject to Italian authority from 1912 until 1951. Egypt, conquered by the Ottoman Turks in 1517 and loosely held for four centuries, became a British protectorate in 1914 and an independent republic in 1953.

Many of the larger cities of North Africa show the European influence in their French-planned boulevards, modern administrative buildings, and elegant hotels and shops, but the most colorful sector of any North African city is the *medina* or native quarter. Its twisting narrow streets often climb to the high point of the city overlooking the sea or the surrounding plain. This hill, ranged with its ascending jumble of boxy steplike houses, is the ancient fortress or citadel known as the *casbah*. To the foreigner or visitor from the European sector, the *casbah* is a place of intrigue and mystery, a labyrinth of passageways lined with beggars and persistent street vendors.

To the residents of the quarter, it is just a place to live. The thick-walled houses are windowless and flat-roofed, permitting the women of the household to take the air on the rooftop in privacy. An outside staircase provides access to the rooftop which is itself surrounded by a parapet. The rooms of the North African house are simply furnished in bare style. Low bolsters, hassocks, or ottomans serve as chairs, couches, *and* sleeping accommodations. Meals are generally served from large trays set on low tripods, with the family members simply squatting on the floor to eat. The men of the household are served separately and always eat their meal first.

In cold or damp weather, heat is provided by a portable

room brazier that burns charcoal, crushed olive pits, or the oily pits of the fruit of the rare argan tree, found chiefly in Morocco. Most cooking is done over a simple charcoal-fueled stove set just outside the doorway of the house.

Sanitation in the *medina* is primitive. For a weekly wash, one may of course go to the public bath. Here, in a large dim room provided with a slatted wooden floor for water drainage, the visitor is charged a small sum for a pail of soapy water, a scrub brush, and a towel. While he bathes, the female members of his household, properly veiled, may be washing his garments and those of the rest of the family at the well or (in a country village) at a nearby stream. One day a week at the public bathhouse, often a Wednesday, is set aside for women only.

The *souk* or native market is the center of North African life. In large cities the marketplace buzzes with activity daily except Friday, the Moslem holy day. In remote country districts the market may be held only once a week, at which time the farmers of the *bled*, the outlying countryside, bring in their produce and the itinerant vendors make their stops. Prices are never fixed in the *souks*, and haggling and bargaining are the order of the day.

Since only a small proportion of North Africa's people is literate, the marketplace is a living newspaper, as well as the social center of the neighborhood or countryside. Public letter writers and those who specialize, for a fee, in reading the daily newspaper aloud do a thriving business here, as do storytellers, sorcerers, and snake charmers.

Melons, oranges, pears, peaches, grapes, and mounds of soft, sticky dates in a halo of hovering bees are on display in the fruit *souks*. Berber children sell the thorny-skinned prickly pear of the cactus. They strip the fruit for the buyer and supply him with a glass of water to counteract the excessive sweetness of its flesh. Onions and peppers, garlic, tomatoes, squash, and leafy greens crowd the vegetable stalls. At the fishmonger's there are sea creatures—anchovies and sardines, squid and tuna; at the butcher's—sheep and poultry, the latter usually sold live.

The spice merchant with his heaps of spices set before him wraps a pittance-worth of saffron or cinnamon in a twist of paper for a customer. Or he selects the spices for a special mixture known as *lekama* that is used in *herrira*, the mutton-and-vegetable soup that is eaten almost nightly during Ramadan. There are cooked-food shops, too, where hot porridge, charcoal-grilled spitted lamb, meat balls, and even roasted locusts may be obtained and eaten on the spot. Hashish, for both smoking and chewing, is sold openly. Derived from the top leaves and tender parts of the Indian hemp plant, hashish is a narcotic drug used by many North African men.

Because coffee tends to be expensive, mint tea is the national beverage in Morocco and Algeria, and sipping it at a native café appears to be the national pastime for men. Mint tea is prepared in a brass pot into which tea leaves, lump sugar, and bruised, pungent mint leaves are stuffed. The mixture then steeps for some minutes in boiling water. Mint tea is served steaming (regardless of the weather), fragrant and *very* sweet, in a glass so hot it must be held with the middle finger on the rim and the thumb against the bottom. Street vendors, too, sell mint tea, for it is the substance of the North African "coffee break."

The *souk*, however, is not all food and talk. Expert craftsmen work in Moroccan leather, in brass, in mother-of-pearl and gold-thread inlay, and in textile weaving and rug making. And not far off, barbers and dentists, many of whom still practice bloodletting, attend to their clients in shaded outdoor premises.

At a country market in Algeria or Morocco one is likely to see a great many more Berbers than in the city *souks*, for these original inhabitants of western North Africa are a rugged people who prefer to live in the mountainous regions and in the remote countryside, often working as shepherds. They have their own tribal dialects, and their gypsy-like women go about unveiled, dressed in brilliant colors and wearing masses of gold jewelry, their faces tattooed with tiny blue dots and crisscrosses in varied patterns according

to tribal custom. These marks are considered by Berber women to be flattering, as false beauty marks were thought to be by the women of the eighteenth-century French court.

Family meals in the homes of the North African poor are of necessity monotonous, consisting as they do of cereals and legumes, vegetables in season, and round loaves of bread baked in beehive-shaped clay ovens. In Egypt the *fellahin* (peasants), who make up three-fifths of the population, subsist on a porridge of dried brown beans or lentils or on rice which grows in the Nile delta region.

A wedding or other feast in North Africa, however, almost always means a whole roast sheep, *couscous* with a rich lamb- or chicken-and-vegetable stew, and a salad of cut-up tomatoes, peppers, cucumber, and mint. Usually, in accordance with Moslem law, no wine is served, but the meal may quite possibly be washed down with Coca-Cola! No spoons or forks are used at the traditional North African feast. The fingers, or scoops of bread, expertly convey the food to the mouth. Slices of melon, or oranges, figs, dates, or grapes are served as dessert, followed by mint tea or Turkish-style coffee. Also popular throughout North Africa are *baklava* and other crushed-nut and *phyllo*-pastry sweets.

A delicacy of Morocco and Algeria is *pastilla*, which is best known in English as "pigeon pie." This dish is made up of a great many layers of paper-thin *phyllo* pastry filled with a mixture of minced pigeon, eggs, vegetables, spices, and nuts, often including chicken and lamb as well. This mouth-melting pie, despite its being crammed with so many ingredients, is only about one inch high. It is served hot, sprinkled with finely powdered sugar! *Pastilla* is often served as an opening course at a festive meal, followed by *couscous* with a lavish stew.

At Ramadan, North Africans like Moslems everywhere observe the month-long daily fast from each day's sunup to sundown. A white flag flutters from the tops of the minarets in North African cities during the hours when neither food nor water, cigarettes nor hashish, is permitted. At sunset the white flag is taken down to signify the end of the day's fast. The vendors who sell steaming, thick *herrira* soup in the streets do a rushing business, and in the homes that can afford it the family sits down to generous helpings of roast mutton and *couscous*.

Life in the oases of the Sahara is quite different from that in the coastal towns or in the villages of the high, grassy plateaus. While most of us tend to think of an oasis as a tiny greensward with one or two date palms springing from it, just large enough for a night's stopover, there are many Saharan oases large enough to support a good-sized village.

The oasis itself derives from an underground desert river or stream, and if the water source is adequate and properly used for irrigation, an oasis may be home to thousands of people and tens of thousands of date palms. It may also include small well-tended wheat fields, vegetable patches, and orchards of tropical fruits.

Contrary to popular belief, the date palm is not a true desert plant, for although it must have its head in the sun it must also have its feet in water and therefore can be cultivated only in the well-irrigated oasis. Nor are dates merely a dessert fruit to the desert people of North Africa. They are eaten as a meal with bread—and are always offered to guests as the symbol of desert hospitality along with a bowl of sheep's milk. No part of the date palm goes to waste in the oasis village. The pits, crushed between stones by women and girls, are mixed with water to be fed as a mash to the camels. The dead lower leaves of the date palm are used as fuel, while the coarse fibers from the base of the leaves are converted into rope and rough cloth.

The oasis dwellers, however, are not true desert people, for unlike the desert nomads they seldom venture beyond the green borders of their villages. They are, in a sense, pris-

oners of the desert, and at the same time defenders of the
oasis which they must not abandon even for a short while
lest the desert sands encroach upon it and reduce its life-
giving productivity. Like islanders in a vast sea, many oasis
villagers live and die without ever traveling out of sight of
the green shores of home.

Between the oasis village and the more fertile lands toward the coast, the desert nomad is the lifeline, often carrying the date harvest of the oasis to market in the cities of
North Africa. In the northern city, the nomad may work as
an itinerant laborer at wheat harvesting, or will trade
sheep's wool, goat's milk, or camel's hair for the pots and
pans, the wheat and rice, he cannot obtain in the desert.
Because he dislikes town life, he will pitch his tent on the
outskirts and stay only long enough to satisfy his needs.
Then, bundling all of his family's worldly possessions into
camel packs, he steals back to the desert.

Most colorful of the North African desert nomads are the
Tuaregs, often called the "veiled men" or "blue men" of the
desert, for oddly enough their skin *is* blue. These Berber-
descended tribes have also been known as the Apaches of the
Sahara. In the days before the French occupation, the Tuaregs on their fine racing camels, trained to unusual silence
and obedience, preyed on camel caravans and raided oasis
towns. Stately and menacing-looking in their long robes, the
Tuareg men wear face-swathing veils that they are said
never to remove even among their families or all-male
groups. Boys begin to wear the face veil, which exposes
nothing but the eyes, at the age of twelve or thirteen. When
eating, the Tuareg man must lift the veil with one hand
while bringing food under the cloth to his mouth with the
other. Tuareg women, strangely enough, go unveiled.

The blue-tinted skin of the Tuareg men and women results from the blue-black color of the loose-fitting wool robes
they wear. Since the Tuaregs seldom if ever bathe, the
greasy blue dye of their clothing rubs off onto their bodies,
and this stain intensifies over the years. The Tuaregs claim
that the dye protects their skins against the harshness of
desert winds. More likely, the Tuaregs prefer to remain blue

since this is considered a lucky color, and the bluer one's skin the more effective his person in warding off evil.

The Tuaregs hunt the desert gazelle and eat camel meat, which tastes a little like poor-quality beef, for it is dry and coarse. They also use camel's milk for both drinking and cheese-making. Camel hair makes excellent tent cloth, and camel hides provide all sorts of leather goods. For dates, wheat, and other food needs, the Tuaregs trade with the oasis villages or trek northward to the fringes of the more fertile North African world.

A NORTH AFRICAN MENU AND SOME NORTH AFRICAN RECIPES

Tamiya

(White Bean Croquettes)

*

Couscous with Lamb Stew   or   Egyptian Roast Lamb with Rice
Moroccan Tomato-and-onion Salad

*

Fresh Dates   or   Sliced Melon   or   Tunisian Nut Pastries

*

Mint Tea   or   Turkish-style Coffee

EGYPTIAN ROAST LAMB

    1 6 to 8-pound leg of lamb, trimmed of excess fat
    2 cloves garlic, put through garlic press
       Salt
       Black pepper, freshly ground
    2 onions, cut up
    1 pound green beans, whole or frenched
    1 eggplant (about 1 pound), peeled and cut into 1-inch cubes
 1½ pounds zucchini, scraped but not pared, in ½-inch slices
    2 green peppers, cut in large chunks

3 to 4 tomatoes, cut into chunks
½   teaspoon marjoram
2   tablespoons minced fresh parsley
2   bay leaves
3   tablespoons tomato paste

Cut tiny slits in the lamb and rub all over with the pressed garlic, spreading it with the back of a spoon or a broad knife. Sprinkle with salt and black pepper. Place in a large roasting pan, fat side up, and put to roast in a 325-degree oven. Allow 30 minutes per pound for roasting from this point.

Two and one-half hours before the lamb is scheduled to be done, add the onions to the pan in which the lamb is roasting and allow them to yellow in the fat that is accumulating. Meantime parboil the green beans in one cup of boiling salted water for 5 minutes. Reserve the green-bean liquid.

Now add the green beans, eggplant, zucchini, green peppers, and tomatoes to the roasting pan, keeping each vegetable in a separate mound. Sprinkle with salt, black pepper, marjoram, and minced parsley. Add bay leaves and tomato paste to green-bean liquid and pour this over the vegetables in the roasting pan. Roast uncovered until lamb is done, basting lamb and vegetables with the pan juices occasionally.

To serve Egyptian roast lamb, carve meat in thick slices and arrange on a large heated platter, surrounded by the mounds of the various vegetables. This dish is excellent with boiled white rice that has been tossed with raisins, sautéed onion, and sautéed slivered, blanched almonds. Makes 8 to 10 servings.

COUSCOUS WITH LAMB STEW

3   lamb shanks (2½ to 2¾ pounds)
    Salt, pepper, flour for dredging
1   tablespoon peanut or olive oil
1   medium onion, finely cut
1   clove garlic, put through garlic press
1   1-pound can tomatoes, with liquid
1   cup tomato juice
1   cup water

1¼ pounds zucchini, scraped but not pared, in 1-inch
    chunks
1½ cups canned, drained chick-peas
 ½ teaspoon thyme
 ½ teaspoon oregano
 2 bay leaves
 1 yellow turnip (1 to 1½ pounds)
 1 large green pepper, cut into strips
 ⅓ cup raisins
 ⅓ cup broken walnut meats
1½ cups *couscous*
 2 tablespoons melted butter or margarine
    Minced fresh parsley, broad-leaf if possible
    Pomegranate seeds (optional)

Trim fat from lamb shanks and season them with salt and pepper, then dust lightly with flour. In a large heavy stew kettle, heat oil and brown shanks on all sides. Lower heat and add onion, garlic, tomatoes, tomato juice, water, half the zucchini, the chick-peas, thyme, oregano, bay leaves, and salt and pepper to taste. Cover tightly and simmer onc hour.

Pare turnip, cut it into quarters, and then cut each quarter crosswise into ⅛-inch slices. Add rest of zucchini, turnip, and green pepper to kettle. Cover and cook one hour longer. Remove lamb shanks and strip meat from bones. It will fall away very easily. Discard bones and return meat to kettle. Add raisins and walnuts.

Prepare *couscous* as follows, during period while stew is cooking. First rinse *couscous* well with cold water. Drain, turn into a large bowl, and stir *couscous* with fork to prevent lumps from forming. Do this quickly. Add 1½ cups of boiling water, 3 tablespoons at a time, to the *couscous*, at 5- to 10-minute intervals to give the grains time to absorb water and swell. Stir frequently.

When the stew has completed cooking, place the *couscous* in a colander or strainer (lined with cheesecloth if holes are large enough for grains to slip through), and set over the cooked stew. Drizzle *couscous* with melted butter or margarine and sprinkle with salt and pepper. Cover *couscous* and simmer stew rapidly for 15 minutes to steam *couscous*. *Couscous* and stew are now ready to serve.

In a large deep serving dish, mound a cone of *couscous* in the center. Spoon the stew into the dish all around the *couscous*. Garnish stew with parsley and pomegranate seeds. Serve hot sauce on the side to be splashed over individual servings of stew and *couscous*. Makes 8 to 10 servings.

Hot Sauce for Couscous:

- 1   cup stew liquid
- 2   tablespoons tomato paste
- ⅛   teaspoon cayenne pepper, or to taste
- ¼   teaspoon ground coriander (optional)

Combine all ingredients. Sauce should be quite "hot" in flavor and should of course be served hot.

Note: If *couscous* is unavailable, this dish may be prepared with rice. Vegetables such as carrots, pumpkin, eggplant, and artichoke hearts may substitute for some of the stew vegetables called for in the recipe, if desired.

Index

ABOUT THE AUTHOR

LILA PERL'S long-standing interest in food encompasses far more than cooking, nutrition, and recipe development. She has looked beyond eating customs and traditions to the background and history which they represent, the culture behind the cuisine. Extensive travel through the United States was the inspiration for her first book for World, *Red-flannel Hash and Shoo-fly Pie:* American Regional Foods and Festivals. A trip with her husband to his native Yugoslavia became a gourmet tour of the Mediterranean countries as Miss Perl compiled the treasury of food lore, tempting sample recipes, and typical menus that became a companion volume, *Rice, Spice and Bitter Oranges:* Mediterranean Foods and Festivals.

Miss Perl holds a B.S. degree in Home Economics and has done graduate work in foods at Pratt Institute, New York University, and Columbia University. Her articles on food, homemaking, and consumer education frequently appear in national magazines, and she has written three other books: *What Cooks in Suburbia, The Delights of Apple Cookery,* and *The House You Want: How To Find It, How To Buy It.* With her son and her husband, who is also a free-lance writer, she makes her home in Beechhurst, New York.